The BEST Angel STORIES 2016

Angels
ON EARTH
New York

The Best Angel Stories 2016

Published by Guideposts Books & Inspirational Media
110 William Street
New York, New York 10038
Guideposts.org

Acknowledgments

Every attempt has been made to credit the sources of copyrighted material used in this book. If any such acknowledgment has been inadvertently omitted or miscredited, receipt of such information would be appreciated.

"A Small Cloud of Witnesses" by Evelyn Bence was originally published in *The Hidden Hand of God: Signs of Wonder* and is used by permission of the author. Copyright © 2002 by Evelyn Bence. All rights reserved.

"Angel in a Pickup" is reprinted from *A Treasury of Miracles for Friends* by Karen Kingsbury. Copyright © 2004 by Karen Kingsbury. Used by permission of Faith Words/Hachette Book Group USA Inc.

"Angel in the Intersection" is reprinted from *A Treasury of Miracles for Women* by Karen Kingsbury. Copyright © 2002 by Karen Kingsbury. Used by permission of Faith Words/Hachette Book Group USA Inc.

"Angels by the River" is reprinted from *To Heaven and Back: A Doctor's Extraordinary Account of Her Death, Heaven, Angels, and Life Again: A True Story* by Mary C. Neal, M.D., copyright © 2011, 2012 by Mary C. Neal. Used by permission of WaterBrook Multnomah, an imprint of the Crown Publishing Group, a division of Penguin Random House LLC. All rights reserved. Any third party use of this material, outside of this publication, is prohibited. Interested parties must apply directly to Penguin Random House LLC for permission.

"Introduction" by Bruce Van Natta originally appeared in *Saved by Angels* and is reprinted with permission from Destiny Image Publishers, Inc. Copyright © 2013 by Bruce Van Natta. All rights reserved.

"Our Angel Tedi" is reprinted from *Gifts of Near Death Experiences* by Denny and Sheila Linn with permission from Hampton Roads Publishing Company. Copyright © 2016 by Denny and Sheila Linn. All rights reserved.

"Rescuing Angels" is reprinted from *Angels by My Side* by Betty Malz with permission from Chosen Books, a division of Baker Publishing Group. Copyright © 1986 by Betty Malz. All rights reserved.

"Two Angels" is reprinted from *My Journey to Heaven* by Marvin J. Besteman with permission from Revell, a division of Baker Publishing Group. Copyright © 2012 by the estate of Marvin J. Besteman. All rights reserved.

"Whoopi at My Door" is reprinted from *The Day I Died* by Steve Sjogren with permission from Bethany House Publishers, a division of Baker Publishing Group. Copyright © 2006 by Steve Sjogren. All rights reserved.

"Wrapped in Light" (originally titled "Wrapped in Light She Flew Out the Open Window") is reprinted from *Whispers of God's Love* by Mitch Finley with permission from Liguori Publications. Copyright © 2015 by Mitch Finley. All rights reserved.

Scripture quotations marked (CEB) are taken from the *Common English Bible*. Copyright © 2011 by Common English Bible.

Scripture quotations marked (KJV) are taken from *The King James Version of the Bible*.

Scripture quotations marked (NIV) are taken from *The Holy Bible, New International Version*. Copyright © 1973, 1978, 1984, 2011 by Biblica, Inc. Used by permission of Zondervan. All rights reserved worldwide. www.zondervan.com

Scripture quotations marked (WYC) are taken from Wycliffe Bible. Copyright © 2001 by Terence P. Noble.

Chapter 1 illustration copyright © 2012 by Yuta Onada; chapter 2 illustration copyright © 2009 by Huan Tran; chapter 3 illustration copyright © 2015 by Marjon F. Aucoin; chapter 4 illustration copyright © 2015 by Marie White; chapter 5 illustration copyright © 2014 by David Grave; chapter 6 illustration copyright © 2012 by Robert Hunt; bonus section "Angels of Christmas" illustration copyright © 2014 by Victo Ngai; bonus section "Glimpses of Eternity" illustration copyright © 2011 by Margaret Lee.

Cover and interior design by Müllerhaus Publishing, Inc.
Cover art by Reed Sprunger. Copyright © 2016 by Reed Sprunger Illustration.
Typesetting by Aptara, Inc.

Printed and bound in the United States of America
10 9 8 7 6 5 4 3 2 1

Contents

Chapter 2
Angels in Our Midst
41

Chapter 3
Orchestrated by Angels
75

Chapter 6
Angels Unaware

SPECIAL SECTION
Angels of Christmas

SPECIAL SECTION

Glimpses of Eternity   273

Introduction

WHAT EXACTLY IS AN ANGEL? It's something I think about every day in my work as editor-in-chief of the magazine *Angels on Earth*. Most people believe angels are God's messengers carrying out His work both in heavenly places and here on earth. The Bible tells us angels have a couple of distinct purposes: to worship and praise God and to communicate with humankind by giving instruction and helping people in need.

I like to think that the stories that cross my desk bring these principles to life. And as surprising as these firsthand experiences with angelic beings are, I know they just hint at the wonder and mystery of God's most magnificent creatures.

The Best Angel Stories 2016 is filled with mysterious occurrences and answered prayers that bring the assurances of God's care through the presence of angels. This annual collection features standout stories from this year's *Angels on Earth*, as well as over three dozen stories never before published and my personal selections from our archive. Threading through these pages is one clear message: God cares for you.

Within each chapter, you'll meet a host of God's messengers, including animal angels and rescuing angels and those who simply offer God's loving-kindness. Like the angel who brings a blanket of comfort to a stranded driver who's been in a car accident. And the camper who dozes off and wakes to find that she is alone in a dark wooded area, until an organized team of fireflies—tiny twinkling angels—lights her path to safety.

You'll read about angels in all shapes, sizes, and colors, from a scruffy, un-shaven man at a bus stop to a mother deer on the fringes of a forest. And you'll discover that some angels have distinct personalities beyond being comforting and polite. In fact, some can be quite abrupt, even a bit discourteous, but helpful nonetheless.

Like you, I am conscious of the daily struggles, tedious tasks, and extraor-dinary tragedies life brings. Sometimes we forget that God is capable of the un-imaginable. This book holds the unimaginable: true stories of those who've been touched by angels through amazing rescues, inexplicable protection, immeasur-able reassurance, and answers to prayer that come in the most unlikely forms.

What exactly is an angel? Psalm 34:7 (CEB) says, "On every side, the Lord's mes-senger protects those who honor God; and he delivers them." I learn more every day about what God's messengers look like, what they sound like, and how they deliver us.

I treasure the trust people have in the editors of *Angels on Earth*. I know that when folks share an experience with us, they are sharing something so meaning-ful and otherworldly that they might have been tempted to keep it to themselves. I'd love to hear your angel story and can help you get it ready for publication. Please send it to *Angels on Earth*, 110 William Street, New York, New York 10038, or e-mail it to submissions@angelsonearth.org.

—COLLEEN HUGHES
ANGELS ON EARTH EDITOR-IN-CHIEF

The BEST Angel STORIES 2016

CHAPTER 1

In the Shelter of Their Wings

"It was undeniably an angel. She couldn't distinguish its face or specific features, but its authority was irrefutable. It was clear to her that he was there to stand watch over them."

—TRISH BLACKWELL

Guarded through the Night

Trish Blackwell

YEARS AGO MY MOTHER-IN-LAW, Marie, encouraged me with a story about how her faith was restored by an encounter with an angel.

The house was dark. Curled up in bed, Marie felt fatigue wrap itself around her like a blanket. Recently separated from her husband, she was already feeling alone and overwhelmed. Now Marie was bedridden, knocked out physically by a virus that had stolen her energy. Her four small children were sleeping in their rooms across the hallway from her. As any sick mother would, she worried about how she would be able to care for her children that night if they were in need, with her youngest being only two and her oldest only seven.

The children's father had dropped them off for the night following their visitation with him. He came and stood in her doorway, silhouetted by the lit hallway. From her darkened room, she begged him to stay in case she needed help. She implored on behalf of their children. He left anyway, the pain of their brokenness overriding his compassion for her. As the door closed behind him, even the house weighed heavy with fear and sadness. The dimness that painted the walls paled in comparison to the darkness Marie felt in her heart.

Dawn arrived with healing and hope. The sickness passed, the children were safe, and daylight had come. Though that long night had lasted only eight hours, the pain of feeling abandoned by someone she once loved and trusted seared her heart with a scar of resentment. She could not forgive him for leaving when she and their children so desperately needed his help. He'd not only let her down, he'd let her children down as well.

The ache stayed with her for twenty years. It haunted her with questions about the reliability of love.

Then one day God lifted the heavy curtain of that memory. What He unveiled changed Marie—her faith and her prayers—forever.

During a contemplative prayer exercise with a counselor, Marie was asked if there was someone she needed to forgive. Her heart knew immediately. The pain in the memory caused by her ex-husband was still undeniable. Guided to ask God a simple question, "Jesus, will You show me where You were that night?" Marie uttered those words in earnest prayer. As her eyelids pressed closed, an image of the memory revealed something she had never seen before. That something was not merely a thing... it was a someone, an army of someones.

Recalling the tearful scene from her bedroom, Marie saw the six-foot-two silhouette of her husband standing in the doorway. This time something different appeared in her memory as well. A much larger and very imposing figure stood behind him, dwarfing him. It was undeniably an angel. She couldn't distinguish its face or specific features, but its authority was irrefutable. It was clear to her that it was there to stand watch over them. God had not abandoned her or the children after all!

As Marie continued to look through the memory of that night, she could see that the house was full of other moving figures. They were hovering throughout other rooms in the house and in the bedrooms where the children were sleeping. Less distinguishable than the large, imposing angel, they were smaller and yet undeniably angelic.

Instantly the pain of the memory melted from Marie's heart, replaced by an overwhelming sense of joy and wonder. God's protective presence became real to her—constant and abiding.

After so many years, forgiveness finally came easy. At last she felt free and peaceful. The revelation of an angel army camped out in her house twenty years earlier assured her of God's love for her. Even through the darkest times God had never left her or forsaken her. As promised in Psalm 91:11, He had commanded His angels concerning her, and they had guarded her, and her children, in all of their ways.

The Smoking Angel
Melody Carlson

I was in Papua New Guinea, spending a year there with SIL, part of Wycliffe Bible Translators. I was eighteen, their youngest short-term assistant teaching preschool on their highland base. With an associate's degree in early childhood education in hand, I was practically fearless.

So when Marilyn Laszlo, a missionary with Wycliffe, invited me to visit her village on the Sepik River during school holidays, I eagerly agreed. Never mind that this place was extremely remote and infested with crocodiles, poisonous snakes, and hairy spiders as big as your palm—or that I hadn't been taking quinine to prevent malaria—I was ready to go. Flying across the island in a single-engine plane with only a small bag containing a spare dress and a few personal items, I felt as free as a bird.

Marilyn was an amazing woman, having faced some tough challenges in her village. She'd even lost her translation partner before going on furlough the year before. Now that she was back in the area, I hoped I could encourage her, and be helpful in getting her settled back in.

After our plane ride, we spent the night at a mission guesthouse. The next day we traveled all day by motorboat down the river, spotting crocodiles, villages, exotic birds ... It was incredible!

By the time we arrived at her village, I understood a couple of things. First of all, this place was really, really remote. And second, Marilyn, the bravest woman I've ever met, seemed a bit uneasy about returning. She'd described her village as "divided." About a dozen people had converted to Christianity, thanks to the message she'd brought them. But the majority of villagers still embraced some pretty dark beliefs and practices—they greatly opposed the influence of Christianity. And they weren't too fond of Marilyn either.

I felt relieved when we were greeted by a group of men who happily helped us carry the boxes of food and supplies up to the house. The house, like the others in the village, was built on tall stilts. Marilyn had already told me it was located on the only piece of land that the headman of the village had been willing to sell. The small hill with a nice view alongside the river seemed like good real estate. But it was also on top of the village's ancestral burial ground and reputed to be haunted. The headman had thought it was a good joke—he would get the money and Marilyn would get the shaft. After all, who'd build anything in a haunted graveyard? But the joke was on him. The one-room house, which resembled a large screened-in porch, was built.

We set to work cleaning the abandoned home. My job was to kill numerous gigantic tarantula spiders with a whisk broom—not for the faint of heart. We also discovered a few poisonous snakes inhabiting dark corners. And I must admit I was grateful for the mosquito netting that we tucked securely beneath our mattresses that night. The next day, I shadowed Marilyn wherever she went in the village. I met her friends, saw how they lived, and watched as she administered medical treatments (she'd been an RN before becoming a translator). By mid-afternoon, the warm air was thick and muggy, and Marilyn challenged me to a swim across the river. Naturally, I agreed. About halfway across she reminded me of the crocodiles. I swam faster. And the men, enjoying tobacco and betel nuts in the men's house across the river, laughed at us, shouting out that we'd make good crocodile food.

Life fell into a comfortable routine during the first week: visiting with villagers, helping Marilyn with all sorts of interesting tasks, and our daily swim across the Sepik.

During my second week there, several missionaries along the river planned for a two-day Christian gathering. Testimonies and food would be shared in the afternoon, and Billy Graham films would be shown in the evening. We traveled a couple of hours by canoe, along with all the other believers, then gathered in an open grassy area with about a hundred villagers. Thousands of hungry mosquitoes were there to greet us. The conference was great, but the next morning I counted more than thirty bites on just one foot. I was getting sick, according to Marilyn, from the bites and possibly the onset of malaria. We decided I should stay home for the second day of the conference.

I slept most of that day, but as the sky grew dark, I heard the low, rhythmic pounding of tribal drums. Steady and intense and slightly foreboding, the sound was the first I'd ever heard of its kind. And then it hit me—the only people left in the village were the headman and his followers, the ones who despised Marilyn and her influence.

But what was going on? Why were they gathering tonight? Suddenly I realized that I was completely alone in one of the most remote places on earth, on top of an ancient and reportedly haunted burial mound, with a group of disgruntled villagers beating on ceremonial drums nearby. Despite feeling sick, I had enough wits about me to know this was a potentially bad situation. But what could I do?

The screened-in house resembled a fishbowl at night, and, feeling safer in the darkness, I turned off the kerosene lamps and climbed in my bed, praying for God's protection. I must've drifted off to sleep, because when I woke up I could still hear the ominous sound of the drums steadily pounding. But what alarmed me more was the smell of smoke drifting up through the loose bamboo floors of the house. As I strained my ears to listen, I could hear the scuffle of footsteps down below the stilted house. I peered down through the cracks of the floor and was able to see the orange glow of an ember. Was someone planning to burn down the house? And if so, what should I do?

As I crouched there praying, I realized that the smoke smelled like the same tobacco that village men smoked in their handmade pipes. But why would someone smoke down beneath Marilyn's house? It made no sense. Still, there was something comforting about his presence. My fear vanished as I fell asleep once again.

The next day, I told Marilyn about the strange visitor. "That's impossible," she declared. "No one in this village—not the ones here last night—would come over here and smoke beneath the house."

We kicked the strange occurrence around some more until I finally decided that, similar to other unexplainable stories I'd heard about protective beings along the Sepik River, my visitor had to have been an angel. A smoking angel, sent by God to watch over me that night.

Lifted

Pam Patterson

MY SEVENTY-YEAR-OLD FATHER-IN-LAW jumped in the water first. But he couldn't get to my daughter. His arms flailed, tangled in the camera strap around his neck.

"Mommy!" three-year-old Jinny cried, her eyes wide with panic. She'd started swim lessons at eighteen months and did fine in shallow water, but she'd drifted into the deep end of the motel pool.

Jinny reached frantically for me. She was in the middle of the pool, too far for me to pull her to safety from the deck. Before I could do a thing, she went under.

I looked around, desperate. My husband, Bob, had gone back to our room to get something. No lifeguard on duty. No one else was close to the pool. Just me. And I couldn't swim. I was terrified of the water.

Some college boys were horsing around on the far side of the deck. "Help us! Please!" I shouted. They didn't even look my way. They were laughing too loud to hear me.

I couldn't wait any longer. I wasn't going to watch my daughter drown. I leaped into the pool. All I could get out before the water went over my head and swallowed me was one word: "God!"

I couldn't see a thing with water in my eyes. I stretched out my arms. I felt a tiny foot against my palm. *Jinny!* I got my hands on her back to try to push her to the surface. At that second, I sensed something pushing against my own back. The pressure of two large, strong hands propelling us to the edge of the pool.

The next instant, I was standing on the deck by the deep end, with Jinny in my arms. We didn't climb any steps or ladder to get out. It was as if we were lifted right out of the water and gently set on dry ground, safe.

A blur flew by me. Bob. He dove in the deep end and pulled his dad out of the pool. My father-in-law coughed and sputtered. Then he caught sight of Jinny and me. "You're okay," he said, wonderingly. "Was there a lifeguard?"

"Yes," I said, catching my breath. One we never saw and never will see on this earth.

Angels on the Fourth Floor

Geraldine Cerrone

My husband, Don, had been sick our entire marriage, suffering from a myriad of illnesses that made even standing up during our wedding ceremony extremely difficult. Years into the marriage, he had suffered a stroke that crippled his right leg. He also struggled with breathing, and most recently he'd suffered a terrible accident and broken his left leg. Don had come to depend on his wheelchair as much as he'd depended on me. For nearly fifty years I'd been his wife and nurse and it was challenging at times. Keeping him close to home was easiest. But we made exceptions for our loved ones.

Don was especially close to his namesake, our grandson who was a mixed martial arts fighter. In 2011, our grandson Don had an opportunity to compete in a UFC fight, a mixed martial arts competition, and we both wanted to support him. We made our plans to attend the event several weeks before my husband broke his leg. But we didn't let the accident deter us.

Two days before the big fight, we arrived at our hotel and settled in on the fourth floor. We needed the extra time to get our bearings so we could enjoy watching our grandson compete.

Around four o'clock the morning after we arrived, my husband and I were suddenly jolted awake in our hotel room. The fire alarm erupted, warning everyone to get out as soon as they could.

I couldn't just leave. I had to get Don dressed and into his wheelchair. He was on oxygen and needed his pills. Being his nurse, I knew the importance of meeting all of his medical needs before we could make a move.

By the time we entered the hallway, everyone else was gone. I started to see the smoke seeping into space only we occupied. Other than the screaming alarm and lights, there was nothing else going on. No one running to the exit. No one screaming or rushing by. No one to help us. We stood there alone trying to figure out what to do.

Despite the smoke I could clearly see the stairs. I thought it was a sign, our only way out! But when we reached the stairs, we realized it would be impossible for both of us to climb down. The wheelchair was too much for me to handle.

Don looked at me. "Go," he said. He urged me to save myself.

"No, that's not how it works," I told him. "You burn, I burn."

As soon as I'd said it, three large males appeared out of nowhere. For a moment, I thought they were UFC athletes in their T-shirts and jeans. They were *big*, at least seven feet tall, and strong, but not muscular like the fighters we'd seen. Then I looked at their faces. They were breathtakingly calm, with ethereal features and kind eyes surrounded by a warm glow that seemed to blanket all three of them. *Angels!* I couldn't believe it! I was awestruck by their grand presence that seemed to fill the hallway.

Before we could speak, they picked up the wheelchair and carried my husband down the stairs to safety. I followed close behind.

When we reached the street, I checked to make sure my husband was okay. Then we both looked around, wanting to thank our heavenly rescuers. But they had already vanished.

My husband looked at me. "They were angels, weren't they?"

I blinked back tears and nodded, overwhelmed that I had been in the presence of God's angels.

King of the River
Jimmy Edwards

INDIAN SUMMER IN MONTANA—the perfect day to float down the Clark Fork River and catch a few trout. My buddy Mike, a Chicago native, had been bugging me to take him on a river float, so he and his sister-in-law, Lagora, met me by the Petty Creek Bridge, about thirty minutes north of Missoula.

As we put my Hyde drift boat, loaded down with fishing rods and other equipment, into the water, I explained that I'd been on thousands of trips down the river in the past as a professional guide and fisherman. "I've never gotten anyone wet," I said. "I could do this trip in my sleep." Even navigating Devil's Tongue, a whitewater chute a few miles down the river, didn't scare me. To say I felt confident about my abilities and knowledge was an understatement.

I realized I'd probably brought too much gear, all of it thrown haphazardly into the boat. The afternoon was getting away from us. I wanted my friends to see as much of the river with the sun dancing across it as possible. There was no time to change into my waders. I just pulled them on over my blue jeans, which I'd never done before.

I was more concerned about Lagora, who was wearing a big, heavy pair of waders. "You need to take those off," I told her. "If anything happened and you got pitched into the river, those waders would fill up with water and drag you right under."

Lagora removed her waders, and we were off. As we floated along, I pointed out otters and giant rocks. I identified trees and birds. I filled my passengers' heads with fishing jargon as I tied a mahogany dun to each of our lines and tried to outsmart the trout. When we weren't fishing, we looked up at that big Montana sky, following the clouds that rolled in.

Eventually we pulled over to the bank for a pit stop. Those clouds overhead had made the temperature drop. "Is there any extra gear?" Lagora asked as she munched on a sandwich. "I'm getting chilly."

I whipped off my favorite Sims Windstopper vest. "Here you go," I said. I dug around the storage area of the boat until I found an old fleece vest. "This will do for me," I said, putting it on. The zipper was a bit buggy, but who cared? I could make do with anything.

We pushed off again for the final leg of our journey. A crisp fall breeze made a late afternoon appearance, letting me know the sun would be setting soon. We tried to coax a big brown or giant pike from the river, then proceeded on toward Devil's Tongue. Some fishermen refused to tackle it in a drift boat full of gear. But I'd never had problems.

We heard roaring water crashing against the rocks before we saw the chute. "Brace yourselves!" I called out. "We're heading into some rapids."

I used my oars to navigate around the worst of it. I glanced about the boat. *We really do have a lot of gear*, I thought. It wasn't even secured properly. *Too late now!* The river pulled me straight into the mouth of the chute. I didn't fight it. I had a better idea. *Mike's in front,* I thought, stifling a laugh. *I'll get him soaked.*

The boat jerked up and down like a seesaw. Cold buckets of water slapped into us, soaking not just Mike but all three of us. The waves were enormous. Adrenaline raced through me. Suddenly the seesaw stopped: the front of the boat was up in the air, and the back was sinking into the river. We'd taken on too much water! A huge rock jutted out of the water on our right. Just beyond it was calm water. "Everyone grab on to that big rock and make your way out of the rapids!"

I shouted, pointing toward our salvation. Mike was so shocked he could barely swim over. Lagora helped him onto the rock.

Back in the boat, my rods and equipment disappeared under the water. The boat sank deeper and deeper with me in it. I let go when it went under. Now it was just me, in the middle of the rapids. *My waders!* They weighed me down. But my bulky blue jeans made them almost impossible to get off. I struggled out of them with the rushing water sounding like a freight train in my ears. I floated with the current, my heart pounding, my body cold and numb and exhausted. Just as I was getting my bearings, I was pulled under. I fought my way to the surface. My waders were floating beside me, still attached to my shoulder by a strap!

I fumbled to release them, but the strap was covered by my fleece vest. I yanked on the zipper frantically as I was pulled under again by the weight of my water-filled waders. That buggy zipper meant to be the end of me! This was it.

Everything under the surface was duller, heavier. Time moved in slow motion. I popped up again, long enough for my burning lungs to take a gasp of air before going back down. In my delirium I thought that if I sank to the river bottom I could push up with my feet—but the bottom was forty-five feet below. I fought with the zipper, my body aching and throbbing, as the river pulled me deeper under.

And then I saw them, shining underwater in the darkness like two beacons: a pair of blue eyes. They were big and beautiful. A woman's eyes. *An angel's eyes,* I thought. They were kind and calm. My aching muscles relaxed. I was as peaceful as the gaze that penetrated me. The darkness underwater was replaced by brilliant white light. Suddenly I was clear-headed, able to focus. An image of my three children flashed through my mind. *I have to make it for them,* I thought. A burst of energy surged through me. I tugged on the zipper of my vest one last time—I was free!

I got the vest and the waders off and made my way back up to the surface. I struggled toward the bank until finally I crawled to land and passed out. Later, after a rescue team arrived, a woman who had been camping near Devil's Tongue lifted a cup of hot cocoa to my lips. "I called 911 and told them you drowned," she said. "You went under so many times, and that last time you were below the surface for so long."

My friends were shaken up but not hurt. They requested a less dramatic adventure next time. And me? I changed after that trip. My faith is stronger, I cherish every moment with my kids, and I'm kinder to loved ones and strangers alike. I gained a new respect for the river, preparing and planning every trip, no matter how often I've traveled it before.

I made mistakes on the river that day—potentially fatal ones. Luckily I had a guide to save me.

Saved by Angels

Bruce Van Natta

THE EVENTS OF NOVEMBER 16, 2006, changed my life forever. I will never forget what happened on that day; it will be with me as long as I live. Many of us can think of defining moments in our lives. Sometimes they are marked by tragedy, sometimes by triumph; rarely are they marked by both. But this was one of those uncommon days.

I was a self-employed diesel mechanic who performed on-site repairs. On this particular day, I was at a customer's shop about forty-five minutes from my home. The vehicle that I was working on was a Peterbilt logging truck. I had worked nearly twelve hours that day in order to complete my portion of the engine repairs, and I was just finishing up. I had been working with the driver of the truck, and after we put the engine back together, we began checking it over and testing the repairs. The rest of the truck had not been completely reassembled, but the driver planned on finishing the remaining work the next day.

I began to put my tools back into the toolboxes on my service truck as the semi engine ran up to operating temperature. The driver asked me, since I was there, if I could also diagnose a non-related oil leak before I left. I was in a hurry to get home, but I thought this task would only take a few extra minutes.

I rolled underneath the front of the truck feet-first on a creeper and started wiping off the area that appeared to be leaking. All of a sudden, the truck fell off the jack and crushed me against the concrete floor. The front axle had come down across my midsection like a blunt guillotine, the five to six tons of weight nearly cutting me in two. From my viewpoint, it looked and felt like I was cut in half as there was less than an inch of air space between the axle and the cement on my left side and about two inches of space on my right side. In a moment of panic, I tried to bench-press the ten-thousand-plus-pound mass off of me. When reality set in, I realized the gravity of the situation and called out "God help me!" twice.

I listened as the truck driver called 911. When he got off the phone, I begged him to shut the engine off because the vibration of the engine directly above me was transmitted through the axle and right into my body. Small amounts of blood started to come out of my mouth when I tried to talk. I watched as the driver repositioned the jack and raised the truck up off of my body. I was scared of it falling again, and I wanted to get out from underneath that truck in the worst way. The large chrome front bumper was just behind my head, and I reached both hands back and grabbed the bottom of it. It took all the strength I had for me to pull myself far enough so that my head was out from underneath the truck. I stayed conscious long enough to see the first person who responded to the 911 call.

The next thing I remember, I was at least ten or fifteen feet above the scene, looking down at myself and the whole situation. The strangest part about my "out of body" experience was feeling like I was just an observer to what was happening below me. It was as if I was watching a movie. I felt no emotion, only a sense of peace. I heard one man say to another that there was no way I was going to live, and it didn't matter to me one way or another. From my viewpoint, I could tell that my body was still mostly under the truck, but that my head was sticking out from under the front bumper. I could see that my eyes were closed and that my head was turned toward the driver's side of the truck. The man I had been working with was on his knees above me, crying and patting me on the head as he was talking to me. I could hear and understand every word he said.

The most incredible thing wasn't that I was having this experience; it was what I saw next. On either side of my body were twin angels, also on their knees, facing the front of the truck. From my vantage point, I was watching from above and behind them. The driver of the truck was over six feet tall, yet the heads of these angels were at least a foot and a half taller than his head. If they would have been standing up, I think they would have been close to eight feet tall. They had very broad shoulders and looked to be extremely muscular. There were no wings. Each angel had positioned his arms under the truck, angled toward my body. The angels had ringlets of long blond hair that fell at least halfway down their backs. They were wearing white or ivory robes. It was hard to tell the exact color because of a yellowish light surrounding each angel. They seemed to be glowing.

I also noticed that the fabric of their robes was very unusual. It was a woven material, but the thread size was very large, like miniature rope. It appeared to be very strong and durable. The angels never moved; they were as steady as statues. I couldn't see their faces because my view was from behind them, but from what I could see, they were identical in appearance.

More people began to come to the scene of the accident, and I continued to watch from above. A red-haired emergency worker arrived, talked to someone, and walked up to the driver's side of the truck. She moved the truck driver out of the way and asked him my name. She held my head, patted my cheeks, and told me to open my eyes. She kept repeating herself in a loud voice, and the next thing I knew, I was no longer watching from above but was looking at her through my own eyes. She told me that it was very important for me to keep my eyes open. I thought about what she was saying and realized that I had been out of my body until she got me to open my eyes. This made me believe that what she said was true and important; I was on the verge of death! Then I thought about the angels that I had seen. I looked to where they had been, but I could see nothing there now with my human eyes.

As I lay there, I heard a voice in my head telling me to shut my eyes and just give up. When I did shut my eyes, the incredible pain stopped, and I could feel my spirit drifting away from my body again.

But there was also another voice; this one was quieter, more like a whisper. It told me that if I wanted to live, I would have to fight, and it would be a hard fight. It was almost as if the red-haired emergency worker could hear that voice too, because she then asked me what I had to fight for. All I could think of was my wife and four children.

These two voices, or conflicting thoughts, volleyed back and forth in my head. If you think of that old cartoon with the devil on one shoulder and an angel on the other, you can use it to picture what was happening. The louder voice that was telling me to give up and die was not from God, but the whispering voice that told me to fight was. As always, the devil promotes death and God promotes life. It's also interesting to note that God will always tell us the truth. He warned me that it was going to be a hard fight, and it has been. It seems that, most often, the right choice is not the easiest one.

I was transported by ambulance to a local hospital and then flown to our state's largest trauma center. I stayed awake the whole time, fighting to hang on and refusing to close my eyes. When the emergency doctors starting scanning my body, they were astounded.

There were so many injuries that they couldn't decide where to start or what to do. They had given me several units of blood, but it just kept leaking out into my stomach cavity. As they were sliding me back in for another CAT scan, everything started to go dim for me, and although I hadn't been able to talk for quite a while, the Lord gave me the strength to tell them that I was going to die and that they had to do something right now. The doctors told me several weeks later that, as soon as I said that, both numbers in my blood pressure reading dropped out of sight! They removed me from the machine and rushed me to the operating room.

The doctors operated on me only long enough to reattach the veins and arteries that had been severed. The head trauma surgeon had been called in from home. He told my family that in all his years as a trauma doctor, he had never seen anybody so badly traumatized who was still alive. He told my family that he was going to cross his fingers and wait at least six hours to see if I was still alive before he would operate on me again. My wife told him that he could cross his fingers but that she and others were going to pray for my life.

The prayers were answered, and the doctors resumed operating on me the next morning. They had to remove most of my small intestine and perform various other repairs to combat my several internal injuries. They decided not to do anything with the two vertebrae that were spider cracked in my spine; they would try to let them heal on their own.

The next thing I remember was waking up a few weeks later. I had had three operations during that time, and my wife never left my side. The night of my accident, she was at our children's school for parent-teacher conferences. When she got home and heard the news, she dropped to her knees and turned it all over to God, knowing that He would give her the strength to get through whatever lay ahead. The only thing that she took with her to the hospital that night was her Bible.

To everyone's amazement, I was sent home a little more than a month after the accident. But after a few days, I was back in the hospital with severe complications stemming from a damaged pancreas and spleen.

I spent a few more weeks in the hospital, but I got out long enough to spend the Christmas holidays at home. Then I returned to the hospital. This cycle repeated itself a few times, before the doctors decided that they would have to perform another major operation.

They had to remove another section of my small intestine that had died and was almost completely closed off. We were told that an adult needs a minimum of one hundred centimeters of small intestine to be able to live by eating food. I was already down to this critical minimum length before my fourth operation, and then they removed more. Before the accident, I weighed over 180 pounds; three months afterward, I was already down to 126 pounds because of the inadequate amount of small intestine left in my body.

Nine months after the accident, I was at the hospital for some tests in preparation for my fifth operation. While performing the procedure, the radiologist and his supervisor found that I now had at least one-third, or around two hundred centimeters, of small intestine. (We have since found out that there is actually even more, about one-half, or three hundred centimeters.) When they looked at the doctors' notes from the previous operations, they found that they had recorded a total length of one hundred centimeters several times during the first three operations and this was before removing more in my fourth operation. It was hard for them to believe that the head of the trauma department and other doctors had made multiple mistakes on my chart and in their calculations, since these men are at the top of their field and have a spotless reputation.

Upon further research, the before and after X-rays and CAT scans show that they didn't make any mistakes. Something had happened that the doctors couldn't explain. Intestines had come out of nowhere but how?

What the doctors didn't know was that several people had been praying for me and that a man named Bruce Carlson had flown in from New York to pray over me after my fourth operation. This man has often displayed the gift of healing, and the Lord has used him to heal hundreds of people. The Bible tells us that we, as Christians, are to pray with expectation for sick people to be healed. Sometimes God chooses not to heal someone in the method or time-table that we want, but that is His decision, not ours. As believers, we are told to pray with expectation, and the results are up to God. When Bruce Carlson prayed over me that day, he put one of his palms on my forehead. He asked the Lord to answer all of the prayers that people had been praying for me, and when he said that, I felt something like electricity flowing from his palm and into my body.

He prayed for my small intestine to supernaturally grow in length in the name of Jesus, and as he did, I could feel something wiggle around inside my stomach. Of course, I didn't know for sure that my intestine had lengthened until the radiologist told me a few months later.

It has now been a few years since my accident and I have almost no side effects or physical problems at this point, despite the tremendous amount of trauma that my body experienced. My weight has also climbed back up to about 170 pounds, thanks to the added intestine. Now that more time has passed, the doctors have also told me just what a miracle it is that I am alive. They said that, because of the arteries and veins that were completely severed, I should have bled to death internally in about eight to ten minutes or less. But it was over two and a half hours from the time that I was injured until they started to operate on me! They also told me that according to an extensive study that had been done on the subject a few years before my accident, I am the only case that doctors know of in which a person has had major arteries severed in five places in the chest and still lived. All other cases have come in dead on arrival. I told my doctors that I know why I am still alive: I got to see the two angels that saved my life!

Angel in the House

Bonnie Wilson

BY NOW THE KIDS AND I were used to Steve's being on the road. His trucker job sometimes kept him away for a month at a time. We were glad to have him home for Christmas, but just after New Year's he had to go out on the road again. Steve loved his job. But that didn't make it any easier for him to say good-bye.

"I think about you when I'm out there," he said as he hugged me at dawn that January morning. "I pray for God to watch over you all. Sometimes it doesn't feel like enough."

"Don't you worry yourself," I said.

The kids and I quickly fell into our daily routine without Steve. But nights were another story. One cold Monday evening I got ready for bed. I imagined Steve driving along a stretch of roadway. I wished he was home with us instead.

I walked into the girls' room. Kimberly, age ten, and Carrie, age eight, were ready for bed. "How about I sleep in here tonight?" I asked.

"What about Ray?" said Carrie.

Their brother Ray's room was right next to the girls' with a connecting door between the two. *Yes, Ray should be in here with us.* What a strange thought. Ray was twelve, almost a teenager. He would not want any part of this. *Ask him.*

I stuck my head through the doorway. Ray was sitting up in bed. "We're all sleeping in here tonight," I said. "Why don't you join us? Come on, it'll be fun."

Ray thought about it. "Okay," he said. "If you want."

The four of us got settled in. "This is kind of nice, all of us together like this, isn't it?" The kids and I traded jokes and talked about what Steve might be doing. He'd called home earlier from a truck stop in Missouri. *Lord, keep him safe on the road*, I prayed. No matter where he was, I knew Steve's prayer was a mirror of mine: "Lord, keep my family safe at home." I said good night to the kids and shut off the light.

It was still dark when I woke up. Someone was shaking me. "Kim?" I murmured. "Go back to sleep."

Kim shook me again and pointed at the open door to Ray's room. I sat up. I rubbed my eyes, straining to see. Something was in the doorway. *What is that?* In the dim light I could make out a tall figure, with wings. The figure had one hand on the door frame. The other motioned us out. An angel was telling us to leave the house? Why?

I craned my neck to look past the angel into Ray's room. The walls were alive with an orange glow. *Fire?* I couldn't see any smoke. I didn't smell smoke. But the room was definitely on fire. And then I realized: the angel was holding back the flames and smoke.

"Kids, wake up! We have to get out." The kids jumped out of bed, grabbed blankets, and we all hurried outside.

A policeman met us at the door. A fire truck came screaming up the street. When I looked back at the house, I saw the kids' bedrooms in flames. The windows exploded and the fire roared out. *We barely made it*, I thought.

The kids and I went to my parents' house, and I left word with Steve's trucking company about what had happened and where we were. "Thank goodness you were awake," my mom said as we got the kids settled down.

"Kim woke me," I said. "She pointed at…" I looked over at Kim, already asleep. Had she seen the angel too? Could I have imagined it? "Kim pointed at the fire," I finished.

The next morning we learned that the fire had started in the light switch on the porch, traveled up through the wires, and burned through the wall in Ray's room. That's where the flames had first appeared. I drove over to take a look. The kids' rooms were gutted, the walls black and charred. The ceiling had burned away, leaving a few beams and the roof above it. Nothing was salvageable. Then I saw our Bible, the pages unburned. I took it with me when I left.

When I got back to my parents' house, Kim was waiting to talk to me. "Mom?" she asked. "Did you see anything strange in our room last night when you woke up?"

My heart beat a little faster, but I didn't want to influence Kim's story with my own. "What did you see?"

"I think I saw an angel," Kim said, "standing in the doorway holding back the fire."

I gave Kim a hug. "I saw it too."

Steve drove home from Missouri without stopping. I threw my arms around him. "I'm just sorry I wasn't here to protect you. I meant to ask," he said, "what was Ray doing sleeping in the girls' room?"

I remembered my strange urge to ask Ray to sleep with us.

"Thank God," said Steve. "He heard my prayers."

Steve's back on the road now. But I sleep just fine. It's still hard for us to say good-bye, but Steve and I both know he doesn't have to be at home for us to be safe. Our prayers are always enough.

Fireproof

Paul Archambault

"THE ROAD IS IMPASSABLE," the fire chief warned us. "You'll never make it." We'd pulled up next to his firefighting team in a snow of ashes, staring at Highway 39, the only route into the San Gabriel Canyon of Angeles National Forest, thirty miles northeast of Los Angeles. Thick smoke and bright orange flames roared from the trees beyond. My partner, John, and I, deputies for the Los Angeles Sheriff's Department, exchanged glances. "We've got no choice," I muttered. I wheeled our SUV around the roadblock, into the jaws of the fiery beast.

The firefighters had their job to do. We had ours: to save seventy-year-old Sigrid Hopson. She lived in a remote cabin in the woods and had stubbornly refused to evacuate. Refused, that is, until the massive forest fire reached her house. She'd placed a frantic call, begging for help. John and I both knew her. We couldn't leave her there.

We peered through the soot on the windshield, picking our way through plumes of black smoke and flames that danced across the road. "Watch out!" John shouted. I swerved to avoid a chunk of burning tree that exploded in front of us. The SUV's air conditioner was on full blast, but still the crackling heat singed the hair on my arms. I pulled on work gloves so the steering wheel wouldn't burn my hands.

The stench of burning rubber, plastic, and paint filled the cab. "My God," John gasped, "the dashboard's starting to melt!" The next instant, the engine stuttered, starved of oxygen. I kept nursing the accelerator. Somehow we chugged on.

Then we reached "the Narrows." The road became one lane, with a granite wall on one side and a three-hundred-foot drop on the other. At the bend of the road stood a stark reminder of how dangerous this stretch was even in normal conditions—a five-foot-high white cross, a memorial for someone who had veered over the edge. It wasn't hard to do.

I eyed the smoke and flames rising from the canyon. Any minute now, we wouldn't be able to pass. We'd be trapped. The firefighters' warnings echoed in my ears. *Last chance to turn around.*

The cross made me think of Mrs. Hopson. I couldn't let her become another memorial. We'd have to risk it.

Sweat streamed down our faces. Sparks blew across the fiery sky. We could barely breathe. Finally we reached a little parking area and spotted the goat path that led to Mrs. Hopson's cabin. "Wish me luck," John said, jumping out. He disappeared into the smoke. Moments later, a flaming tsunami rolled across the road ahead. We were as good as trapped.

I radioed our command post at the base of the canyon. "The fire's surrounded us. Send a helicopter. Or a water-dropping plane to clear a path . . ."

"Can't," came the commander's crackly voice. "Updrafts are too strong. Flying in isn't possible."

Then the radio died.

Where's John? I wondered, fighting off the thought that I was the only one alive up here. Could he even see? Breathe? The ground itself was aflame!

I was ready to jump into the firestorm and find him. You never abandoned your partner. All at once, a movement on the trail caught my eye. John appeared through the smoke, carrying a frail, frightened, white-haired lady—Mrs. Hopson. He put her in the rear seat, and dove in front. "Let's go," he said, choking.

I turned around quickly and headed into the deadly smoke. It was our only chance, and not much of one at that. I could barely see the road. What would happen when we reached that three-hundred-foot drop?

Near the Narrows, the smoke enveloped us completely. I inched the SUV forward into darkness, waiting for that sickening moment when I'd feel the tires slip and we'd plunge off the edge. Would anyone even know how we died?

Then, suddenly, the billowing clouds of smoke parted. A blinding light filled the vehicle. Were we burning up? I recognized a shape, glowing fluorescent white in front of us, as if illuminated from within, like a beacon. The cross! Flames licked at shrubs around its base, yet it wasn't burning. *I'm here to protect you*, it seemed to say.

Guided by the glow of the cross, we rolled safely through the Narrows and on down Highway 39. Close to the bottom, the tires melted completely. We emerged from the worst of the smoke and coasted to a stop—just yards from the roadblock. The firefighters looked shocked. "We were sure you were dead," the chief said, while his crew attended to Mrs. Hopson.

"It was like someone was watching over us," I told John later as we gulped down water. Neither of us could figure out how that wooden cross was still standing while everything around it burned. Or how our half-melted SUV had even made it out.

"We *should* be dead," John said, shaking his head.

The fire burned for thirteen days, torching twenty-one thousand acres. After it was extinguished, John and I drove back up the mountain, in a new

SUV, to see if Mrs. Hopson's place had survived. The forest along the way was nothing but ash. The cross at the Narrows was singed but somehow still standing.

Finally we reached the start of the goat trail winding between the charred skeletons of trees. John and I climbed out. The trail itself was indistinguishable from the rest of the black, scorched earth, save for a line of tiny patches of healthy green grass, evenly spaced, leading from the old woman's cabin. John's footprints, where he had carried Mrs. Hopson to safety.

Catch of the Day

Bill Logue

IT WAS LABOR DAY WEEKEND. I was motoring across Lake Eufaula with my kids and friends George and Stanley. The kids laughed and pointed at fish jumping, birds sailing in the air, and frogs by the dozens leaping from the shore. But what they laughed at the hardest were the boats going full throttle and then hitting a sandbar. *Bang!* Each time it happened the boat would stop dead in its tracks.

The drought had taken its toll on the lake, and hazards increase when the water goes down. I couldn't help grimacing at the sight. It was dangerous. I knew my wife was back on shore watching and praying. I figured she was asking God to send an angel. I believed in prayer, but I wasn't sure if I believed in angels. While I figured they existed in heaven, I wasn't convinced angels intervened in our lives here on earth. My motto had always been that God helps those who help themselves.

The kids wanted to go see the sandbar for themselves, so we took Stanley's pontoon out. As we pulled up onto the sandbar they scrambled out. "Be careful and stay together!" I warned. The water levels ascended from ankle-deep to knee-high.

We weren't there long when the wind kicked up. "Come on, kids, get back to the pontoon!" I yelled.

As I turned back, I noticed that the waves had dislodged the boat from the sandbar and it was drifting away. *No problem*, I thought, as I dove into the water, surprised at how hard the waves were pounding me. Though I swam fast, the boat continued to float farther away.

The wind and waves grew stronger, and the battle grew harder, as I drifted away. I lost sight of the kids. Halting mid-stroke, I searched the horizon, but saw nothing except whitecaps. Then a flash of red...Stanley's ball cap! I found my target and swam toward it.

Within seconds, I was exhausted. Fighting the whitecaps grew harder. Waves sapped more of my strength with every stroke. *What am I going to do?* I worried.

No longer able to fight the waves, I felt myself being pulled under. Instinct told me to hit the lake bottom hard and push myself to the surface. My feet sank into mud and I bent my knees and pushed. Kicking my legs and feet as fast as I could, I surfaced to find I still had no strength. Staying above the water was impossible.

One more deep breath and down again.

As I descended the second time, panic engulfed me. I had less energy now, and realized that I might not return to the surface again. Feeling mud between my toes, I pushed off and kicked. Breaking the surface, I gasped for air, catching a glimpse of the sky, but I knew I wouldn't be able to stay on the surface.

One more deep breath. My last?

My heartbeat pounded in my head. My chest was about to explode as I sank deeper into the dark, murky water. The water weighed heavy on my shoulders, pushing me farther and farther down. My strength gone, I felt the bottom of the lake under my feet again.

I'm done, I thought. *Is this how it will end?*

All at once I felt my knees bend, and with unimaginable strength I pushed, propelled through the water by some invisible hands. I torpedoed upward so high above the surface that my arm hooked the side of a boat and I collapsed in exhaustion.

"Hold on!" someone yelled as the boat motored toward shore.

Back on land, the man in the boat towered over me. "Beau Chandler," he said, shaking my hand. Beau explained that he'd been at home about to watch a football game when he felt restless. Giving up on the game, he went fishing but the waves soon pounded his boat, rocking it hard. He was about to go home when he saw a man and three children waving like crazy and pointing to a man in a red hat. He shot over there, thinking the man needed help. But the man in the red hat pointed toward the open water.

"I didn't see anyone," Beau explained. "I slowed the motor as I approached the area, but no one was there. All at once your arm lunged out of the water and latched over the side of the boat."

With me hanging on to the side of the boat, he trolled over to the man in the red hat, Stanley, asking if he was all right. "Yeah, but I'm sure glad you showed up. I was tiptoeing just to keep my head out of the water."

That's when Beau looked down at his depth finder and realized the man was tiptoeing in twelve feet of water.

All my life people have told me that angels were around us, but I never thought much about them until I came in contact with three. One placed his hand under Stanley's toes to keep his head out of the water. The second propelled me out of the dark depths of the lake. The third, well, the third introduced himself as Beau Chandler, and I was his catch of the day.

Come Back to Me

Stuart Reininger

A MAN STRODE TOWARD ME across the dock in Charleston, South Carolina. I didn't recognize him, but he sure seemed to know me.

"Stuart!" he said, clapping a heavy hand on my shoulder. I only had a second to look at his face before another meaty paw clasped me to his breast in a rib-cracking hug. "It's me, Fred. From Bequia. Don't you remember? You saved my life!"

Saved a life? *That* I would remember! The only saved life I knew of was my own. A life I almost lost as a hopelessly drunk sailor. Which made me think twice. I *did* know a Fred once back in those days. And it was in Bequia. But he wasn't this guy. This man was clean shaven, dressed in immaculate whites. On his shoulders gleamed the four stripes of a yacht captain. I glanced again at the elegant boat docked next to my own. But that didn't help me ID the man in front of me.

"Yes, I'm her skipper," he said. "And I wouldn't have this job—I wouldn't even be here—if it wasn't for you, Stu. Do you really not remember me at all?"

"I knew a Fred," I said. "But you're not...you can't be..."

I tried to imagine the smartly dressed captain in front of me with a dirt-flecked beard that hung down to his waist. That was the Fred I knew, a hulking man with an equally filthy and long-reaching ponytail. That Fred had no yacht. He lived on an old, wooden sailboat, wandering around the Caribbean and Bahamas. His life, like mine, was the sea.

We shared another passion: drinking as much and as often as possible. The last time I'd seen Fred, in Bequia a couple of years earlier, he'd been out of work for a long time. I reassured myself that I wasn't as bad off as him. I, at least, could sober up long enough to get a boat from one place to another. I had no idea how Fred supported himself or paid for his liquor. How could *that* guy have turned his life around?

The new Fred nodded, as if he knew what I was thinking. "Same guy," he assured me. "Hard to believe, isn't it? Now, do you remember the last time we saw each other?"

It was off-season. Fred's boat and mine were among only a few in the anchorage that night. The two of us pulled off a gargantuan bender at a dockside gin mill. It was after midnight when I stumbled toward the door.

Fred was still in the process of hoisting himself off his stool. On either side of him, ready to grab him if he fell, were the bartender and a waitress. Neither of them looked big enough to support him. But what really struck me was the look on their faces: a mixture of pity, disgust, and loathing. *That's what they think of Fred,* I thought. *Because he's a drunk.* They both turned and noticed me standing at the door. They looked at me with the same expression.

I hurried as fast as I could to my dinghy, revved the engine, and motored out to where my boat floated. I wanted to get as far away from Fred and those judgmental faces as I could. A haze had come in from the sea while we'd been at the bar. A near full moon cast an ethereal glow over the water. My boat appeared a ghostly gray ahead of me. I looked over my shoulder at Fred's boat on the water. The tranquility of the scene cut through my alcoholic haze. I was transfixed. The waves lapped in the moonlight like a familiar lullaby. I remembered why I'd become a sailor to begin with. I wanted to live my life surrounded by God's work.

So why was I spending most of my time blind to it? What was I doing to myself? Maybe Fred was beyond hope, but I wasn't. Not yet.

That night wasn't the last time I had a drink, but it was the start of the big change in me, a change that eventually led me to quit. It was an important night for me, and Fred would always be part of it. But Fred knew nothing about it. What did he mean about *my* saving *his* life?

"All this time I've wanted to thank you," he said, grabbing my hand and giving it a vigorous shake. "You disappeared before I had a chance to that night. But I never forgot you."

"Thank me for what?"

"For being my angel!" he said.

"You've got the wrong angel, dude," I said. "I don't know what you're talking about!"

"Listen. After I left the bar that night, I started up my dinghy to get back to my boat. I got a little ways out. Then my engine quit."

It was every sailor's nightmare. The water in the anchorage in a place like Bequia is full of strong currents and wind, all pushing out to the open sea. It was too strong to row against. A sailor whose engine quit would quickly find himself floating fast out into the open Caribbean, too far out to swim back. Nobody would see him again until fishermen found his mummified body floating somewhere at sea.

"I drifted right past my boat," he said. "I knew I couldn't make it back—rowing or swimming. I remember calling out as I drifted past the headland of the anchorage. I was sure I was done for. I felt calm. And sober. And I prayed for the first time in a long time. I prayed mostly for you, Stu. I prayed you wouldn't end up like me.

"Then, out of nowhere, your dinghy came tearing around the headland with a humongous white bow wave—like you were throwing open the very gates of paradise! I had never been so happy to see anyone in my life. Next thing I knew, you had tossed me a line and were towing me back to my boat."

"You saw *me* in the dinghy?" I said.

"Didn't I?" Fred said. For the first time he looked unsure of himself. "I guess I couldn't actually see your face. All I could see was the stern light as you towed me. The haze made a halo around your head. It had to be you. When you left me at my boat, I asked you to come aboard. You didn't answer. But a few seconds later, when you'd motored a few yards away, you called over your shoulder, 'Come back to me.' I always wanted to ask you what you meant by that."

A chill ran down my spine as I realized who had really spoken to Fred that night. He was rescued by an angel, all right. We both were.

The Guardian of Highway 277

Cynthia Bilyk

CLICK! I BUCKLED MY SON, Gregory, into his car seat and hopped into the driver's side. Gregory had a pediatrician appointment, and I was running behind schedule. I glanced at the dashboard clock. *Please don't let us be late.* I followed the speed limit, going not a mile over or under, and headed for the highway.

Since the Eagle Ford shale oil boom, the roads near my west Texas town were busy. Highway 277 used to be wide-open for miles. Now it was packed with eighteen-wheelers. It got a little crowded on that tiny, two-lane Texas highway. I said a prayer every time I got on it. Just in case.

As I came up on the ramp, I pressed on the brake to yield for a van. *Lord, look after us.* I pulled out behind it. *Come on, buddy.* He was doing fifty. The speed limit was seventy. The oncoming lane was clear of traffic, and my foot itched to hit the accelerator so I could pass this pokey driver, but the sight of my son in the backseat reminded me why I said all those highway prayers. I had to do my part to keep us safe as well.

When the van slowed down to a crawl, I craned my head to look around it—only to see another slowpoke in front of him. *Ugh!* Soon, traffic halted completely. While I waited to get moving, I glanced at the oncoming lane. A car was stopped there too—a sedan. Stopped for no reason I could see. A second car eased to a gentle stop behind the sedan. He had plenty of room to leave a safe distance between them. Maybe the sedan was stalled, and the other was coming to the rescue?

The road ahead curved into a small hill, and with all the traffic in my own lane, I couldn't see a thing. I was stuck until the situation cleared up.

I glanced at the clock, wondering how late we were going to be. With my eyes off the road, I sensed something shining outside. I leaned into the steering wheel and looked up.

Overhead, behind the two stopped cars in the other lane, was a tiny pinprick of light. I squinted, and before my eyes it burst into a being composed of pure, white light. He towered above the highway and glowed with such intensity that I could not make out his face, only his strong shoulders and windblown hair. In one lightning-fast movement, he threw out his arms and unfurled his great wings over the entirety of the road, radiant as a blinding sun. The car behind the sedan in the other lane was gently nudged forward about a foot, suddenly repositioned nearer to the other car.

Before I could process what I was seeing, I heard screaming brakes. A truck was coming up fast behind that pair of unmoving cars. *He's going to hit them!* There was no time for the massive truck to stop. Just as the eighteen-wheeler passed beneath the glowing wings, the being vanished, snapping out of sight. The truck driver swerved off the road to avoid the cars. I held my breath as I watched it miss them by barely a foot.

No one was hurt, and traffic returned to normal. I looked back to the sky and replayed the vision over in my mind, imagining the terrible collision that could have occurred, how my son and I could have easily been caught in the wreckage—if not for the guardian of Highway 277.

We arrived late, with apologies, to the pediatrician, but we arrived safely, with all my just-in-case highway prayers answered.

CHAPTER 2

Angels in Our Midst

"It wasn't only me who made Sally well," Mamaw said. "Angels came and stood beside her all night. They guided my hands."

"Angels?" I said. "In the cabin last night? Really?"

"Of course, child," she said. "Angels are all over these old hills. They tend the plants, the trees, the roots—all the abundant vegetation God put in this part of His good, green earth."

She paused for a moment and looked me in the eye.

"You'll cotton to that idea soon enough. All it takes is faith and willingness to believe."

—DOUGLAS SCOTT CLARK

A Poultice and a Prayer
Douglas Scott Clark

MAMAW CLARK'S FADED HOMESPUN skirt trailed in the leaves as she walked along the creek at the forest's edge. Mamaw bent down beneath a cedar sapling and picked a handful of wild mint.

I took a handful myself and breathed in the sweet, cool scent.

"Don't go eating that there mint," Mamaw warned me. "It's still green as grass and will upset your innards. You can chew on a sprig, but don't swallow a drop or you'll be sorry."

Mamaw was a fourth-generation medicine woman. Her own mother was full-blooded Cherokee. Mamaw didn't talk about that much, because when she was growing up a lot of people looked down on her heritage. But she did learn all her mother's secrets about home remedies and nature's healing. Deep in the Great Smoky Mountains, professional medical care was scarce and expensive. People swore by Mamaw's cures, even if they didn't understand how they all worked.

I thought Mamaw could cure just about anything. She was a small woman, but even in her late sixties she held herself as straight as a young hickory sapling. She wore her long black hair, streaked with gray, up on her head, emphasizing the high cheekbones she'd inherited from her Cherokee ancestors.

I tried to pay close attention as she gathered up yarrow, sassafras, and spicewood for the sack I carried over my shoulder. What was so special about the plants she chose? How would they be used? What was her secret? It was a mystery to me.

Back home Mamaw settled in her rocking chair on the porch and set me to washing all the dirt from the roots and laying them out to dry in the sunlight. Once they were ready they'd go into her fixin's bag, the one she took with her when she went to heal people. I'd just about finished when Jim Reed, one of our neighbors from over in Hickory Holler, came up the path. He rarely made it over.

"How's Ida Mae and all your little ones?" Mamaw asked him.

"That's why I came to see you," Jim said. His face looked grim. "Our little Sally is powerful sick and ain't getting any better."

Mamaw frowned. "What signs is she showing? Is she eating or drinking at all?"

"She's wheezing like a steam engine and coughing her little head off," said Jim. "She can't keep a thing down. We don't know what to do."

Mamaw turned right to me. "Doug, get me my fixin's bag and put your shoes on. We're going with Jim."

I could hear Sally wheezing before we even got inside Jim's cabin. Ida Mae sat beside her bed, dipping a rag in cold spring water and pressing it to her face.

Mamaw examined Sally. She handed her mother some herbs and told her to boil them in water. "Cover the pot to make sure no wellness gets out," Mamaw said. She told me to gather firewood. "We're going to sweat the poison from her body."

All afternoon we sat with Sally, who was wrapped in blankets next to a roaring fire. She didn't seem to be getting any better, but surely Mamaw had some secret way of helping her. I waited and watched.

Late in the day, Mamaw sent me home to tell my father that we would be spending the night—and to collect stump water from a chestnut tree on my way back. This she used to make a poultice for Sally's chest. "Now we wait some more," she told me. "And, of course, pray."

As the sun set outside and the cabin grew dim, the only sound we heard was Sally's labored breathing. The moon rose and set. I struggled to stay awake, but the heat of the cabin made me so drowsy I dozed off.

I woke up just after daybreak. Sally was sleeping peacefully, her fever broken, and breathing as if she had never been sick at all.

But how had it happened? I had missed the secret!

Ida Mae wanted to do all of Mamaw's cooking and cleaning to repay her, but Mamaw refused. As we walked back home, I just came out and asked her how she had managed to make Sally well.

"It wasn't only me who made Sally well," Mamaw said. "Angels came and stood beside her all night. They guided my hands."

"Angels?" I said. "In the cabin last night? Really?"

"Of course, child," she said. "Angels are all over these old hills. They tend the plants, the trees, the roots—all the abundant vegetation God put in this part of His good, green earth." She paused for a moment and looked me in the eye. "You'll cotton to that idea soon enough. All it takes is faith and willingness to believe."

I had finally discovered Mamaw's secret. And of course, I believe.

The Angel in the Corner

Johanna Sturlini

"LET'S GO OUT TO THE AIRPORT," Chuck said as he gazed out the window. He was sitting in his favorite chair in the family room. The recliner was the only place where he was comfortable. "Just one last time," he continued, looking up at me. His face was gaunt. Chuck had lost so much weight since he had been diagnosed with lung cancer five months earlier.

I sighed. I knew I couldn't take him out to the airport. My husband loved planes and flying them. Sometimes we went to the airport just to watch the planes land and take off. Chuck loved that.

But it was a frigid January afternoon. I knew he couldn't handle that weather. Even if I could have lifted him!

"Not today, my darling," I said, sitting down on the couch right across from him. Chuck had his chair, and the couch was my seat. This was our room. It was the coziest spot in the house with its comfy seats, large windows, and family photos all around. During our thirty-nine years of marriage, this was the room where we discussed our two daughters, our jobs, and everything else under the sun. This was the room where we laughed. This was the room where we *lived*.

We rarely sat in the living room, and now Chuck's hospital bed was in there. The hospice workers had just moved it in, but he wasn't using it yet.

He just didn't feel ready. And I wasn't ready! But we both knew that time was coming.

I was determined to savor every moment I could with Chuck. But I couldn't stand to see him suffer. We had a few minutes of alone time before his nurse, Susan, came back to check on him. She was in the kitchen talking on the phone with his doctor.

I handed him a cup of coffee. It was a familiar routine. His hands looked frail as he took it. I regretted it almost immediately. The cup dropped to the floor. The hot liquid spread across the carpet as my eyes met his. Neither of us knew that he was too weak to grasp the mug.

"I'm not ready for this yet!" he said. "I've got too much to do!" Chuck was the one who took care of all of the details in our household, and he was filled with anxiety about how I would manage on my own once he was gone.

I had tried to be strong. When his doctor gave him six months to live, I didn't think I could handle it. But Chuck took the news like a champ. He put together a to-do list: "Fix the leak, teach Johanna to do the bills, get a new computer mouse, write letters to my daughters." That's just the kind of man he was. Always taking care of everyone else. He had a repairman service the furnace, and I heard him say, "If my wife calls you, please come right away, day or night." Chuck made him promise. "I'm dying," he told the man. "I need to know she'll be okay if the furnace goes out."

I considered it an honor to be the one taking care of him now. And I wasn't going to let him see my tears.

But we both knew that losing the use of his limbs was a sign that the end was close. Most cancer patients would have felt hopeless after that. But Chuck actually rose out of his recliner and sat down next to me on the couch. Using every ounce of strength he had, he lifted his arm. As soon as I saw him struggle, I helped him place it around my shoulder.

"I don't want to be a burden," he said.

"You're not, my love," I told him. I could see it was painful for him to sit there with his arm around me. I helped him back to his recliner.

"I don't want to not be able to move," he said. I looked into his eyes and felt so much love but also fear. I could not bear to watch him suffer. That was the hardest part.

Dear God, I prayed, *please have mercy on him. Please don't let my love suffer.*

Just then, Chuck put his hand to his forehead as if he were shielding his eyes from the sun.

"It's that light." He looked up toward the corner of the room, squinting. "There's a big angel standing in the corner."

"Where?" I asked. "Where is it?"

"Right there. Can't you see it?" Chuck said, pointing again to the corner.

I looked up. All I saw was an empty corner near the ceiling.

Chuck was not a man given over to fantasies. He had lived the life of a scientist. He was a Christian but also a pragmatist. This was the first angel he had ever mentioned.

He was calm and peaceful as he stared toward the corner. All the stress left his eyes. I could see his worries, and his to-do list, fade away.

"I wish it would turn down that light," Chuck said, matter-of-factly.

I gazed up again at the empty corner of our favorite room, stunned. Chuck was still shading his eyes.

Susan walked in. "I got your new prescription," she said. I wanted to ask Chuck more about the angel, but Susan was tending to him and I needed to clean up the spilled coffee.

By the time we had another moment alone, Chuck had fallen asleep, exhausted.

I never got the chance to ask Chuck about the angel in the corner, but I didn't need to. I knew that it was the answer to my prayer. Chuck and I wanted to take care of each other, and not let the other one suffer. I took his angel sighting as confirmation that Chuck was in God's hands. And that gave me peace even through my grief at his passing.

A Small Cloud of Witnesses

Evelyn Bence

WE BURIED MY MOTHER in a rural cemetery in northern Pennsylvania alongside my two brothers, who'd died before I was born. Without Mother, Dad seemed to lose his bearings. They'd been married sixty-three years, utterly dependent on each other. Dad never learned to cook. Mom never learned to drive. Dad was the handyman. Mom was the seamstress and laundress. Dad grew the vegetables. Mother froze them. But one thing they did together—church visitation. As a pastor, Dad believed in "calling" on his parishioners and prospects. And nearly always, Mother went with him.

Exactly a year after Mom's death, Dad left us to join her. We buried him next to her. My siblings and I tried to come to grips with the reality of our loss. Our parents were gone. I couldn't quite shake the sadness of it.

Before leaving town to head south down Route 15 to my own home in Virginia, I stopped at the local Mobil station to buy gas. Since I'd replaced the alternator at this very station on my trip north to see Dad through this transition just ten days earlier, the car had been grinding more and more with each start. "Could you please check the battery?" I asked.

"Low, precariously low," the mechanic said.

"It's the original, seven years old."

"Bad, very bad," he said, shaking his head.

"I'm on my way to Virginia, will I make it?" I asked.

He shrugged.

"Surely if I drive several hours before stopping, the juices will run. I've got jumper cables in the bottom of the trunk—not that I know how to use them."

"Good luck," he said.

Every spring for more than ten years my sister had driven my parents down this route to visit me. Dad insisted on making one particular stop, at a McDonald's on the south side of Williamsport, Pennsylvania. As if it were new information, he'd always say, "Best cup of coffee I ever had—right here."

Seeing the yellow arches now, I pulled into the lot. Before I turned the ignition off, in case I needed a jump, I backed into a parking place next to an empty handicapped space.

I locked the door, stepped toward the restaurant, and noted the neighborly smile of a dark-haired stranger in his thirties. He looked into my eyes and said a firm hello as if he knew me. I smiled back and walked past. He got into the white pickup truck parked next to my car on the driver's side.

When I came back out, that white pickup was gone. I slipped behind the wheel, turned the key, once, twice, three times, and heard the dry, impotent grind. I groaned. *Not even noon—hours till dark. Just need a jump. And someone who knows how.* I released the hood and got out of the car. Another white pickup had pulled in and parked on the other side of a small curb, perpendicular to and behind my car. A man in his forties sat in the driver's seat. *Maybe I'll ask him for help—after I open the hood.*

But before I got front and center, I heard a man's voice. "Do you need a jump?" he asked. I looked up, surprised. A third white pickup, driven by a woman, had pulled across the empty handicap space, nose to nose with my white Chevrolet.

"I think so," I said with grateful relief. "Do you have cables?" I was happy not to have to unload my trunk.

"Yes." Both the man and woman, maybe fifty years old, climbed out of the cab, teamed for mission. As my fingers fumbled to release the lever inside the grill, the woman nudged in and popped the hood. The man picked up jumper cables from the truck bed. We threw around key words: *positive, negative, red, black*. I'd heard that getting it wrong could be disastrous.

The man tentatively clipped metal to metal and sparks sputtered. He quickly disconnected. "Hmm. Maybe it's the other way," he said.

You aren't sure? This is trial and error?

I pointed at the plus sign on the right battery pole. "Positive to positive. I'm pretty sure." He reversed the connection. All looked calm. Nothing flashed bright.

"Okay, go ahead," he said. "Try it." *God, let it be right.*

Smooth turn. Quick catch. I reached into my purse, squeezed a ten-dollar bill in my palm, and returned to the front bumper. The man rolled up the cables. The woman urged me to stop at Walmart—down the road a few miles on the left—and replace the battery.

"Thank you," I said. "Please." I tried to hand them the ten.

They adamantly refused.

"Bless you," I said softly.

I quickly drove away, not thinking to look back—to see if they actually parked and went into the restaurant.

I didn't stop at Walmart and was on top of the next mountain before I puzzled about the help scene. My keen awareness of two men kindly perceived, each in a white truck. A third white pickup that I didn't see until after I'd heard the man's offer of help. Three men and a woman who seemed present on my homeward journey.

Who were those guys?

Then suddenly it felt like an uncanny representation of my four family members on the other side. A small crowd of heavenly witnesses watching, waiting, working. Aware of my grief and my physical need. Pulling for me on my journey.

To lighten my spirit on the rest of the trip, I imagined they even were having a little fun. Why did *he* connect positive to negative? Why did *she* drive the truck?

When I drive through central Pennsylvania, I still stop at that McDonald's. In the parking lot I'm always comforted by the memory of that "pastoral visit." Thank you, Mom. Thank you, Dad, for your care.

Whoopi at My Door

Steve Sjogren

DURING MY STAY IN THE ICU, my condition bounced from one state to another depending on the numbers of infections that I was dealing with and the complications that my body was fending off at the moment. I was not in an induced coma at this point, but physically I was still critical. My charts weren't looking good, and everyone on my medical team was concerned.

To make matters worse, I was far from the model patient. Unaware of how grave my situation was, I was fighting the efforts of the doctors and nurses at every step along the way: I was tired of being in the ICU and pleaded with my wife and others to grab each end of the bed and roll me out of the hospital. In addition, although I was given pain meds and sleeping meds, I had not been getting enough real sleep.

One morning at about two thirty, a stern-looking individual showed up at my doorway. Although she looked every bit the part of an ICU nurse, she stood out in several ways. She wore jeans, an oversized rainbow-colored sweater, and leather tennis shoes. Her hair was arranged in short dreadlocks. She looked a lot like folk singer Tracy Chapman. Her attitude was another matter—with her sharp and cutting remarks, she reminded me of Whoopi Goldberg. In short, she was rude.

When this nurse spoke, I listened. "Look, Mr. Sjogren," she stated firmly. "You are not cooperating with the healing process. If you don't start listening to the doctors and nurses and what they are trying to do, you aren't going to make it. It's that simple. You have to get on board with your own healing. I want to see an attitude adjustment in you, and I need to see it immediately. Do you hear me?"

With that, Nurse Whoopi turned and walked out of my room.

Wow, I thought. *I didn't realize how sick I was. I guess I'd better start being a better patient.* It was a good thought, but as I already confessed, I was not such a good patient. In the back of my mind, I entertained the idea of complaining to the hospital staff for sending such an in-your-face nurse.

The following night, Nurse Whoopi came by my room again—at two thirty. Precisely. I was wide awake. She gave me the same talk, word for word. *Okay*, I thought, *I get it already.* (I couldn't respond to her because I still had the ventilator tube down my throat.)

Nurse Whoopi came by my room yet a third night and gave me a third tongue-lashing—again at precisely two thirty. I didn't know if that was the time she came on duty and I happened to be the first bed on her list to visit or what. Each night she had been dressed in the same attire. Each night she had showed the same sassy attitude. Each night she had scared me.

By this third night, I thought, *I'm definitely going to be a good boy from now on. No more resisting the doctors and nurses. No more going crazy on them when I'm frustrated.* Surprise. My healing process began to improve from that night forward. Not long after, my ventilator was removed. The doctors thought I was making remarkable progress.

Once I was able to talk, one of the first things I asked about was the Whoopi Goldberg nurse. I described her in great detail: her dreadlocks, what she wore, the time she approached my room each night. The nursing staff was baffled. They told me there was no African American nurse on night shift duty during that time frame. Further, they said it was strictly against hospital policy to wear jeans on duty. I suggested that maybe she was a volunteer. The nursing staff said that there was no way a volunteer would be allowed in the ICU, especially at night.

It took me a couple of days to put the pieces together, but I finally figured out (with the help of a couple of friends who were interested in my recovery) that this must have been an angel who had visited me. Imagine that, an angel visiting little ol' me. I couldn't believe it. God loved me so much that He sent an actual angel from heaven to deliver a message to me at the precise moment when I absolutely needed it.

Since getting out of the hospital, several people have asked why God chose to send me an in-your-face angel. Why didn't I get a happy-go-lucky angel like Clarence in *It's a Wonderful Life*? That angel drank a little too much, was very human, and seemed to understand the human struggle. He was almost an uncle figure to George Bailey. Why didn't I get an angel with that sort of persona?

I can only conclude that a more direct approach was needed to get my attention. I am high-strung, so I needed a slightly hyper angel who would face me head-on. When God sent me Nurse Whoopi in blue jeans, He sent me exactly what I needed.

The Three Angels of Quito

Lina Prasad

FROM HER PERCH ATOP El Panecillo Hill, the 148-foot winged Virgin kept watch over the city of Quito. I lingered in her shadow long after my classmates had snapped their photos and left. When the coast was clear, I stuck a crumpled note into a crack at the base of the statue.

I'd scribbled five simple words across it, my heart's deepest desire: *Please send me an angel.*

It was week two of my college study abroad semester in Quito, Ecuador, six thousand miles from my home in Norway, and I was desperately homesick. Maybe I wasn't cut out for travel. In fact, at twenty-one, I still really didn't know *what* I was cut out for.

My parents were very logical, by-the-book people. They wanted me to pursue a practical career in economics or finance. While I studied numbers, I dreamed of becoming an artist, writing and painting, but I couldn't tell my parents. I didn't want to disappoint them.

Grandmother thought a semester in Quito might be just the thing—a complete change of scenery, a whole new culture, an opportunity to assert my independence. "Follow your heart," she always said. "God has so much in store for you." But I didn't know how to do that. Especially not in Quito, surrounded by American exchange students, unable to speak much Spanish with the locals. I couldn't even get a good night's sleep in this strange city. If ever I needed an angel, it was now. Not a giant angel like Quito's. A tiny angel would be enough for me.

I walked back to the tour bus, hoping no one had seen me leave my note. As we pulled out, I took one last look at the statue. A beam of sunlight caught on the metal, and Quito's angel sparkled back at me, as if to say, *Give our city a chance.* I guessed that she and my grandmother had something in common.

The next day I determined to get to know the city a little better. I visited a market with some girls from my class. We found stalls brimming with treasures. I bought a turquoise scarf for my mother and a carved wooden jewelry box for my aunt. Just as we got ready to leave, I noticed one last booth at the back. I had to see it. "Lina, where are you going?" one of my classmates called after me.

"I'll be right back," I said, not sure what drew my attention. *Follow your heart,* I reminded myself as I reached the run-down stall selling silver bangles, flasks, and rings. I was examining a bracelet when the vendor shook her head and placed something else in my hand instead. "*Para usted,*" she said with a cryptic smile. It was smooth and cool to the touch—a little guardian angel!

"For me?" I wished I could tell the woman just how perfect the angel was, but my Spanish was too poor for that. When I pulled out my wallet to pay, she waved me off.

"*Muchas gracias,*" I managed to whisper. I looped the angel on the chain around my neck. That night, for the first time since arriving in Quito, I slept like a baby.

Instead of going to class the next day, I followed my heart to Quito's historic center. I fingered the angel necklace and walked the cobblestone streets. In the distance, I could make out the winged outline of the Virgen de Quito. From a café, I watched the locals going about their business while I took a lunch break. As I was about to dig in, someone approached me.

"That's a beautiful necklace you have there," a young man said. He was tall and blond, and he spoke with an American accent. "I'm Ty."

"I'm Lina," I said. "Would you like to join me?" My own words completely shocked me. I *never* spoke to strangers. But today my heart—or my angel—had other ideas.

Ty asked me what I was doing in Quito. Before I knew it, I'd told him my life story. We talked about my grandmother and my secret dream of pursuing a career in art, despite my parents' wishes.

"It's your life," he said. "You have to live it."

"I dunno . . ." Ty really didn't know me at all. How could he imagine I could do something so brave? "You're much stronger than you think, Lina," Ty said, getting up from the table. "Your dreams are what make you, well, *you*."

And with that he said good-bye and left me to finish my lunch.

I returned to my dorm feeling like a new person. Before I lost my nerve, I ran to the pay phone outside. Was I ready to do this? I'd never be more ready! Gripping my angel charm, I called home. Mother answered.

"Mom," I said, "I'd like to make some changes in my life."

We talked for over an hour. *Really* talked. I explained that I was bored and lonely at my college in Norway, that I didn't like my financial studies. "I want to transfer to a new school, switch majors, do something artistic," I confessed. Everything tumbled out. "Do you think that's possible?" Mother was quiet. Was she upset? Disappointed? Was she crying? I waited anxiously. But when Mother finally broke the silence, there wasn't a trace of sadness in her voice. "Lina, your father and I just want what's best for you," she said. "But in the end, only you know what that is. We would never want you to give up your dreams."

In my remaining weeks in Quito, I took every advantage of my adventure so that I had many stories to tell when I got back home. Since then, I've traveled all over the world, just like Grandmother imagined.

Today, I live in India with my husband and write children's stories. No matter where I go, though, I'll always have a special spot in my heart for Quito. Right over my heart, in fact—that little angel charm given to me in the marketplace still hangs around my neck, a reminder of my answered prayer. And angels who gave me wings to follow my heart.

Blanketed with Peace

Eileen Jurain

"NEITHER SNOW NOR RAIN nor heat nor gloom of night stays these couriers from the swift completion of their appointed rounds." As a letter carrier for the town of Hamburg, New York, I had to get to work no matter how slick the roads were that dreary December morning.

Driving across the Eighteen Mile Creek Bridge in Derby, my tires hydroplaned. Bright headlights bore down on me—the Metro bus headed to Buffalo. There was the sound of crunching metal, the burst of the air bag. The world spun around me.

Next thing I knew, the road was full of policemen and paramedics. I was so cold, colder than the winter chill should have made me. I tried to move, but I was pinned in place. "Get me out of here!" I yelled. No one seemed to hear me.

Then a tall man appeared outside my window, dressed in a long coat and a wool hat. "Would you like a blanket?" he asked. He pushed one through the broken window and draped it around my shoulders. Immediately I felt better.

"That paramedic is going to turn around and see you," the man said. "You will be fine."

With that, the paramedic rushed over. My blanket kept me warm as rescue workers cut me out of the car and carried me to the stretcher for the airlift to the hospital. "Where's the man who gave me this blanket?" I asked before getting aboard.

"Blanket?" the paramedic said.

Only then did I realize the blanket wasn't there. Letter carriers aren't the only ones working rain or shine.

Lost and Found in Paris
Aminda Parafinik

MY HEART POUNDED. My hands were clammy. I was on the verge of panic. The tangle of multicolored lines on the Paris Métro map made my head spin. I asked a ticket-booth attendant for help. He shot me a dismissive look. How could I have been so careless? The world never felt so big, and I never felt so small, so lost. I'd come to Paris in hopes of finding myself. Now I couldn't even find my way back to my hostel.

"If you're lost in Paris, just look for the Eiffel Tower," another traveler told me when I arrived from Arizona. If only there was a guidepost to help me find my way in life! Two months earlier, I'd been downsized from my job as an editorial assistant, my second job since graduating from college with a degree in communications. I'd thought I would be climbing the ranks by twenty-five. Instead, I was out of work. I felt like a loser.

I dreamed of getting away. That's when I got the idea for this trip. I'd been fascinated by the "City of Light" ever since I was a little girl. I had some money saved up. What better place was there to be inspired again?

I took in the awesome views from the top of the Eiffel Tower, gawked at the luxury shops along the Champs-Élysées, saw the magnificent Palace of Versailles. Today, though, after exploring exhibits at the Louvre and visiting the gargoyles at

Notre Dame, I'd taken a wrong turn. The narrow streets surrounding the cathe-
dral were like a maze. In the spirit of adventure, I kept going…until it got dark. I
could see the Eiffel Tower, a finger of light impossibly distant. I searched for more
than an hour until I found what I thought was the right Métro stop, but it was for
a different line than the one that let off near my hostel.

I turned away from the ticket booth, and the reality of my situation hit me.
I'd been crazy to spend my savings on this trip, trying to "find myself." When—or
if—I got home, then what? "Lord," I whispered, "please help me. I am so lost."

"Excusez-moi." A tall, brown-haired man startled me. A little older than me,
clean-cut, dressed like a businessman. "Can I help you?" he asked, with just a hint
of a French accent.

"I need to get to Félix Faure," I said, trying to keep my voice from quivering.

"Follow me," he said. Normally I wouldn't, but there was something about
him. He seemed trustworthy. Confident. Besides, did I have a choice?

Striding through the dark streets, we made small talk. "Where are you from?"
he asked. "The United States, obviously," he added, smiling. "But where?"

"Phoenix," I said. "It's in Arizona, the Southwest—"

"Really?" he interrupted. "Have you heard of the Thunderbird School of
Global Management?"

I vaguely remembered that name from a billboard near my freeway exit. Of
all the things in Phoenix to ask about…"I don't really know much about it,"
I said.

He paused, then looked at me quizzically as if he wanted to continue. But
by then we'd reached the Métro line I needed. "Hurry, you don't want to miss
your train," he said. I thanked him, then dashed down the stairs. Before long, I
was back at the hostel. The rest of my time in Paris was uneventful, even restful.
Something about that encounter seemed to calm me.

Okay, time to get back to my life. My first week home, I sent out more résumés.
Nothing.

That weekend, I was scanning the want ads when a position caught my eye. They needed someone with a communications degree, and the responsibilities matched what I'd done in the past. Program assistant for an executive MBA program. I liked the sound of that.

I liked the sound of the employer too. The Thunderbird School of Global Management. Suddenly, the world seemed very small. I applied and was called in for an interview.

Guess who got the job?

Angels over Iraq

Brenda Kay Ledford

"HI, AUNT BRENDA! Thanks for the care package. Those brownies were delicious." My nephew John was calling from Iraq, where he'd been deployed with the army for the last five months as a military police officer. I loved hearing his voice, even when the reception was poor. John only got access to the shared satellite phone once or twice a month. Those calls were the only times I knew he was okay. The only times I took a break from worrying about him.

"I'm glad you liked the brownies," I said. "I—" *BOOM! Pop-pop-pop-pop. BOOM!* The sounds of explosives and machine-gun fire rang in my ear with crystal clarity. "John, what was that? Are you okay?"

"I'm fine," he said. "That is nowhere near where I am. But yeah, that's pretty much what it sounds like over here all the time. Someone's always shooting at us. But I have a job to do. I can't let it get to me."

It certainly got to me. All I could think about was the danger around him. I had a job to do too. "I'm praying for you," I said. "And so are a lot of other people. I have called most of the churches in Clay County about getting your name put on their prayer lists."

Day and night I asked God to watch over John, but that didn't stop me from worrying. It was 2004. Soldiers were dying every day in Iraq. "It means a lot just knowing that you and everyone back there is thinking of me," John said. "And sending brownies, of course."

I laughed and we said our good-byes. But even as I hung up the phone, I wished there was something more I could do. *Time for another care package*, I thought. I filled a box with more brownies, packages of Kool-Aid, wet wipes, a long letter, and some inspirational books. At the post office I asked God to ensure it reached its destination.

"Were you praying?" a woman behind me in line asked. I explained about John. "He's going to be fine," she said. But how could she be so sure?

Back at home I stared out the window at the Blue Ridge Mountains in the distance. I never had any children of my own, so all the love I would have given them went to John. When he had visited me in the summer, the two of us had ridden horses all over the mountain trails. Deep in the forest, surrounded by the beauty of nature, that's where I felt closest to God—and to John too. We talked about his dreams for the future, how he wanted to be a lawyer. But when he told me he was thinking of enlisting in the army after graduating from college, that he hoped to one day be a JAG officer, I was terrified. "What do you think?" he'd asked me.

I took a deep breath. "I think you should pray about it and go where you feel led," I said, hoping that God and I were on the same wavelength.

But it hadn't turned out that way. Since the day John left for boot camp I'd never really stopped worrying. It only got worse when he deployed to Iraq. His quarters, he'd told me, a squalid former Iraqi jail, were infested with rats. Nothing like the beautiful mountains we loved. So much of what he was doing he wasn't even allowed to tell me about. He felt unreachable. Even my prayers seemed somehow to fall short, as garbled as the reception on John's monthly phone calls.

That night in my bedroom I read the Bible and prayed for God to shelter John from harm. Like I always did. But in my mind I could still hear the sound of the mortars from that morning's phone call. My hands trembled as I closed the Bible and got into bed.

I tossed and turned for what seemed like forever when…suddenly I was in the desert, nothing but sand for miles around. In the distance I saw a group of men. I walked toward them. They were soldiers, kneeling in a circle. One of them was John. He was holding another soldier in his arms. John was crying. *Why am I seeing this?*

Overhead I heard a sound, like a whisper on the wind. I looked up. A band of angels hovered above. Female angels with wings, in flowing white robes. They encircled the men and danced, their faces joyous, carefree, as if there was no place in the universe they'd rather be.

One of the angels reached out to me. I hesitated, not sure if I should take her hand, but she beckoned me. There was a warmth to her, an incredible feeling of reassurance that put me at ease.

I floated up with her, and we danced. Time stood still. I could feel the tension leaving me. In its place there was only love, unconditional love. Our bond had a strength to it that even an army couldn't break through.

I lifted my head and…I was back in bed. My eyes wide open. I cried tears of joy, and I thanked God for being ever faithful, for watching over all our soldiers, and especially John—the connection between us stronger than ever.

A couple of weeks later I answered the phone. John's voice sounded strained. "We got ambushed the other day," he said. "Someone shot three rocket-propelled grenades at us. But no one got hit. No one. The grenades just flew by us."

In the months that followed there were more calls like that. Mortars and mines that exploded near John but didn't harm him. The danger was still ever present.

Of course I worried but not like before. It wasn't that I thought he could never be hurt. But I knew with absolute certainty that he wasn't alone, that the angels would always be with him.

John served two tours of duty and finally came home for good in 2006. He never got that law degree. Today he's in seminary, but that doesn't mean I pray for him any less.

The Survivors
John Senka

WELCOME, US ARMY 4TH BATTALION, *9th Infantry, 25th Division*. I stared at the sign outside the reception. For forty years I'd avoided these Vietnam vets' reunions. I didn't want to talk about the battle that haunted my nightmares, or how I'd survived.

The Battle of Mole City, December 22, 1968. We were a unit of five hundred American soldiers, stationed in deep bunkers along one of the North Vietnamese Army's (NVA) busiest supply routes. I was twenty. Fit, strong, tough. My three months in 'Nam hadn't been much different from working on our family farm. I spent most days in the hot sun, digging the trenches the base was named for.

There was a holiday truce. After dinner, we opened packages from home with cards, cookies, and miniature trees. It almost felt like Christmas. At 10:00 p.m., we received our orders for the night: patrol, LP (the listening post), or perimeter. I was assigned to defend the perimeter.

All was quiet till midnight. The LP reported some NVA movement. The four of us in our bunker took our positions. Suddenly the night sky lit up. Flares. Mortar fire. A surprise attack!

We returned fire. There was a tremendous explosion. An anguished scream from the soldier next to me. I looked over. He was dead. I was struck too, in my right leg. Another grunt dove out the back of the bunker. I crawled after him.

We squeezed into the next bunker, filled with GIs. Something thudded into the mud. Another grenade! I threw myself as far from it as I could.

Boom! Blood ran from my ears. A third grenade rolled in. Shrapnel ripped into my belly. My rifle was clogged with mud. My injured leg was useless. We were overrun. Guys were falling, crying out for their mothers. One brave sergeant climbed out of the bunker, firing his M16. His silhouette crumpled; his body rolled down past me. All I could do was lie there and wait for death.

I wouldn't have called myself religious, even though I wore a miraculous medal with my dog tags. Still, I shouted above the gunfire, "God, help me!"

Everything went silent. No explosions. No screams. Like I'd gone deaf. At the same time, I felt something hover over me. It fell softly upon my shoulders, warm, comforting, like I was a child being tucked into bed. Before I could figure out what it was, I blacked out.

When I came to, it was daylight. I moved to uncover myself, but nothing was there. Feet shuffled outside the bunker. Who had won? The NVA? Would I be taken prisoner? I pulled away a sandbag blocking my view. It thumped to the ground.

A helmeted head poked in. A US Army sergeant. "It's okay, soldier," he said.

I was the only one found alive in that bunker. The army sent me home. The physical wounds healed. My other wounds didn't. Counselors told me that the nightmares were my mind trying to piece together what had happened in Mole City. Even after I learned that we'd been stormed by 1,500 NVA, outnumbered three to one, the survivor's guilt remained. Why had I been wrapped in that cocoon of safety, while others died?

For forty years, that guilt kept me away from reunions. I wasn't sure why I'd come now. But I took a deep breath and entered the reception hall. I put on my name tag and scanned the room.

A man came up, saw my name tag. "You're the guy I've been looking for."

"I'm sorry," I said. "Who are you?"

"Bob Chavous." He shook my hand. "I heard you were in the perimeter bunker near where I was supposed to be. I survived, the other guys didn't. It's not easy to talk about."

I understood all too well. Bob said he'd been assigned to the LP that night, one of the men who called in the warning about the enemy soldiers.

"Before we could withdraw, the sky lit up with a hundred mortars. We were pinned down in a rice paddy," Bob said. "I made my peace with God, and prayed He'd let my family know that I loved them."

He paused for a moment, searching for the right words. "Then it was like… a blanket settled over me and put me to sleep until the fighting was over."

A blanket of protection. I'd never know why it had covered me. But I hadn't been the only one. How many others at this reunion had felt the same thing? Been touched by the same inexplicable warmth that we told ourselves couldn't possibly be real?

I was ready to talk then. Ready to tell everything I'd held inside. I wasn't alone. Bob needed to know he wasn't either.

Angels by the River
Mary C. Neal

THE KAYAKING ADVENTURE of Dr. Mary Neal in southern Chile had gone terribly wrong. Her husband, Bill, their friends and traveling companions Tom and Anne Long, their son Kenneth, and Kenneth's teenage son Chad, tried mightily to save Mary from what seemed to be imminent: her death.

I became aware of my body and opened my eyes to see the faces of the Longs looking down at me. There seemed to be a sense of relief and excitement as Tom and Kenneth started telling the others what to do for me. They arranged a kayak to be my lift and secured my body to the top. The rocky riverbank was adjacent to an extremely thick bamboo forest. The incline of the hillside was steep and appeared insurmountable.

As the Longs considered their options, several young Chilean men materialized out of nowhere. A couple of them helped lift and begin to carry the boat to which I was secured, and the others began to push a path through the bamboo. No words were ever spoken to them or by them; they just knew what to do. It was slow going through the forest, and I faded in and out of consciousness. Kenneth has always been filled with the qualities typical of an oldest child, and his drive pushed everyone else. Despite their increasing fatigue, no one was going to stop unless he did.

During my intermittent interludes of consciousness, I would confidently blurt out instructions for them to give me steroids; I knew I couldn't move my legs and, as a spine surgeon, I assumed that I had broken my back and injured my spinal cord. If such were the case, the timely administration of steroids could lessen my degree of paralysis. This seemed like rambling to them, but it was difficult for them to ignore. Eventually they found a single-track dirt path, which led to a dirt road.

Our entourage slowly trundled along this dirt path, moving forward but not really knowing what they would do when they eventually found a road. The nearest village was too far to reach by walking and any road they came upon would be infrequently traveled. They vaguely hoped to find someone with an old tractor or other farm implement that could transport me more quickly to the village. At the time, ambulances were essentially nonexistent in this part of Chile, so it was a great surprise when we emerged from the forested hillside and saw an ambulance parked on the side of the road. The driver didn't speak, but he seemed to be waiting for us.

After Bill had waved us off at the river put-in earlier in the day, he drove the truck to a sunny spot, parked, and pulled out a book in preparation for a leisurely day of reading. He planned to meet us later in the day at the river take-out. During my resuscitation, one woman sort of "freaked out" and ran away from the scene at the river. With what I am sure was God's leading, she ran to the exact spot where Bill was reading. After a quick explanation, they both jumped into the truck and rapidly drove along the road in search of our group. They found us just as I was being loaded into the ambulance.

Tom and Chad drove in the truck while Bill and Kenneth rode with me in the back of the ambulance. The driver careened down the road toward the tiny first-aid station in the village of Choshuenco, and Kenneth was somewhat reassured about my condition and my degree of comprehension when I began insisting that the driver slow down before he killed us. When we finally made it to the first-aid station, Kenneth and Chad returned to the chaos at the river. Tom stayed with Bill and me.

When Kenneth and Chad returned to the river, they first tried to find the young men who had been such a great help in carrying me through the forest. These young men were nowhere to be found and the people from the village had no idea whom they could be talking about. They didn't know of anyone fitting their description in the village, so the people thought Chad and Kenneth must be mistaken. Angels? Chad and Kenneth found their return trip through the bamboo forest to the riverbank was even more difficult than when they had carried me out. They found the forest to be even thicker and the hillside even steeper than they remembered. It made the success of their earlier efforts seem even less plausible, unless one accepted that the process of my rescue was almost entirely a result of divine intervention.

Once all of the remaining boaters were accounted for, Kenneth and Chad tried to recover the two boats that were still trapped at the bottom of the waterfall. It was nearly impossible. The rock upon which they had been standing when they fished me out of the water was gone. It was not possible for them to stand in the current of the steep waterfall. It was impossible for them to reach or even touch the boats. It took more than an hour of dedicated working and suffering through multiple snapped ropes to get the first boat out. In order to achieve this, they had to first bend and fold both boats in half by securing lines to the boat ends and rotating them such that the current could do this work. When they finally retrieved the lines they had been using, they saw that there had been enough friction and force between the lines to melt the knots together.

As they returned to Pucón, they were exhausted and overwhelmed by the absolute impossibility of my rescue and the supernatural aspects of what had occurred. God's presence and purposeful intervention were clear to all those who were present on the scene. Tom, Kenneth, Chad, and Anne have all told me they feel that the situation went from one of total and absolute failure and hopelessness to one of success without any meaningful input from them. They have described it to me as a choreographed performance in which they were each just playing their roles. To this day, they continue to feel that ours is not just a good story. It wasn't just one miracle; it was a constellation of miracles for which there is no possible explanation other than God's intervention. As Chad later said, "Let's not let life muddle what happened. We were all part of a miracle."

Anne has reported that she was overwhelmed by the simultaneous and contrasting feelings of being so helpless and small in the universe and of being so loved by God that He chose to be present. She, and I think all of us, are still feeling undeserving of His intervention. With all of the suffering and people in need, it is difficult to understand how or why He intervened that day on the Fuy River in Chile, but He clearly did.

Anne has also described feeling both helpless and remarkably liberated. She knows that God is in control and she feels that she now understands the verse in the Bible that describes how you must give up everything in order to gain everything: "For those who want to save their life will lose it, and those who lose their life for my sake, and for the sake of the gospel, will save it" (Mark 8:35, NRSV).

CHAPTER 3

Orchestrated by Angels

"We moved quickly through the wood, clinging to one another.

The light kept up with us faithfully,

illuminating the space directly around us, but no more.

I peered beneath the trees as we walked,

scanning the ferns and underbrush,

but saw nothing that could be producing such radiance.

How does it know where we're going?"

—NELL GOODWIN

Heaven's Lights
Nell Goodwin

NO MOON. NO STARS. I had never seen a night so dark. My mother reached down and grasped my hand. *How will we make it back to the house?* I thought. The familiar walk home suddenly felt like a trek across an unknown world.

There wasn't a lot of outdoor lighting back in 1940. We didn't even own a flashlight. When it got dark at night, we relied on heaven's lights to guide us. Where were those lights now? "Let's pray," my mother said. We'd just come from our Wednesday prayer meeting. The pastor gave us a ride in his car as far as the highway would take us. He dropped us at the gate on the far side of our thirty-acre property. From there my mother and I would walk the dirt path that stretched through a field, then a forest, before reaching our doorstep.

"God, walk with us," Mother said. She took my arm and we set out.

"I've never seen it so dark!" I said, pressing my mother's arm in mine. I searched the sky for familiar pinpricks of starlight or the gentle glow of the moon, but tonight held a new moon and clouds hid every star. We walked blindly, each step careful and precise, with only the dirt path under our feet to reassure us.

"I can't even see my hand in front of my face," my mother whispered. I put my own hand up and waved it around. Mother was right. If God himself was walking with us, I would not be able to see Him.

We stayed on course through the field until we heard the last crunch of dry earth beneath our feet. We'd reached the forest!

Mother and I lingered at the edge of the wood, feeling helpless. Even though we were already in the dark, the woods seemed to hold even greater dangers, more chances to get lost, with no path to guide us. *We can't go a step farther.*

In that moment, a soft light appeared. *The moon?* I thought. But there was no moon, and this light wasn't silver. It was golden and ethereal, surrounding and embracing us. It came from nowhere and everywhere all at once, and cast no shadows as it glowed brighter and brighter, and brighter still. It was as though someone had lit three lanterns around us. Now I could see, but there was no one in sight.

"Hurry," my mother whispered. "Let's go while we have the light."

We moved quickly through the wood, clinging to one another. The light kept up with us faithfully, illuminating the space directly around us, but no more. I peered beneath the trees as we walked, scanning the ferns and underbrush, but saw nothing that could be producing such radiance. *How does it know where we're going?*

When we reached the end of the forest, the comforting shape of our house rose up in the gloom. I thought the light would be confined to the woods, but it accompanied us all the way to the doorstep.

I went up to my room on the second floor, my head swimming. *Was any of that real?* I felt as though I'd just stepped out of a dream, and I went over to the window. There was the light, just below, glistening golden in the yard, but it had already begun to fade. I watched until it blinked out entirely and the world outside my bedroom window was dark once again.

Heaven's lights had led us home.

Finding Ziggy

Nitza Wagoner

THE FIRST PRESENT MIKE EVER GAVE me was a small plush Ziggy doll. Ziggy. That short, bald, down-on-his-luck pants-less character from the funny pages. Back then that lovable little guy was everywhere, on coffee mugs, T-shirts, you name it.

"I like this dude," I remembered Mike saying. "He's all right."

Memories of our complicated relationship had flashed through my mind often in the two weeks since Mike's funeral. He died unexpectedly in his sleep. One day there, one day gone. I'd never had the chance to say good-bye.

Now, trudging through Brooklyn to the subway stop for the F train, it was all I could do not to turn around and run home, to the cozy place Mike and I had bought together back in the 1970s with help from the GI Bill. But I had my job, processing claims for a health insurer, and I had to go back to work. People hurried past me. I barely had the energy to walk down the stairs to the subway platform.

I'd met Mike the summer I graduated from high school, playing stickball. He was older than me and incredibly handsome, just back from serving in Vietnam. He liked to dress sharp. I liked what I saw. We started going out, and it didn't take long for me to see that his Puerto Rican machismo masked a great deal of sensitivity. He acted tough but was really a sweet, hapless guy. A bit like Ziggy, you might say.

Our first Christmas together, Mike gave me a polar bear sporting a Ziggy sweater. And for Valentine's Day another Ziggy, with the words *I love you* emblazoned on his tummy. At every special occasion I couldn't wait to open my Ziggy card. I treasured them all because I knew how much it meant to Mike to make me happy.

After we were married, every Christmas I arranged all my Ziggys under the tree. We had two sons and they came to love Ziggy as much as we did. Ziggy was practically a member of our family!

So many wonderful memories: taking the boys to Coney Island, skipping stones on the river under the Brooklyn Bridge, quiet walks along the promenade. But nothing came easily for Mike. He liked to drink, and at first I didn't think much about it. He was never mean or violent. The years went by and Mike's drinking got worse. He blacked out on more than one occasion.

"I can't go on like this," I told him. "You need to get treatment."

He sought help but couldn't stick with AA. We went for counseling. Nothing changed. After nineteen years of marriage, I filed for divorce. It broke my heart. I prayed he'd find the help he needed. Our marriage was over, but I still loved him.

He married a woman with three children. And by the grace of God he got sober through a program with the VA, but the marriage didn't last. The insecurities he tried to drown with his drinking were still there. And I lost track of him. Eventually our younger son, Charles, called to say his father had been staying with him some nights. Where he stayed other nights, Charles didn't know.

One day ten years after our divorce, I answered a knock on the door. It was Mike. "I need a place to sleep," he said.

I had the basement finished. A place he could call his own. He agreed to do some chores and pay a small amount of rent.

We'd lived in the house as friends for the past decade. He'd bring me soup when I was sick. I always checked in on him after work. He seemed to be finding himself. As far as I knew, Mike was in good health, though he still smoked cigarettes. In a few years I hoped to retire. I thought we'd grow old together, ex-spouses but best friends.

Then came that terrible evening when I got home and knocked on Mike's door, and he didn't answer. I found him lying on his bed, holding a gray teddy bear. I stroked his hair, told him I loved him. It felt like he'd been stolen from me. I hoped he'd found peace, but how does one ever know such a thing? All I knew for sure was that he was gone.

Now I was finally going back to work, though the grief still hung over me. I stepped on to the subway platform, staring down at my feet, too tired to even look up.

For an instant I thought I was seeing things. Maybe I was losing my mind. Scrawled in white chalk on the ground was the word *Ziggy*. I stared at it in disbelief. Who would have done such a thing? I raised my head slightly, and saw *Ziggy* written over and over again across the entire platform. At least a hundred times. It was crazy, whimsical, just so completely over the top. *Ziggy*s everywhere! They continued right up to the spot on the platform where I always waited for my train.

Over the next few days I looked forward to seeing this outburst of *Ziggy*s. Then, just as suddenly as they had appeared, they were gone. I even wondered if I had imagined them. I wondered if life made any sense at all.

A few weeks later, Charles dropped by, back from a trip to Israel for his boss's son's wedding. I quizzed him about his trip and the sights he'd seen, but he seemed anxious about something.

"What's wrong?" I asked.

"I just don't know what to make of it," he said.

"What? Tell me what's bothering you."

"I was at the Wailing Wall. I wanted to slip a prayer into one of the crevices. The wall is filled with slips of paper with prayers written on them. But I was drawn to one particular crevice. It was weird, like I was led to that spot. I reached in. I didn't want to desecrate such a holy site, but I just couldn't help it. Something was in there, an object. I pulled it out. It was a cigarette lighter!"

"So?" I said, confused.

Then Charles, smiling but choking back tears, said, "There was one word on it. Engraved. *Ziggy.*"

Next Stop, Heaven

Karen Krone

I CAN SEE BILL NOW. *Running up to the train, excited at the journey ahead. The next big adventure. He's ready to take a trip with the "Great Conductor." For a moment, he hesitates. Smoke billows from the engine. A whistle blows, one long, mournful cry. Bill glances back. But the train is leaving and it's time to hop aboard that big red caboose to heaven....*

The words of the eulogy Bill's friend Larry had delivered were still on my mind when the huge Hummer limo pulled up to the ranch-style house on Estates Drive. Our former home, where we'd raised our boys. I couldn't help but wonder: What had Bill's journey really been like?

I tried to picture Bill healthy and free, as Larry had described in his eulogy. No longer bedridden. God greeting him with a locomotive and a shiny red caboose. Oh, how Bill would've loved that! For as long as I'd known him—since high school—he was crazy about model trains. His parents had surprised him and his little brother with a brand-new train set one Easter morning, brightly painted eggs hidden in each of the boxcars. It wasn't until we were married, though, that I found out I'd be sharing my house with dozens of pre–World War II trains and endless feet of track. We hadn't been able to take a proper honeymoon because Bill had to teach a class at Washington University. But the day after our wedding we paid a visit to the Museum of Transportation in St. Louis. Bill spent hours crouching beneath full-size engines, asking questions and taking pictures. That's when I knew for sure—I'd married a train nut!

We planned several vacations around the National Train Collectors convention. We traveled from Illinois to Pennsylvania to Florida. Our three boys loved to brag that their dad was the "train guy." Their school classes took field trips to our basement train room, where Bill had laid out a complex labyrinth of tracks and towns, complete with miniature trees, benches, and lampposts. A whole other world.

Bill was diagnosed with pancreatic cancer in 2009. I was devastated. I couldn't imagine life without Bill. And his trains.

The trains soon became more than a hobby. That other world became an escape. The minute we returned home from a chemo treatment, he'd go downstairs. He was at peace there, sitting at his workbench tinkering with engines. In those quiet moments, he was transported to a place where the pain was remote. Later, he was too weak to go up and down the stairs. I'd bring up a few old Lionel trains and set them out on a TV tray, so Bill could work on them in the family room.

Now that Bill was gone, the house was so quiet. I missed the hum of the trains going around the tracks. I'd always been able to hear that *clickety-clack* from the kitchen upstairs. I never realized how familiar and comforting that sound was...until now.

I wanted to do something different to celebrate Bill's life. We'd always been a no-frills kind of couple. Never splurged on new cars, always bought dependable used models. But for the day of the funeral, I rented a twenty-five-seat, triple-axle Hummer limo to take our closest family and friends on a tour of all the places Bill loved most in our hometown. It wasn't a train, but it was the next best thing.

After the funeral service, and Larry's beautiful eulogy, we'd piled into the Hummer—all twenty-two of us, including our three sons, three daughters-in-law, and eleven grandchildren. We put on the 1950s music Bill and I had listened to when we were dating and shared our favorite memories.

The first stop on the tour was Faith Salem Church, where Bill and I were married all those years ago. Then Bill's elementary school. His childhood home. Jennings High School, where we met. And, finally, our house on Estates Drive. We'd downsized after the boys moved out. What an ordeal, cleaning out the stuff we'd accumulated over the course of thirty-seven years. Even though we'd sold it six years before, it still felt like home.

"We should knock on the door and ask to go inside," my son Brad said.

Just then, a car pulled into the driveway. A man got out and walked briskly toward us.

"Did I win the Publishers Clearing House sweepstakes or something?" he asked, taking in the Hummer.

Brad explained.

"Why don't you come inside?" the man offered. "Take a look around." We followed him into the foyer.

"You're lucky," he said. "I came back because I forgot my briefcase. Listen, I'm glad I caught you. I have a gift for you."

He disappeared into the garage. What could it be? I doubted we'd left something behind. On moving day, we'd searched the house from top to bottom to make sure we hadn't forgotten anything.

The man came back with a large framed picture.

"I found this when we moved in," he said, turning it to show us. "My wife kept bugging me to throw it out, but for some reason I just couldn't."

A painting. A beautiful painting. It had once hung in Bill's train room. Something he'd found at a garage sale years ago. But that wasn't all.

The scene in the painting... a train with a red caboose, on its way out, chugging through a landscape unlike any on earth. Exactly the picture Larry had painted in Bill's eulogy, down to the smallest detail. And for an instant I heard the faint sound of a train whistle, echoing in the distance.

Mom's Promise

Lynda Taylor

FRESH-BREWED COFFEE, a wet dog, a pot of stew on the stove. Those are the kinds of odors that awaken people's sense of smell. Well, most people—but not me. For fifteen years I'd struggled to detect even the strongest scents. The doctors couldn't confidently explain what my problem was, much less fix it. I'd taken medication for my sinuses, had surgery for polyps. I'd even tried acupuncture. But nothing worked. Sometimes I'd get a few weeks when I could catch a whiff of somebody's perfume. Then suddenly I'd go nose-blind again.

"I really don't think there's anything more we can do," my latest otolaryngologist told me.

I thanked him for his help and drove to my mother's house. *There are far worse things you could have to deal with,* I told myself. But that didn't make my condition any less maddening. Worst of all, the ability to smell is closely tied to the ability to taste. Even spicy food tasted bland to me. I was stuck in a tasteless, odorless world, and there was nothing I could do about it. I smelled and tasted in grainy black and white while everyone else was doing it in HD color.

"I give up," I told my mother. She knew how frustrating this was for me. I visited with her nearly every day and kept her up-to-date on all my doctors' appointments. "I just need to accept it," I said. "I'll never be able to smell properly again."

But giving up wasn't Mom's style. She didn't get to be an independent, vibrant ninety-seven-year-old without a fighting spirit. "That just isn't right," she said. "You should be able to smell and taste like everyone else!"

"What can we do about it?" I said.

"I know what *I'm* going to do," Mom said. "When I get to heaven I'm going to ask God about this issue. I'm going to get to the bottom of it!"

That was the other thing that kept Mom going at ninety-seven: her total trust in God. She talked about Him like an old friend. When I was growing up, I went to Mom with all my problems: trouble in school, trouble with boys. She listened without any judgment. "We'll figure this out," she'd assure me, no matter how hopeless things seemed. And sure enough, with Mom's help and a lot of prayer, I found a way to pass the test or get over the boy.

Even now Mom was sure she could work out a solution with God. I didn't like her talking about sitting down with Him in person—as much as she believed in heaven, how could any of us know for sure? Yet I could not deny mortality. Even my invincible mom would not live forever, though it was impossible to imagine the world without her.

Only a few weeks later, on Easter Sunday, Mom's heart gave out. My husband, Glen, and I were with her at the senior living apartment where she spent her last few days with hospice care. Afterward, Glen went home with some of Mom's things. I stayed behind to take care of everything with the hospice center. It was evening by the time I called Glen and told him I was on my way home.

"Do you want me to fix dinner?" he asked.

"I'll stop somewhere," I said. I wasn't particularly hungry, but I knew I should have something. Mom wouldn't want me to skip a meal on her account.

I pulled in at the first place I saw—a pizza parlor. I got out of my car, pushed open the door to the restaurant, and nearly fell over.

The smell! Freshly baked bread and pungent garlic. It was so strong my eyes watered, to say nothing of my mouth. I ordered a slice and could barely wait for them to heat it up. I was practically trembling.

I sat down with my pizza and took a minute to just breathe in the aroma before I took a bite. What a bite! Warm, yeasty crust; sweet tomato sauce with a touch of basil; and thick, gooey cheese! It was as if I'd never tasted food before. I hadn't—not like this.

I was afraid to finish, worried that each taste would be my last. *How is this possible?* I thought. Then I remembered Mom's promise. "When I get to heaven..."

I haven't had a problem smelling or tasting since.

Heaven's Trail

Mary Louise Hillyard

BROKEN SUNLIGHT FILTERED through the ceiling of branches high above our campsite near the Eel River in Humboldt County, California. I worked at the camp stove cooking dinner for my husband, Arland, and our teenage girls, Maureen and Cheryl. Some potatoes I'd boiled that morning sizzled in a big cast-iron pan. Roasting alongside were hot dogs and a batch of squash we'd picked up earlier at a vegetable stand on the Avenue of the Giants, the famous scenic road that runs through a stretch of particularly huge California redwoods. "Warmed-over potatoes," Dad called them, back when he cooked up meals for my brother, sisters, Mom, and me on the camping trips we took as children.

The woods always made me think of Dad—but this summer that was especially so. It was almost a year to the day since he'd suffered a severe stroke, transforming him from the vital, energetic person I'd known all my life into someone who could no longer do anything for himself. He was in a nursing home in Erie, Pennsylvania, just down the road from my brother, Bud. "Dad doesn't even know me anymore," Bud had said before we left on our trip. I wondered if we should go cross-country instead.

"You're doing the right thing," Bud told me. "You know how much Dad loved taking us to the woods when we were kids. He wouldn't want the girls to be stuck in some hospital. He'd want them to be sitting around a campfire and walking trails, the way we used to with him."

Dad always made sure we were the first campers out in the spring and the last ones to leave in the fall. No one loved nature more than he did. I promised Bud we would phone every couple of days.

I pushed the food around the pan with a long spatula, feeling a rush of second thoughts. The last time I'd checked in, Dad's condition had been stable. *God, I hope I did the right thing coming out here.* I felt someone behind me. Dad? I turned around. Nothing there but the massive, silent trunks of the redwoods.

"Arland, Maureen, Cheryl!" I called. "Supper's ready."

Arland and the girls came running. Dishing out the food, I looked up and noticed a forest ranger coming toward our campsite, clipboard in hand.

"Good evening," I said. "Would you like some dinner?"

"No thanks, ma'am," the ranger said. He removed his hat and sat at our picnic table. "I'm doing a little research for a field report. Would you mind if I joined you?"

The ranger asked us a few questions—where we were from, how long we were staying—while we ate. "We love this area," I said. "The trails are gorgeous."

"We have a brand-new one, on the Avenue of the Giants. You won't find it on the maps yet, but it's magical." The forest ranger gave us directions. The trail was right across from the vegetable stand we'd stopped by earlier. The ranger stood up, put his hat back on, and bobbed his head good-bye. "It was real nice talking to you folks." Campers were set up here and there among the trees around us. I was surprised that he didn't stop to talk to any of them for his field report. Just us.

After dinner we drove to a pay phone. I could immediately hear in Bud's voice that something was wrong.

"Mary Louise, Dad's gone. He passed away just after I talked to you last. The funeral was this morning. I've had the Highway Patrol trying to find you. I'm sorry."

Back at the campsite we spent the rest of the evening gathered around the fire, sharing memories of Dad and crying. I told the girls how much I'd loved being in the woods with him when I was their age—how he was always ready to scout out a new trail or find a perfect fishing spot no one else knew about.

Finally, we all went to bed. But I couldn't sleep. *Lord, I should have been there to tell Dad good-bye.*

"Let's go on one more walk before we head home," I said to Arland the next morning. "For Dad." We got on the Avenue of the Giants and drove to the vegetable stand.

There was the new trail, just as the ranger had said. I was surprised we hadn't noticed it before. The trailhead was clearly marked. We got out and set off into the woods.

Delicate flowers and ferns sprang from the forest floor. Redwood trunks rose like columns up to the leafy canopy, where birds flitted—their faraway calls the only sounds in the woods. This really was another world.

Deeper and deeper into the forest we walked, the girls in front, Arland and I holding hands behind them. We came to a spot where a redwood trunk lay across the path, illuminated by a single ray of light. "You and the girls go on," I said to Arland. "I want to sit awhile."

Arland touched my cheek. "We'll see you on the way back."

The three of them disappeared down the path. I sat in the circle of light and ran my hand along the rough bark. *Dad, I'm sorry I wasn't there with you. But you know how much I love you, how much I always will.* The sun wrapped me in warmth and held me. I looked up into the blinding light and listened in the perfect silence.

"Good-bye, Dad."

Arland and the girls got back and joined me on the log. My sadness was still there, but something was different. In some strange way, I felt it was okay I hadn't been there with Dad after all.

We walked along the peaceful path out to the edge of the forest. "It's hard to step back into the real world," I said at the trail opening.

By that afternoon we were packed up and on our way home. Again and again in the weeks that followed, when Dad came to mind, I'd immediately think of that spot in the woods. I liked to imagine Dad full of his old enthusiasm as he explored heaven's trails.

When Arland's vacation rolled around the next year, we went back to the Eel River. "Let's go to the special trail," the girls said on our first morning there. I couldn't wait to see it again.

We got on the Avenue of Giants, and slowed down at the vegetable stand. "This is the place, but where's the trail?" Arland said. Across from the stand there was no sign of a trail entrance. We got out of the car and looked around. The underbrush was so thick you could hardly even step into the woods. We asked at the vegetable stand.

"Trail?" the man said. "There's no trail over there. Never has been."

We drove up and down the road, looking for some sign of a trail entrance. Finally, we stopped by the ranger station. When the guys on duty didn't know of any such trail, we described the ranger we'd met.

"I'm sorry, ma'am," one of them said. "We know every ranger in the area. We don't know who you're talking about. And there is no such trail."

Arland and the girls looked as confused as the rangers did. But I wasn't. We had walked on a heavenly trail, and Dad had heard my good-bye.

Dad's Last Gift

Ashley Kappel

I HEARD THE CRASH from the bridal suite where I was getting ready for my big day. The photographer and I exchanged shrugs and went back to taking a few final photographs before I walked down the aisle.

We heard a knock at the door. "It's time!" I said when my dad walked in.

"Not quite." For a man full of jokes who was seeing his daughter in her wedding dress for the first time, he looked awfully sheepish. "I've got some bad news. I backed your car into a pole in the parking lot. It dented the fender pretty badly and broke the taillight. I promise I'll pay to get it fixed after the wedding."

He couldn't have been more contrite, but I almost had to laugh. Here was my dad, who was footing the bill (gladly!) for my dream wedding and he was apologizing to me for something that could be fixed? On a car that he himself had purchased for me years before? The look on his face told me this was no laughing matter, so I held in my giggle.

"Dad," I said, "are you okay? Nothing hurts?"

"No, no. I'm fine. It's just your car. I can't believe I did that," he said.

"It's nothing money can't fix," I said, quoting one of his favorite lines back to him. My parents weren't flashy. They believed that so long as their kids were okay—happy and healthy—nothing else really mattered. Sure, the car was banged up, but we could pay for a new taillight later. Now it was time to exchange some vows!

The wedding went off without a hitch, unless you count the priest mispronouncing my new last name four times and losing the second page of the ceremony. We toasted at the reception and headed off for a honeymoon.

But just ten days after the wedding, the bottom fell out of my world. My mom called to tell me that something was wrong with my dad.

I raced home, getting updates as I drove. But before I could get to my parents' house, they told me that Dad had died. Nothing exceptional had happened. He had felt poorly and called 911. He was unconscious when the medics arrived.

The next three days moved at a snail's pace. We planned a funeral, wrote an obituary, and mourned my dad, whose smile had filled a banquet hall only a week and a half before.

Afterward, I headed back to my in-laws' house, where my car was still parked.

"Ashley," my mother-in-law began, "we don't know when it happened, but your car got hit while it was at our house. I don't know how—it's been in our driveway the whole time!"

Fresh grief washed over me. That same silly ding that had caused Dad even a moment of pain now tormented me.

"That wasn't you guys," I said. "Dad had a little accident before the wedding. We'll get it fixed now that we're home."

We walked out to the car to take a look. The same chip in the taillight was still missing, but the dent in the bumper was gone. Where there had been scratches and a large gouge, nothing remained. If not for the dirt, I would've sworn it was a new fender.

"Am I crazy?" my father-in-law asked. "It was here, wasn't it?"

"It definitely was," I replied.

I found comfort in knowing that Dad was watching me still. I keep the before and after photos as a reminder that he's always there.

Abuela's Roses
Carmen Escamilla

MAYBE GARDENING WASN'T THE BEST PLAN for today, after all. The sun was broiling. "Let's go to the movies," my son, Juan, said, "where it's air-conditioned." Monica held up her doll. "It's too hot for us too!"

I wasn't any more enthusiastic about tending my mother's garden than they were. What was I thinking even suggesting it? We'd been living with Mom since my divorce, and the memory of our own garden was still fresh in our minds: the red and yellow snapdragons, orange zinnias, and best of all, the beautiful rosebush in the front yard, a gift from my mom when my daughter was born. I'd never seen such delicate flowers, pale with the slightest hint of pink around the edge of each petal. My roses, my garden, that home, that *life*—all of it was gone now.

I'd hoped the planting would be comforting, but the rocks, weeds, and hard ground were anything but. How could something grow from that? I looked down at the shriveled carrot seeds in my hand. "Maybe we *should* go to the movies. We can help Abuela with her garden next season. . . ."

Before the children had a chance to reply, Mom came out the back door with a tray of iced glasses topped with red cherries. "Look what I have for my three farmers!" she said. "Lemonade and cookies!"

Leave it to Mom to find just the thing to encourage us. She handed me a napkin. "*Dios es bueno*," she reminded me as she so often did.

"God is good." Mom was always saying that, especially in my despair. She truly believed it would pull me through this terrible time. "Come back home and heal," she told me when the kids and I moved out. What better place? But it had been weeks, and I wasn't doing any better. Sadness and guilt overwhelmed me. I felt like a failure. I stared again at the carrot seeds in my hand.

"Let's get started," said Mom. "Just think of what this garden will look like come fall."

I grabbed a hoe and chopped at the ground. "Lord, till my own heart, and remove the hard places within it," I whispered. Juan and Monica picked out rocks and churned up dirt. Who could resist Mom's hopeful spirit?

She tipped some more seeds into my gloved hand. "*Dios es bueno*," she said.

The children lugged out additives for the soil and helped me mix them. Monica practiced counting out the right number of seeds for each row. Juan made sure each would-be plant was labeled: squash, pumpkin, zucchini, carrots. Monica started singing a song she'd learned at school. Soon all of us were singing along as we worked, digging in time to the music, patting the soil back over the seeded holes.

When we finished we had several rows—and four sweaty farmers. We grabbed hands, and I breathed in the smell of fresh, wet earth. *It's done*, I thought. *A new life for the garden and a new life for us.*

The thought was fleeting. Weeks later, I still mourned my failed marriage, our family of four all together in what appeared on the outside to be a happy home. I still missed my own garden, my delicate pink rosebush. I still worried about the future. It was still hard, some days, to get out of bed. But every morning Juan and Monica pulled me out to the garden to search for signs of new life poking out of the ground.

"It's taking too long," Juan said impatiently one day in late August.

Monica stamped her foot. "The plants will never grow," she told her doll.

"Maybe birds pecked all the seeds up!" said Juan.

I kneeled and touched the soil. "It may not look like anything is growing, but deep in the soil there's a lot of activity," I said. "A gardener has to be patient. We will water and watch and wait. God knows the right time for these plants to come up."

Juan and Monica went back into the house. I looked down at the empty ground, as impatient as they were. Nothing was growing. Nothing was getting better. For all my talk of watering and waiting, I still felt as helpless and hopeless as those tiny, shriveled seeds I'd held in my hand.

Then one day in late September, Monica yelled from the garden. "Mom! Something's growing!"

We all ran to the garden. There, poking through the soil, were green tips that would become pumpkins, squash, carrots, and zucchini. Now each morning we couldn't wait to get outside to see the surprises: green tendrils curling out of the ground, tiny pumpkins hiding in leaves. Soon we had a fall harvest. Mom and I carried the vegetables to the kitchen. Zucchini bread, carrot cake, pumpkin empanadas—there was no end to our bounty. I no longer had my pink roses, but Abuela's garden had sown seeds of hope in my heart.

"Let's bring in one more pumpkin for a pie," I said. Juan chose a beauty.

"Come see!" Monica called from the back corner of the garden.

Mom, Juan, and I ran over. "What is it?" I asked. Monica pointed me to a spot nearly hidden in the shade of other plants. I gasped. There, in the back of our vegetable garden, was a rosebush. A pink rosebush, just like the one I'd left behind.

"Mom, did you plant roses for me?" Mom shook her head. "Then where did they come from?"

"How come we never noticed it growing?" the kids wanted to know.

"*Dios es bueno*," Mom said with a smile. God *is* good.

Stairway to Heaven
Sylvia Gardner

WHEN I WAS GROWING UP back in the Berkshire Hills of Massachusetts, Mother prided herself on preparing us kids for anything life might send our way. Her own mother had suffered a massive stroke when she was only five years old. As the oldest of four children, my mother professed that it was hard work and a strong faith in God that got her through those rough years. She was a shining example of Yankee faith and fortitude, and she passed along those values to each of us.

Still, nothing could have prepared me for the void that Mother's death on October 14 would cause. She'd lived ninety-six healthy years and passed quietly in her sleep after enjoying a wonderful visit with the four of us. I was grateful for that. But now the person who'd helped me get through everything was gone. Never again would I dial her telephone number after a difficult day on the job as a nurse practitioner at the VA Medical Center. Never again would I hear the dearly familiar pearls of wisdom that had shaped my life.

Sometimes when a patient was going through a trying time, one of Mother's little sayings would come to mind and I'd share it with them. I remember the first time I met Mr. Sampson, a World War II veteran with emphysema and arthritis. I'd just moved to Appalachia from upstate New York, and my accent quickly branded me as a northerner and the new kid on the block. Mr. Sampson wasn't at all happy I'd been assigned to his care. "I'm short-winded and can't get around good anymore," he practically barked at me. "It takes me twice as long to cut the grass as it used to. And then they give me some foreigner like you."

After an introduction like that, I said a quick prayer, and all of a sudden a memory of Mother and me on our dairy farm back home came surging back. The minister had stopped by for a visit; our big black and white Berkshire pig that thought he was a watchdog had gotten loose from his pen and wouldn't let the minister out of his car. Mother and I leaped over the barbed-wire fence to catch it. I didn't quite make it.

I had a six-inch gash in my left knee after my attempt. Mother rubbed some of the same Bag Balm we used on our cows on my cut, taped it up just so, and pronounced me as good as new.

"Can't someone else milk the cows, just for today?" I pleaded.

"You can do it, Sylvia," Mother replied in her no-nonsense voice. "It may take you a little longer, but you can still do it. The angels will help you." The message was simple, and it had gotten me through more than a few hard times in nursing school.

That memory of Mother and the Berkshires was all I needed. I shared the story with Mr. Sampson and even showed him the scar I still have on my knee. Turned out, he, too, had been raised on a farm and had a mother whose practical faith was a lot like *my* mother's. When he left my office, he was still laughing about that pig and was reciting Mother's words and promising to put in a garden. Next time I saw him, he was loaded down with tomatoes and green peppers for our entire department. The only thing he requested in return was another installment of Mother's faith-filled counsel.

But with Mother gone, her words of wisdom seemed empty. The evening of her funeral, my husband and I drove through a misty rain just as the sun was setting below the trees somewhere between Chambersburg and Harrisburg, Pennsylvania. I felt completely overwhelmed. "God, where are You?" I prayed. "Please let me know that Mother is with You."

All at once, the rain stopped and the most spectacular neon light show arced across the sky. Vibrant red, orange, yellow, green, blue, purple—the colors were every bit as brilliant as the highlighter pens I used to mark points I needed to remember in my nurse practitioner journals.

The display reminded me of a time when I was nine years old. Mother was driving us kids to the Eastern States Exposition to show our Holsteins when this huge, beautiful rainbow lit up the sky. She pulled our 1936 Buick off the road, and exclaimed: "Kids, whenever you see a rainbow, that's God's angels dropping down His stairway to heaven for someone who has died."

As I recalled that unforgettable day, tears fell down my cheeks, blurring my vision. I did a double take, stunned by the sight, for there was not one, but two, rainbows spread across the sky. It was so spectacular that cars began parking along the side of the road to take pictures. My husband and I kept on driving, seemingly forever, toward Mother's double neon staircase and God's unmistakable sign for her doubting daughter.

When I returned to work after Mother's funeral, one of the nurses tapped on my office door. "There's a man out in the waiting room," she said. "He keeps telling everyone he's got to talk to Sylvia." She pointed to a gray-haired man in khaki slacks. I recognized him right away: Mr. Sampson. I hadn't seen him since he moved several years earlier and he looked terrible. *He must have gotten some really bad news*, I thought.

When I called his name, he looked at me and began to sob. I wrapped my arm around him and led him to a chair in my office. "My mama died October fourteenth," he told me. "I came back home for her funeral and to get the farm ready to sell. She was my best friend in all the world, Sylvia. I know how you loved your mother, so I knew you'd understand." Tears glistened in his eyes as he fixed his glance on an educational poster hanging on my wall. "I've got to have one of your stories, Sylvia...one of your mother's sayings about God's angels."

My words came out barely above a whisper. "*My* mother died the very same day as yours did, Mr. Sampson. But there's something she used to say that I believe might help you."

When I told him what had happened and Mother's angelic philosophy on rainbows, Mr. Sampson's face lit up. "You're not going to believe this, but I was driving to my mama's funeral that same day. And there were two rainbows in the sky for me too. I didn't know rainbows meant anything. I just thought they were pretty. I guess God must have thought He'd better send us a pair of them, as hardheaded as we can be. Huh, Sylvia?" He paused, his eyes filled with peace. "Can you imagine what a great time our mamas are having in heaven right now? While we're down here worrying how God's going to take care of us. We've got to start living what our mamas taught us. We've lived off their faith long enough."

And that's what I've done ever since. For I know firsthand that no matter how far away we are from our loved ones, God and His angels are always near. And whether by a spectacular show in the sky or a whisper to my heart, He will find the perfect way to send me a mother's comfort and guidance when I need it most.

Until my time on earth ends, and His angels drop down His stairway for me.

Promise of the Painting

Ann Mulligan

IT WAS JUST A WATERCOLOR PORTRAIT of a family at the beach. A mother and father barefoot on the sand, looking out over the ocean with their four children, the youngest perched on the father's shoulders. Yet this painting had somehow taken a powerful hold over my husband, Tim. He claimed it had saved him twice.

It wasn't hanging in an art gallery. No, it was in Oakwood Hospital in Dearborn, Michigan. The same hospital where we'd spent the saddest day of our lives.

That morning, sixteen weeks pregnant with our fourth child, I'd had a miscarriage. I lay in the hospital bed, staring at the bare white walls, as stark as my family's future seemed after this terrible loss. I needed Tim to be strong, to help get us through this. But he sat in the chair next to me, his eyes red from crying, looking just as torn apart as I felt.

"I could use a cup of coffee," he finally said, standing up wearily. "Be back soon."

I thought of our three young children, who were at home with the babysitter—seven-year-old Timmy, six-year-old Katie, and Liam, who'd just turned one. My husband and I had hoped to bring another little Mulligan into the family. Now that seemed unlikely.

Tim didn't return for a full hour. I was starting to get concerned. "I thought you were just getting coffee," I said when he came back. Then I glanced up.

His eyes were clear and bright, and he had an air of confidence. He sat down beside me, clasped my hand in his, and smiled. "We'll get through this," he said. "I know we will."

"And you know this how?" I asked.

He took a moment to gather his thoughts. Big, deep breaths. "I saw something in the hallway," he said.

Tim explained that he'd wandered the hospital corridors. He didn't even really want coffee. He needed somewhere to think. He ended up at the hospital atrium, found a low ledge, and sat down.

Framed watercolor paintings lined the wall across from him. One painting caught his eye, a beach scene of a family, a mother and father and their kids. *Four* kids. He stared hard at that youngest child, enjoying the view from his father's shoulders. *Our family will never bring our fourth child to the beach,* he thought. He closed his eyes and prayed, asking God to help him through this loss.

"That's when I heard it," Tim told me. "A voice." His eyebrows furrowed in disbelief. "You know me. I don't hear voices. This was like an inner voice, a thought with sound. I couldn't ignore it: *You will have a fourth child.*"

He tried to dismiss it, he said, but he couldn't. He looked at that painting again, and suddenly, it seemed like a divine promise. "I believed it."

I listened to the story wide-eyed. Tim believed that a painting had talked to him? It sounded crazy. Maybe it was the stress. Yet he seemed so certain. We went home late that afternoon, tired and still grieving.

Before we knew it, I was pregnant again. Nine months later, we welcomed baby Joseph into our family.

Tim and I were ecstatic...but soon we had something new to worry about. Tim was losing weight, fast, more than fifty pounds in three months. His face grew pale and gaunt, like an old man's. Every morning he woke up exhausted. He was too weak even to lift little Joseph. We feared the worst. Cancer?

Finally Tim's doctor gave us a diagnosis: Graves' disease, an overactive thyroid. A quick, noninvasive procedure at the hospital would shut Tim's thyroid gland down, the doctor said, and he'd have to take hormones for the rest of his life. Within a few months, though, he would feel better again. I was relieved. But Tim still seemed worried.

The day of the procedure arrived. Tim drove himself to Oakwood Hospital while I stayed home with the kids. When he came home, he had a strange look in his eyes, a calmness I'd seen before.

"I saw that painting again," he told me. "I wasn't even looking for it, but I got there early and was wandering the halls." Again he found himself sitting on the ledge in front of the watercolor of the family, fixated on the boy held by his father. Suddenly, Tim felt an overwhelming sense of peace. He heard that inner voice again, passing through him like a gentle breeze: *You will soon have the strength to hold your child just like that.*

I looked into his eyes. They blazed with hope and certainty. I didn't understand the painting's power over him, but I got an idea. What if I bought the painting for him? His birthday was just two days away, and I'd racked my brain for the perfect gift. This painting was it. I knew it would mean so much for him to have it. I *needed* to get it. But how?

First thing the next morning, I called the hospital about the painting. It wasn't for sale, but the hospital staffer who ordered the art offered to put me in touch with the artist. Would she even respond to such a crazy request?

Within the hour, my phone rang. The artist! Her name was Jan Mayer. I told her our story—my miscarriage, my husband's operation, and the voice he'd heard both times while looking at her watercolor.

"Do you have another copy of it?" I asked.

"I'm sorry," Jan said. "Each of my paintings is unique. Before I make a brush-stroke, I stare at the blank canvas and pray for inspiration. I ask God to use the finished work in whatever way He chooses to help whoever is in need.

"It was odd. For that painting, I prayed for days before I knew what direction to take. Then it came to me. It's a portrait of my son, my daughter-in-law, and their four children. The boy on my son's shoulders is my youngest grandson, Joseph."

"Joseph?" I blurted out. "That's *our* youngest son's name!"

Jan was silent for a moment. Then she whispered, "I believe God wants your family to have that painting."

Jan contacted the hospital and cut a deal to exchange the beach scene for another painting. I met her outside the hospital the very next day and we made our swap, just in time for Tim's birthday.

Not long after, we took a Mulligan family trip to Pawleys Island in South Carolina. We couldn't resist posing for a photograph on the beach, with Joseph in his father's arms. A reminder of the painting that had assured us our family's dreams would come true.

More Than Coincidence

Heather Smirnoff

I STOOD BEFORE THE FULL-LENGTH MIRROR in the church's bridal suite, look-ing past myself in my wedding gown, searching for a blessing. The secret blessing I'd prayed for. My soon-to-be mother-in-law fussed with the train on my gown, and the reflection got blurry as my eyes welled with tears. Not even my fiancé, Paul, knew the sadness that weighed on my heart, the longing I had for the pres-ence of the five people missing from my special day.

My mom, my aunt, Grandma and Grandpa, and my sister, Audrey. Five people I'd adored. My aunt and grandmother had passed away many years before; Grandpa, Mom, and Audrey had all died within four years of each other. I didn't know how the rules of heaven worked, but I'd asked God for a travel allowance, permission for all five to be in attendance. The Wayfarers Chapel in Rancho Palos Verdes, California, designed by the son of Frank Lloyd Wright, had a beautiful glass sanctuary—nothing blocked the altar from the sky above. *A perfect view from heaven,* I thought. I had asked for a very specific sign—something fluttering into the church, a sign I couldn't miss. On that chill November evening, though, I'd finally accepted that it was unlikely to happen. It wasn't that God didn't care, but that I'd asked for too much.

"Don't cry, dear, you'll ruin your makeup," Paul's mother said, noticing the tears trailing down my cheeks. Her English-bred politeness and charm usually eased my nerves. But no one could distract me from the absence I felt today.

"I see that I should give this gift to you now." She reached into her bag and pulled out a slim box. "I found this lovely handkerchief in a little English shop in Santa Monica. It was such fine-quality linen. There was another I liked even more, but this one spoke to me. It has little butterflies on it."

Butterflies? Paul's mother couldn't have known—I hadn't told a soul but God. The sign I'd prayed for was a white butterfly.

She handed me the delicate square of white cloth. Sure enough, it was embroidered with butterflies. *Five* white butterflies.

A flurry of blotting tissues and powder brushes had me looking radiant in almost no time. Finally ready to walk down the aisle, in front of everyone—*everyone*—I loved.

Road Trip Angel

Teresa Olive

WE WERE ONLY AN HOUR into our three-thousand-mile, cross-country trek to my family reunion in North Carolina. Already, bored voices from the backseat of our old, un-air-conditioned Dodge Dart were pleading: "Are we there yet?" Driving wasn't the fastest route to our destination, but it was the cheapest.

My husband, Jeff, and I had planned this trip for months, mapping it from our home in eastern Washington, highlighting campgrounds along the way. I couldn't wait to catch up with relatives and show off Christy, our newest addition at eighteen months old. At least she wasn't crying in her car seat—yet. Her sisters, LeeAnne, age seven, and Kellye, age five, were already complaining.

Even reaching this point—doing laundry, packing, planning snacks and car activities—hadn't been easy. We'd left right after church, midday on a Sunday, the minister's sermon on turning our worries over to God still fresh in my mind. That might have worked for someone who wasn't carting three kids on a road trip in a car with 165,000 miles on it and an unsettling tendency to slip out of gear. The Dart rode so low to the ground that we held our breath over speed bumps. Plus, I had to watch our pennies and keep us on schedule. All those breaks for the girls to potty could really add up. These were my worries for now. God could take over the worrying once we made it to the reunion.

We stopped for a quick lunch by a big pond in northern Oregon. "Who wants to watch Daddy skip rocks?" Jeff asked the girls.

"Not now, Jeff. We're still ten hours from your mother's house," I called after him. We'd planned to spend our first night in Reno with her.

"Just a couple more. I have to beat my record!" he said. At this rate, we would never make it to the reunion.

"Try this one, Daddy!" Kellye yelled. "It's perfect."

Jeff fingered the pebble, nodding his approval. He pulled his arm back and released the rock with a practiced flick of the wrist.

Plop! Plop! Plip! The last skips came so fast we could barely keep up with them. Sixteen skips in all! Each sent a swell of ripples out through the water. It always amazed me what one pebble could do. This one had left its mark for sure. It was so beautiful I nearly forgot my worries. "Okay, everybody. In the car!"

By late afternoon southern Oregon's soaring temperatures made the Dart feel like a blast furnace. The girls were whining and arguing. "I guess we need a break," I said.

We found a park in Klamath Falls with a wading pool. After we cooled off, we loaded up again. Jeff threw the car in reverse. But the Dart slipped out of gear and lurched forward, its bottom scraping over the concrete parking strip. The underbelly of the car ground against the barrier as Jeff got us free. Heading down the road, Jeff looked in the rearview mirror. "Uh-oh!" he said. I looked out the back. A trail of oil snaked behind us.

Jeff groaned. "Busted oil pan." He coasted to a spot behind a gas station, jacked the car up, and crawled underneath. When he finally wriggled out, even the oil couldn't hide the concern on his face. "It's fixable, if I can find someone to weld the hole in the oil pan. Plus, I need more oil and a gasket. But who're we going to find at five o'clock on a Sunday?"

Jeff and I stared at the Dart, not knowing what to do. A gravelly voice startled us. "Howdy, folks!"

We looked up at a tall man with a thatch of silver hair poking out from under a black cowboy hat. "Name's Phil," he continued. "Anything I can do?" We explained the situation. "Let me make a call," Phil said and strode to the gas station.

When he returned he said the owner of the auto parts store had agreed to stay open for us. "He's a friend," Phil explained.

He led the girls and me to his air-conditioned van while Jeff got the bolts off the oil pan. "I'm hungry, Mommy!" Christy said.

"Me too!" her sisters chimed in.

"I know a cure for that," Phil said. Before I could protest, he was headed up the road to a Dairy Queen. Hamburgers and milk shakes for everyone, including Jeff. I pulled out my wallet. "Your money's no good here," Phil said. Munching on my hamburger, I couldn't resist peeking at him. *Is this guy for real?*

When we returned to the Dart with Jeff's burger, he had a question for Phil. "You don't happen to know anyone who welds, do you?"

"You're looking at him," Phil said.

Once again the girls and I jumped into the van. We rode to a big metal building across town. When Phil opened the place up, we gasped. A row of classic sports cars sat in various stages of restoration. "You're welcome to look around," Phil said. "I'll be done in a jiffy."

It had been a long day. Normally, the girls would be inventing new ways to annoy one another. But they were entranced. "Wow! This is cool," LeeAnne said, running her hand over the shiny red hood of a 1959 Porsche. We lingered there studying every car until Phil returned.

"Sorry that took so long." Funny, I hadn't looked at my watch once. It was 7:00 p.m. Phil must have had his own schedule for the day, but when he saw we were in trouble he put his entire focus on us.

The Dart looked forlorn sitting in its puddle of oil back at the station. All that time wasted. We were still six whole hours away from Reno.

"Anyone around here like to swim?" asked Phil. "A friend of mine owns a nice little motel nearby."

I glanced at Jeff. It would throw us a day off schedule, and we had intended to avoid motels. But then again, Phil had saved us so much.

At the motel the girls squealed when they spotted the corkscrew pool slide. I tried to give Phil some money, but he just shook his head. "Do a favor for someone else," he said.

In our motel room, Kellye looked at me seriously. "Was he an angel?"

"Not the kind you're thinking of," I replied. "But he's an angel."

That night we bowed our heads and thanked God for sending Phil into our lives. I still couldn't get over the attention He'd given us. The wading pool, the garage full of hot rods, the corkscrew slide, skipping rocks in the pond—who had time for worries?

I called Jeff's mom to say we'd be there a day late. As I fell asleep I saw the surface of the pond again, ripples spreading ever outward, like angels spreading God's radiant, never-ending love. We were prepared to pass along the kindness Phil showed us and make our mark like a skipping stone. I'd let God worry about the schedule.

No One to Save Them

James Nelson

LIKE ANY FATHER, I was concerned for my daughter's safety. During college, Lori moved to a remote area outside Spokane with her horses and dogs, to a rustic cabin amid hayfields and pine forests, a mile and a half from her nearest neighbor. The vista from her home was achingly beautiful. But she was so isolated. I called a lot to check on her. "What if something happens?" I asked. "If you need help, there's no one around."

Lori laughed me off. "Oh, Dad," she said, "I'm fine."

I wanted to believe her. But every night I'd think about the coyotes out there in the woods, or of some unsavory characters she'd once seen around her cabin. "Dad, I'm okay," she assured me. "Clancy barks if he sees strangers. We can handle ourselves." Still, I worried. When I worry, I pray. *God, my daughter thinks her black Lab keeps her safe. Protect her, Lord, when he can't.*

One day, Lori called. Her voice didn't sound quite the same. "I have something to tell you," she said. "I don't want you to worry." As if that were possible. "I think you should know." I grabbed a chair and sat down.

A spring rain had been pelting her cabin all day, she said. She'd crawled into comfy clothes and snuggled on the couch with a good book and a cup of tea. But Clancy got restless. A bit of canine cabin fever. He needed exercise.

Finally, in the afternoon, the rain stopped. Lori laced up her heavy boots and pulled on a down jacket. "Come on, Clancy," she called.

Lori opened the door and Clancy nosed past her outside. He loped down the road toward Dead Man's Creek, about a third of a mile away. He knew the way. He swam the creek all the time while Lori watched from the one-lane bridge above.

The road was empty. They were almost to the creek, she said, when ominous black clouds rolled in. "I knew what that meant," she told me. The sky began spitting rain. She called to Clancy.

But he had other ideas. He had reached the embankment. "Clancy, no!" Lori yelled.

There was no stopping him. Labs are like that when it comes to water. He leaped into the creek.

Lori yelled for Clancy to come back. The rain and snowmelt had turned the shallow, slow-moving creek into a raging torrent. Clancy was nowhere in sight. Lori ran to the middle of the bridge and yelled his name.

Then she heard whimpers and cries. She spotted Clancy downstream. Normally a powerful swimmer, he struggled to keep his head above water.

The barbed-wire fence! There was pastureland on either side of the creek, and the owner had strung a line of fencing the length of his property, crossing the creek. Usually it hung two or three feet above the waterline. Clancy would swim right under it. But now, with the water so high, the fence was hidden beneath the surface. Clancy was snared on the barbed wire.

"Dad, I had to save him," Lori said.

She hit the water and used her sleeve to grab the fence, figuring she'd pull herself to Clancy. But the weight of her boots and jacket, and the force of the current, nearly dragged her under. By the time she reached Clancy, she was neck-deep. The barbed wire dug into her jacket. She couldn't work herself free. Clancy kept going under, losing stamina. Running out of time.

"I grabbed Clancy around his chest and lifted him so his head was above water," Lori said. Every movement sank the barbs deeper into the dog's flesh. There was pain in his whimpers, fear in his eyes.

The creek was freezing, sapping her strength. In a few minutes she'd have a terrible decision to make: let go of Clancy or risk drowning herself.

She trained her eyes on the bridge, her only chance for rescue. Not a vehicle in sight. "Dad, I kept thinking of you worrying about me and praying." She looked to the sky and said a word of prayer herself.

She glanced back to the road. There was a pickup truck, the first car she'd seen since she and Clancy had set out. The truck crested the bridge. She yelled as loud as she could. But the truck continued down the road.

"I knew it was a long shot," she said. How would the driver have seen her? In this weather, he was concentrating on the road. As for hearing her yells—his windows were up, the rain was blowing, and he was probably listening to weather updates on the radio.

Exactly what I was afraid of. No one out there to look after her.

She must have been heartbroken, saying good-bye to her beloved dog. All the times he had protected her! "I'm so sorry about Clancy...," I said.

"Dad, listen," Lori said. "I looked back to the road. The pickup. It stopped. And then backed up onto the bridge."

Two men piled out. "Hang on! We're coming!" one of them shouted. They climbed down the embankment, worked Clancy and Lori free, and pulled them from the water.

"I'm not going to stop worrying," I told her. "And I'm not going to quit praying."

"I hope you never do," Lori said. And then she told me the rest.

The men hustled her and Clancy into the truck to warm up. "Are you ever lucky!" the driver told her, as he drove them back to her cabin.

"I know," Lori said. "Thank you."

"No, it's not that. See, we never take this road," the driver said. "It's out of our way. For some reason, today we took this route to town. I can't explain it. I just got this weird sense about it."

A Perfect Match
Staci Almager

ACCORDING TO JOHN, I drove up to the front entrance of his favorite San Antonio coffee shop in a BMW convertible nearly every morning, flung my long blonde hair over my shoulder with a confident air, and strode up to the counter to buy a cup of coffee and the newspaper, seemingly without a care in the world.

I remember that time differently. It might have looked like I had it all together, but that couldn't be further from the truth.

The Saturday morning I first met John, my five-year-old daughter, Jennifer, and I were sitting in the coffee shop. She sipped a smoothie; I had the paper spread out across my lap. But it was only a breather before a difficult afternoon—a doctor's appointment that I hoped could save my daughter's life.

In truth, I was the twenty-five-year-old single mom of a chronically ill little girl. We'd left our home in Kansas to come here to Texas for six months of medical tests and observation before a specialist would agree to perform a risky surgery. I'd told Jennifer that everything would be okay, that we'd be back home in Kansas before she knew it—but the fact was I didn't know anything for sure. From the outside, my daughter seemed fine. A bit small for her age but your typical curious, happy-go-lucky kid. You could barely see the outline of the colostomy pouch under her clothes, the most visible sign of the disorder that wreaked havoc inside her body.

Jennifer slurped the last of her strawberry smoothie. A little boy with brown hair, right around Jennifer's age, walked across the coffee shop in our direction. He marched up to Jennifer and whispered something in her ear.

I straightened up in my chair. *Who is this boy?* Then Jennifer giggled. I relaxed. *She knows him. Is he a friend from kindergarten?* The boy turned to me and said something through a heavy lisp. I smiled tentatively, not able to understand a word.

A tall man with the same brown hair appeared from behind the boy. "Sorry about that," he said, smiling. "My son is a loose cannon." I'd never seen him before, but he gave me such a familiar look. . . .

"Do I know you?" I asked.

"Well, Adam is in your daughter's kindergarten class," he said. "Maybe you saw me at school. I'm also in this coffee shop every morning." He smiled. "Just like you. My name is John." He extended his hand.

"Staci," I said, extending mine.

He was a single parent too, he said, recently divorced. I felt a bit awkward. How long had he been watching me, this random stranger in this random coffee joint in the middle of Texas? I remembered Jennifer's appointment and quickly gathered our things.

"Jennifer and I have to get going," I said. "See you around!" We waved goodbye and hurried out to my car, the hand-me-down convertible I'd driven here from Kansas. I wasn't looking to meet anyone. I was only in San Antonio for one reason.

From birth my daughter had struggled with health problems. Her pediatrician diagnosed her with a rare birth defect called VATER syndrome. Many of her organs hadn't developed properly. She was missing a functioning bladder, her digestive system hadn't formed normally and she suffered frequent life-threatening infections. She'd grow terribly weak, her fever would spike, and I'd rush her to the emergency room. Jennifer's father and I had split up when she was only two, so it was up to me to take care of her. Between college classes and a part-time job, I sought out the best treatment available.

Jennifer's condition only worsened. She was becoming immune to antibiotics. I found myself driving her to the hospital in Kansas City nearly every other day. *Lord,* I prayed desperately, *help me find some way to save my daughter's life.*

I looked up doctors across the country who specialized in treating congenital syndromes like my daughter's. Only one, a doctor in San Antonio, had extensive experience successfully operating on children with VATER syndrome. I called him and described my daughter's case. "Give me six months," he said. "If you bring your daughter to Texas for six months, I can monitor how she responds to testing and see if she is eligible for the surgery that has helped other patients."

It was a long shot. A team of specialists would have to reconstruct her internal organs. There was no guarantee that the operation would be successful. How was I supposed to uproot us and move across the country for the next six months? Yet it felt like our only chance. I dropped out of college, quit my job, and piled our belongings in the car. Only one thing mattered—saving my daughter.

I rented half of a duplex close to Jennifer's new school and found a job at a clothing store that paid just enough to cover our expenses. Every morning, I'd get up early and make breakfast. Wake Jennifer and get her dressed. Drop her off at kindergarten. Sit at the coffee shop until the store opened for business. Work until five, pick her up, and make dinner. Then get ready for bedtime. Only Jennifer's medical appointments broke up the routine.

I thought about the man from the coffee shop and his son while we waited at the doctor's office, running my hands through Jennifer's blonde hair. I felt bad. *Maybe I should have been nicer. Especially to a friend of Jennifer's. She can use all the support she can get right now.*

Based on Jennifer's response to testing, the doctor said he was willing to green-light her surgery. "It's a risky procedure," he said. "We might never be completely out of the woods. But it's her best hope."

We set a date for her surgery and spent a month preparing, physically and emotionally. I was hopeful and scared all at the same time. One Sunday afternoon, I stopped in at the coffee shop with Jennifer on our way to the movies. We sat on the couch by the window and looked through the paper for movie times.

There were John and Adam. They sat at a table on the other side of the shop. I buried my head in the newspaper, trying to hide—but Jennifer caught my glance in their direction.

"Mommy," she whispered. "Can we invite Adam and his dad to come to the movies with us? Please?"

I shook my head. "I don't think so, honey," I said. But I couldn't resist the pleading look she gave me. How could I say no to this simple request when she'd been through so much and the future was so uncertain?

I stood up and walked over to their table.

"Jennifer and I are going to the movies later. Would you and your son like to come?"

John looked at me and then at Adam. He smiled. "Would you like that, buddy?" he asked, patting Adam on the back. Adam nodded enthusiastically. "We'd love to," John told me. We arranged a time to meet at the theater.

The two kids sat between John and me. Every so often, I looked over their little heads at him. Feelings whirled within me, feelings that were trying to form into something coherent. I sensed something I hadn't felt in years: peace. More than that, contentment, as though this was something we'd done a thousand times or could do a thousand times. As though we were a family. Then the credits rolled and the lights came up, but the feelings stayed.

After that first movie we arranged another. That one turned into lunch afterward. Soon John, the kids, and I had a little tradition. We were growing inseparable.

On the day of Jennifer's surgery, John came with me to the hospital. He kept me from going crazy during the seventeen hours she was on the operating table.

Finally the doctor emerged with good news. The procedure had gone even better than he had hoped. Jennifer needed time to recover, and there could be complications down the line. But eventually, she wouldn't need my help for daily functions anymore. She wouldn't be prone to infections and fevers. She could have a normal, happy childhood.

Jennifer and I had gotten the miracle I'd prayed for, and it was time for us to go home to Kansas. I kept putting it off, though. Jennifer was making more friends; she seemed content here. Then there was John. From the beginning, he'd known my plans to leave, but he never put the brakes on, never held back his feelings for me.

One day, John took me out to dinner and asked if I would marry him. I looked into his eyes and said yes without having to think about it.

Things were going great for us. That feeling that I got in the movie theater, that feeling of contentment—it was the norm now. We really had become a family.

We took Jennifer for follow-ups, and she seemed to be thriving, though she experienced periods of weakness. A year after her surgery, the doctor called us in, troubled by what he'd found in recent lab tests. John sat at my side.

"Your daughter is experiencing acute kidney failure," he told us. "She will need a transplant, the sooner the better. I'm sorry."

The room spun. I could hardly breathe, as if the air had been sucked right out of me. I'd been able to prepare for her other health issues, but this one was a shock. After everything Jennifer had been through, now this? *Why, God?*

"She can go on the transplant list," the doctor said, "but the wait for a kidney could be five years, or more. Unless someone volunteers to be a donor."

"What about me?" I asked.

A donation from a blood relative increased the odds of a match, the doctor explained, but my being Jennifer's mother was no guarantee that my kidney wouldn't be rejected by her body. The testing protocol would be comprehensive. I would have CAT scans and X-rays. The doctors would check everything from heart health and liver function to exposure to drugs and past viral illnesses. Additional testing was required to determine whether my blood type was compatible with Jennifer's. And still there would be no guarantee.

John reached for my hand. "Don't worry," he said. "I'll get tested too." Of course he'd volunteer to go through this with me. But it was even less likely that he would be a match. *Way* less likely.

We both took the tests. I was a good match…but John was perfect. John was the ideal donor.

Today our daughter is twenty-two—John's kidney saved her life. I'm now the executive director of Transplants for Children, a nonprofit organization based in San Antonio that supports organ donors and recipients.

From the moment he first saw me in the coffee shop, John says, he knew we were meant to be together. That day with John and the kids at the movies, a feeling I'd never had before assured me that we were meant to be a family. It couldn't have been a more perfect match.

Sometimes life seems to be made up of random events and encounters. Then again, sometimes it is anything but.

Long to Live

Jackie Clements-Marenda

"GOD, IN THE NAME OF MARY, be with us, give us hope." That's what I had started praying before my grandson Patrick was even born. When we were told the amniocentesis was abnormal. When his high-pitched, catlike cries drew the attention of the maternity ward staff. When at barely a day old, he stopped breathing. On every harrowing trip to the emergency room we'd made in the years that followed. Every time I flashed back to that terrifying moment in the delivery room, when my daughter and I listened to the pediatric specialist's grim prognosis: "He may not survive childhood."

Then the day came. The day I believed God stopped listening, stopped caring. I stood outside the isolation room at Staten Island University Hospital, staring through the glass at my daughter, Tara, and Patrick, seven years old. If the results of Patrick's MRI were what the neurologist suspected—an inoperable brain tumor—it was almost certain: Patrick would die. I wasn't just isolated from them, I felt isolated from God, from His goodness and His love. My grandson was a sweet, gentle child. *Why,* I screamed silently, *why must he endure all this?* I tried to pray for understanding, but the words stuck in my throat.

A nurse, chart in hand, touched my arm. "Sorry for the delay," she said. "There's another patient ahead of your grandson, so it'll be a while." Another minor cruelty, making Patrick wait, making us all wait, for confirmation of the worst. I signaled to Tara that I was going to the ladies' room. Patrick waved and blew kisses to me, his hazel eyes opening wide. "I love you, Boo Boo Bear!" I mouthed back. I barely made it to the bathroom before the tears spilled over.

Tara was a single mom, living with my husband and me, so I felt bonded to my grandson even before he arrived. I was standing right there when he entered this world, and I immediately sensed that the amnio was right. The doctor called it cri du chat syndrome, or cat cry syndrome, because of the distinctive sound of an affected child's cry. It occurs in one birth per fifty thousand, when a portion of the short arm of chromosome number five is missing. Most doctors go through their entire careers without seeing a case of it. Although Patrick was born without many of the problems that often go along with the syndrome, others he had: folds beneath his eyes, low-set ears, poor growth and muscle tone, and a hole in his heart. Torticollis made it difficult for him to move his head, and he was unable to suckle. At twenty-four hours old, his lungs gave out. Because he was already in the pediatric intensive care unit, quick-acting nurses were able to revive him.

The pediatric specialist didn't sugarcoat Patrick's prognosis. His life would be a struggle, and likely shortened.

I had drawn upon a tradition of my Irish family when I appointed Patrick a spiritual guardian. He needed someone loving and strong. Who better, I'd decided, than Mary, the mother of Jesus? "Mary is a mother," I implored God. "She knows a mother's love. Give Tara and me Mary's strength to return Patrick to You if You call, and please don't let our little one suffer."

Over the years, Patrick had many health scares. Worry and panic often overrode my faith. It got to the point that even a simple case of toddler sniffles had me begging God: *In the name of the Blessed Mother, please not today.*

I hoped the bathroom would be empty. A sanctuary. But a gray-haired woman with beautiful skin the color of creamed coffee stood by the sink, blotting her tears with a paper towel. Our eyes met in the mirror. "Are you okay?" I asked, trying to swallow my own tears. No need for two of us to be blubbering.

She turned, looked at me for what felt like a long moment. Then she said, "Depends on what you consider okay. These are tears of gratitude."

"Happy tears?" I asked.

"You could say that. We were on our way home to Florida from a wedding in Boston when our daughter got terrible pains in her legs. This was the nearest hospital. The MRI confirmed it was only a pinched nerve this time, so we're going home today. She's out in the car now with her father."

I passed her another paper towel. "That *is* great news!" I said. "She's had health problems before?"

"Many," the woman said. "She's an adult, but she has the mental age of a five-year-old. She's nonverbal, which makes it hard to express how she's feeling. I understand her signing but most people don't."

"She has a hearing impairment?"

The woman dropped her paper towels into the trash can. "No. She has a condition called cri du chat syndrome."

I stared at her, my heart pounding and the room spinning. "She has cri du chat?"

"You've heard of it?"

"Yes," I said. "My grandson has it. We were told that he would have severe health problems and a shorter life expectancy."

"We were told the same," the woman said. "Years ago, when they knew nothing about it. Doctors say a lot of things, but they forget that God has His own timetable. My daughter? She's fifty years old."

"Fifty! She's fifty?" My words came out in a burst of astonishment.

The woman smiled and nodded, then checked her watch. "I have to get going before my husband leaves without me, but I will pray for your grandson. What is his name?"

"Patrick," I said, "thank you. Running into you helped me more than you'll ever know. What's your daughter's name? I'll pray for her too."

"Mary," she replied. "Her name is Mary."

The woman left the bathroom. I followed shortly after. I returned to Tara and my grandson just in time to hear the results of his MRI: no tumor. A false alarm.

"God, in the name of Mary, be with us, give us hope." I still say those words every day, and I know Someone is listening. Today Patrick is eight and getting stronger. Not just surviving but thriving.

Wish You Were Here

Danielle Eliska Lyle

'TWEEN WATERS INN ON CAPTIVA ISLAND in Florida started out as a cluster of fishing cottages in 1931 and grew into a good-size resort. Yet in its eighty-two-year history, the resort had never done a promotion as big as the Vacation of a Lifetime contest it launched in January 2013. The prize was a free three-night stay for two at 'Tween Waters Inn every year for the next twenty-five years.

Entries poured in—fifteen thousand before the deadline. On May 1, the resort's general manager, Jeff Shuff, randomly drew a number between one and fifteen thousand. He picked 6,723. Emily Kettner of the resort's marketing team found the corresponding entry: Deborah Tilson of St. Paul Park, Minnesota. *A snowbird,* Emily figured. *She's going to love this.*

She couldn't wait to call Deborah with the good news. "Congratulations, Ms. Tilson!" she said. "You're the winner of 'Tween Waters Inn Island Resort's Vacation of a Lifetime contest."

Deborah gasped. "I really won?" she asked, her voice breaking.

It sounded like she was crying. Not happy tears, either. *What's going on here?* Emily wondered. She said carefully, "Yes, ma'am, you won."

"You have no idea what this means to me," Deborah said. She told Emily that she had been to 'Tween Waters Inn only once—three years earlier, with her husband, oldest daughter, and grandson. It was such a beautiful place, a slice of heaven on earth.

"But being there was bittersweet," Deborah continued. "We'd come to 'Tween Waters to say good-bye to my youngest daughter, Kristine."

Kristine was the spark in their family. She had a laugh that could fill a room. The only thing bigger than her laugh was her heart. She was always looking out for other people. Her family. Her friends. Even strangers. She wouldn't think twice about giving her last dollar to a homeless person. She had just enrolled in nursing school when tragedy struck. Kristine was killed in December 2007, a victim of domestic violence. Her ex-boyfriend was convicted of her murder and sentenced to life in prison.

Deborah had never talked to Kristine about going to Florida, let alone heard of 'Tween Waters Inn. One day in March 2008, Deborah was home watching Kristine's son, who, at age two, was a real handful. He begged to go outside. Deborah cleared off their deck—it was covered with snow, being March in Minnesota—so he could play.

She found a notepad with Kristine's handwriting stuck in a stack of patio chairs. On the first page was a monthly budget. Kristine had jotted down what it would cost for nursing school, what she would make if she worked nights, and so on.

There was an arrow pointing to the next page. Deborah flipped to it. Across the top were the words *Mom. Me. Florida.* Below, Kristine had listed three resorts, but her number-one choice was 'Tween Waters Inn on Captiva Island.

"She wanted to surprise me," Deborah explained to Emily. "Kristine wanted to get me to Florida, to 'Tween Waters Inn. She'd been putting a little away every month. But she never got a chance to take me."

Deborah and her husband had held on to Kristine's ashes, not knowing where to lay their daughter to rest. The notepad changed everything. "It became my project to get her there," Deborah said. "We saved up and made the trip in 2010."

Deborah talked to the resort manager and told him about her daughter's death. She asked if it was okay for them to scatter Kristine's ashes on the beach. "He told us to go right ahead. Like I said, it was a bittersweet time for us, but it was a release. I felt like I was telling Kristine in heaven, *Here we are now, in Florida together, just like you wanted.*"

Deborah was a little sad, though, knowing that Florida was too far for her to visit often. She found the resort on Facebook and when she saw their contest, she thought, *What are my chances?* But she entered anyway. "Thank you," she told Emily. "Now I can come back every year and be close to my daughter."

It was Emily's turn to cry. She hung up the phone and knocked on Jeff's door to tell him about the winner.

Before she could finish, he interrupted. "I remember her! She was the one who scattered her daughter's ashes on the beach."

A winner chosen at random? Deborah Tilson doesn't think so.

Still Life

Deborah Walz

A DOLL. A HANDFUL OF BLOCKS. My two-year-old daughter's old baby shoe. I'd grabbed the items at random to bring to my art class, where I'd use them in a still life.

"Compose a scene," the teacher said, "then start painting."

I sat Raggedy Ann up with the shoe beside her. Now for the blocks . . . I turned one a little to the left so I could see one letter and one number. Another had a picture of a cat facing out. Where I put things didn't really matter, it was just to have something to paint.

"Looks good," Sandy said. It was Sandy who'd gotten me into the art class—at a time when just leaving the house seemed impossible.

Four months into my second pregnancy, I'd miscarried. In one terrible night I lost my baby along with my confidence and hope. I had no energy, no appetite. I passed day after day in a haze. I no longer wanted to try for another baby. I couldn't endure another miscarriage.

Until then, Sandy was just my next-door neighbor, with three lively children. Her youngest boy was the same age as my daughter, Mary. Sandy helped her husband run a lawn mower and bicycle shop. She had her hands full, to say the least. But she became a lifesaver. She looked in on me every day. She watched Mary while I slept, washed dishes, did laundry. She taught me what it meant to be a good neighbor.

Sandy encouraged me to get out of the house. She signed us both up for the oil-painting class. "It starts this week," she said one afternoon. "I've bought all the supplies we need."

I didn't have the heart to say no.

Week by week, thanks to Sandy's enthusiasm and the teacher's patience, I'd come to love the class. For the first time since losing my baby I had something to look forward to.

So why did I choose baby things for my still life? I wondered now, uncapping my paints. I couldn't say. I just let my instincts take over and painted. I worked quickly and self-confidently, as if the haze that hung over me was clearing. Finally I sat back and admired my work. It looked like a scene from a nursery, the nursery that could have been. Strangely, it didn't make me feel sad. I was proud of my work. So were Sandy and my teacher.

The art class was like a door back to my life. Gradually my depression lifted. My fear of trying for another child didn't, though. One night I dreamed I was pregnant and woke up troubled. The next day I was having my wisdom teeth removed. When the anesthesiologist asked if there was a chance I was pregnant I said no. Two weeks later I found out I *was* going to have a baby—and I was terrified.

"What if the anesthesia hurt the baby and causes another miscarriage?" I asked my obstetrician. "Just relax, and have trust," he said.

Trust. It was the one thing I hadn't gotten back in the two years since my miscarriage. I didn't trust my body. I didn't trust God. I lay awake at night imagining all the things that could go wrong. I tried to convince myself this was God's plan and not a mistake, prayed the baby would be healthy. But the fear never completely left me.

As my due date drew near, I got the nursery ready, hoping to chase away my fears. Searching a closet for some of Mary's old baby things, I came across a painting—my still life! I remembered with fondness the kindness of my friend Sandy and thanked God for her help through such a difficult time. I hung the painting above the crib. The colors matched the room perfectly.

At last I gave birth to Katherine Anne—happy and healthy. My husband, Marshal, and I brought her home, wrapped in a pink blanket. I laid her in the crib. Staring at my newborn girl, I felt nothing but joy.

Then I looked up at the still life, as if I were seeing it for the first time. There was the doll, next to a baby's shoe. At her feet was a block with an image of a little girl and the letters *K* and *A*—for Katherine Anne. It was between a block with *M* for Marshal and one with *D* for Deb. Another block showed a cat—like "Kat"— along with *O*, her blood type. Three more blocks showed a little clock set at 4:02, the time she was born, and the numbers six, one, and seven—June 1, 1977, my new daughter's birthday! She was born right on time.

The objects were anything but random. They'd been chosen with a careful hand by an artist much greater than myself, with a vision I was only now beginning to see.

CHAPTER 4

Angels in Fur and Feathers

"The old doe was already waiting on the deck. Her fawn stood at

her side. Four more deer crowded in behind them.

They weren't the rescue team I'd imagined, but they were all I had.

'Look, I have to get to a doctor,' I said. 'Now.'

The deer flicked their ears, watching.

If I can just get to the road at the top of the hill, *I thought,*

I can flag someone down. *Could I make it that far?*

I had to try. The longer I went untreated,

the worse the damage could be.

I moved stiffly off the deck and on to the lawn,

forcing my left side to move.

The deer were close behind me."

—PATRICE VACCA

Deer Crossing

Patrice Vacca

MOVING FROM URBAN NEW JERSEY to the Pennsylvania woods was a dream come true for me. The land around my house was a campground in the summer. My nearest neighbor was miles away, and there was no phone service to my house. Didn't bother me a bit.

Back in New Jersey I'd worked as a rehab nurse. I saw people all the time. Some predicted I would soon tire of my new solitary life, but I hadn't so far and didn't expect I ever would. My whole life I have felt connected to nature, and I could never feel lonely with animals nearby. Thankfully the woods were full of them.

"I call that one Scarbelly," I told a visiting friend when a deer tiptoed out of the woods one afternoon. She was a doe, easily recognizable by the old wound running from her shoulder to her hip. "She had a fawn last year. She brings her baby around too."

"They sure seem to like you a lot!" she said as the doe inched nearer to me. We stayed very still so as not to startle her.

"I'd like to think so," I said. "Deer aren't easy to get close to."

Each day I woke up in my house in the woods was a pleasure—until one April morning. I heard the birds singing as usual, saw the pale sun through the window, smelled the fresh air. But something was wrong. I tried to sit up. My legs felt like lead. They refused to cooperate with me. I had to struggle just to swing them over the side of the bed.

I managed to stand. *Get to the bathroom,* I thought. Just turning in the right direction almost knocked me over I was so off-balance. I managed to shuffle toward the bathroom door.

Thud.

My shoulder hit the doorjamb. *How could I miss the door?* I took a step back and tried another time. Once again my shoulder hit the door.

I didn't feel it at all. In fact, I couldn't feel my shoulder, my arm, my fingers on the left side of my body. It was like a great emptiness hung where my arm should be. I tried to squeeze my fingers together. They wouldn't budge.

Stroke! I thought, my nurse's training kicking in. My mother and grandmother had both died from strokes. Could that be happening to me—at forty-six? I had to get to a hospital fast. But how? No neighbors, no phone . . .

"Well, God," I mumbled, "we've got to do something here. I need help. Fast!"

I pulled on the easiest clothes I could find and slipped my feet into a pair of sandals. I moved carefully to the door.

"Scarbelly!"

The old doe was already waiting on the deck. Her fawn stood at her side. Four more deer crowded in behind them.

They weren't the rescue team I'd imagined, but they were all I had. "Look, I have to get to a doctor," I said. "Now."

The deer flicked their ears, watching.

If I can just get to the road at the top of the hill, I thought, *I can flag someone down.* Could I make it that far? I had to try. The longer I went untreated, the worse the damage could be. I moved stiffly off the deck and on to the lawn, forcing my left side to move. The deer were close behind me.

The lawn stretched out before me like an ocean. *I'll never make it all that way!*

I put my hand to my face, ready to cry. *That won't help!* I told myself. I rubbed my eyes and looked down at the gravel road. I was standing at the edge of it. I looked over my shoulder at the expanse of lawn and my house in the distance. *How in the world did I get here?* I didn't remember walking that significant distance—and it would have taken ages. But here I was, and so were the deer—right beside me. Scarbelly's deep brown eyes looked into mine. "Did you carry me?" I said.

She blinked her long lashes. She was so close I could have touched her.

A cloud of dust in the distance! I waved frantically as the car got closer. The driver smiled and waved back, but he didn't even slow down. *He can't even tell I need help!*

Another car went by. The same thing happened. Again and again.

"I have to go out to the middle of the road," I said. "They'll either stop or run me over. If I don't get help, I might not make it anyway."

I pulled myself into the road. The herd of deer walked forward, keeping pace with my own tortured steps. They huddled close around me, surrounding me with a protective circle in the middle of the road. The heat from their bodies warmed me. Their soft sides rose and fell in a calming rhythm. I felt their gentle breath on my skin.

A truck appeared in the distance, moving toward us. *If this one doesn't stop, I don't know what I'll do.*

I raised my hand and held it straight out in front of me. The deer stood still as stone, not budging even as the truck came at full speed. Thank goodness, it slowed and stopped. The driver stuck his head out the window and stared at me surrounded by a herd of deer.

"Please," I said, "I need to get to the hospital. I think I had a stroke."

The driver's eyes moved to the deer and back to me. He opened his mouth, but no words came out. He shook his head and climbed out of the truck, hurrying to open the passenger door.

The deer parted to let me get to the truck. The driver eyed them the whole time he helped me inside. The deer eyed him too, but they didn't run away as they usually did when faced with people. People besides me, that is. The driver settled me safe in the passenger seat and got behind the wheel. He shifted into gear and beeped the horn as gently as he could. Only then did the deer lower their heads and step gracefully off the road.

I laid my head against the car seat, exhausted. *Thank You, God,* I prayed, *for Your beautiful creatures who watched over me like You do.*

Tests at the hospital proved I had had a stroke. "You should have a good recovery," the doctor told me. "You're lucky you were able to get here as quickly as you did. If you'd waited much longer, you might have had serious long-term damage."

I got lucky, but the situation was nothing short of angelic.

Sunny, My Four-Legged Rescuer

Jennie Ivey

SUNNY WAS "BOMBPROOF." That's a word equestrians use to describe a horse that's safe for anyone to ride. A horse that doesn't kick or bite or buck or rear or run back to the barn with a terrified rider clinging to the saddle horn for dear life.

I'd met Sunny ten years earlier when an elderly neighbor decided to sell his farm and livestock. He needed a good home for his favorite horse, a beautiful champagne palomino with a pale golden coat and matching mane and tail. Even Sunny's eyes were pale gold.

When I looked into those gentle golden eyes, it was love at first sight.

We'd been inseparable companions ever since. No matter how busy my day, I always tried to carve out an hour when I could toss a saddle onto Sunny's back and head for the woods. An abandoned logging road cut years ago on the back of my property had become the perfect horse trail. I loved being out in God's creation, with the solid Tennessee ground underfoot and a thick canopy of trees overhead. Nothing in the woods—be it squirrels, wild turkey, or even the occasional white-tailed deer—ever seemed to bother Sunny.

As summer approached and the days grew long, I'd started routinely packing a sack supper and heading out for a ride after work. That supper always included a sandwich for me and an apple for Sunny.

One evening, our ride was so pleasant that we lingered on the trail too long. It was nearly dark by the time we returned to the barnyard. I looped Sunny's reins over the fence rail, unbuckled the girth, and slid the saddle off his back. I was headed to the barn when he began to neigh in a way I'd never heard before. I turned and was surprised to see him pawing the ground and tossing his head. *Probably just eager for some sweet feed and a bucket of water*, I figured. But before I could step into the dimly lit barn to get the sweat scraper and hoof pick from the tack room, Sunny jerked loose from the fence rail and bolted straight toward me.

What had come over my sweet, gentle horse?

My instincts took over, causing me to step aside just as Sunny charged into the barn. He whinnied loudly and then reared up, pawing the air with his front hooves before sending them stomping to the ground. Again he rose up and came down. Then a third time. Finally, he wheeled and—with nostrils flaring and tail in the air—trotted out of the barn. He nodded his head at me as though urging me into the barn to see what he had done.

I made my way gingerly toward the tack room. In the deepening dusk, I could barely make out something slithering toward the barn's rear gate. As I moved closer, I could see what it was. A four-foot-long snake with a body as big around as my arm. And not just any snake—a deadly timber rattlesnake, its tail shaking ominously as it slipped beneath the gate and disappeared into the tall grass.

Trembling, I whispered a prayer of thanks as I threw my arms around Sunny and felt his velvety nose nuzzle against my neck. My not-so-bombproof four-legged angel had just saved my life.

What Casey Did

Ron Berler

CASEY WASN'T THE MOST popular dog in her owner Carol Baird's neighborhood of Dalton, Georgia. A huge, burly Alaskan malamute, she had a heart of gold but a nose for trouble. She'd slip out the Baird family's back door and trot down the street without a care. Most people gave her a wide berth. That was hardly surprising. From a distance, Casey looked a lot like a wolf.

She behaved like one too, or at least had an appetite like one. Neighbors often stormed over to complain. "Your dog got out again, and ate all of our dog's food!" or "Casey's turned over our garbage!"

So when a man rapped on Carol's door, said he lived three blocks away, and then asked for her dog's name, Carol braced herself. *What did Casey do this time?*

"We have a sliding-glass door that we usually keep open in the summer," the man began, "and every day for the last several weeks your dog has wandered off the street and come uninvited into my house."

That dog, Carol thought. "I'm so sorry," she said. "I don't know why Casey gets herself into such mischief. A lot of it's our fault. We have to start watching her more closely. But honestly, she means no harm—"

"No, you don't understand," the man interrupted. "I came over to thank you."

The man must have seen the confusion on Carol's face. No neighbor had ever said anything positive about Casey before. They usually wanted to know who would fill up the two-foot hole she'd energetically dug in their backyard.

But not this neighbor. He explained that his father, who had Alzheimer's, lived with him and his wife and needed constant monitoring. The father rarely moved from his easy chair in front of the TV in the living room and was often agitated. Caring for him had exhausted the man and his wife. "I couldn't remember the last time we had two hours to ourselves," the man said. "And then, one day, your dog showed up."

Casey wandered into the house through the sliding door and made straight for the man's father. "She sat right beside him, like she had planned to visit him all along," the neighbor said, his voice filled with wonder. He saw his father turn to Casey and begin to pet her. He stroked her and stroked her, and fell peacefully asleep. "He slept two full hours," the neighbor said. "It was the longest midday reprieve my wife and I have had in years."

Casey returned the next day, and every day after that, as if she had an appointment to keep. Each time was the same. She'd pad to the old man's chair and sit by his side, letting him pet her till he dozed off. "To my wife and me," the neighbor said, "Casey was a gift from heaven. That's why I've come to see you today. Is Casey here?"

"Yes, she is," Carol said. "Casey!"

The big malamute trotted up, looking at the neighbor with searching eyes. The neighbor gave a gentle pat. "You must have known, didn't you?" the neighbor said to Casey. "That's why you just stopped coming a couple of days ago."

"Known what?" Carol asked.

"My father died in his sleep the night after Casey's last visit. She knew her job was over."

Last Good-bye

Lourdes A. Bernard

IT WAS AROUND SEVEN in the morning when I made my way to the kitchen. I poured a cup of coffee and sipped it while looking through the glass patio doors toward the backyard. The day was clear, but the air was crisp and cold. I couldn't help but admire the defiant daffodils pushing through yet another dusting of snow. The sun beckoned the flowers to show their first colors, but Bloodroot and Early Star of Bethlehem were holding back.

I loved spring, but I was feeling really restless. My mom had been put in hospice the day before down in Florida. This yearning to see God now was prompted by yesterday's painful call from hospice about Mom's condition. She wasn't doing well, they said. *Lord, I really need to know You're here with both of us*, I prayed.

Suddenly I saw a bird I'd never seen before. He was gloriously beautiful. He wore a shiny blue-black coat with white zigzag stripes and a red head-dress that reminded me of a plume on a Roman centurion's helmet. *Does he know I can see him?* I wondered. I felt an incredible peace, as if he were an angel sent in response to my prayer to tell me everything would be okay. A moment later he was gone, leaving me with an indescribable longing mingled with joy.

After a bit of research, I learned that the new bird was a red-bellied wood-pecker, not uncommon in New York, but uncommon in my Brooklyn backyard.

A month after my bird angel sighting, I traveled to Orlando and stayed at my friend Sue's house. Her home sat empty after she'd moved in to care for her own ailing mother. I stopped at the market to buy lunch, intending to eat a sandwich on Sue's screened-in back porch. I planned to see Mom later, already exhausted by the travel and stress of having to face her rapid decline.

I nodded off briefly, awakening with a surprising sense of peace. Then I saw him! The red-bellied woodpecker was sitting on a scrawny tree right in front of me. It was the same species of woodpecker I'd spotted in Brooklyn the day after Mom entered hospice. I was in awe, thrilled, and strangely happy that he had found me again, here in Sue's backyard.

His markings were just as pronounced, with his mane of vivid red, his striped blue and white wings, and soft yellowish belly. Yet his behavior was rather odd. He hopped up the tree and then proceeded to entertain me as he hopped back-ward down the tree, a splash of red and blue moving down the tree trunk. His shimmying was so funny it made me laugh out loud. I felt my stress lessen as I watched him. He repeated his jerky dance move up and down the tree a few more times, keeping me company for several minutes. I felt refreshed, happier, and more at ease about seeing Mom. Gone was the wave of sadness and grief that had engulfed me. *I am okay now*, I thought as he finally flew away.

I soon went to visit my mom, and we spent a wonderful week together before I had to head back to my home.

It was spring again, a year since I'd first spotted the red-bellied woodpecker in Brooklyn. I had not seen him since the visit in Sue's backyard. I was down in Florida again, sitting next to Mom in front of a large picture window, the entry-way for the golden light that poured into her bedroom. I knew this would be our last good-bye. I went over to raise the blinds all the way up to let in even more light and looked out on to the garden. Then I sat next to Mom and put on some music. Bach serenaded us through the earbuds I'd brought. I held Mom's hand and told her I loved her. I thanked her for being such a good mother and told her I would be okay. She gazed up at me smiling, and I began to feel an incredible peace fill the room. There was complete stillness, and as I took in her expression I glanced up to see the silent wind moving the giant oak trees outside.

The moment was perfect, and in that instant, I thought of the word *Ruach*, the Spirit of God. Then I noticed a rustling movement in the branches of the large palmetto tree that sat outside her window. Palmetto trees look like giant pineapples, and this one was in bloom with large white flowers on its branches. And there on the palmetto tree sat a red-bellied woodpecker. He remained in the shadows a bit longer, then moved out toward the window and stared in.... As the silence deepened, the next word that came to mind was *Emmanuel*, God with us.

The stillness felt vast, nothing but beauty surrounding us. Mom and I sat together watching in a timeless silence. Then our angel flew away. I knew then for certain everything would be okay.

The Dog Who Went to War
Rick Hamlin

WORLD WAR II HADN'T BEGUN YET, but the British gunboat HMS *Gnat* was patrolling the crowded waters of the Yangtze River in China, making sure the Japanese bombers flying overhead, brazenly flexing their military muscle, wouldn't interfere with traffic and trade. The *Gnat* had taken on an extra passenger, a sort of mascot or good-luck talisman, but like the sailors she was expected to toe the line, especially when it came time for inspection. And that November day in 1936 the rear admiral had arrived unexpectedly on board.

All was shipshape, from bow to stern, from galley to engine room, from bunks to bridge, even the ammunition box that served as a bed for this newest member of the crew—an English pointer named Judy. The admiral began one last exercise with the crew when all at once, their canine shipmate raised her head and made an unholy racket, barking madly, drowning out the admiral's commands.

No doubt her companions on board were tempted to silence her, but they already knew to pay attention to Judy's outbursts. A few days earlier, her 3:00 a.m. howling had saved them from crashing into a trap set by a junk-load of pirates. Now the sailors looked up and spotted a Japanese bomber. It swooped down from the sky, strafed the boat, and then rose again in a dangerous display of power.

Judy was bred for hunting in the English countryside, but the coming war would test her almost beyond endurance, as her masters themselves were brutally tested. Again and again she would show her extraordinary ability—her uncanny gift for protecting them and helping them. Her story is told in captivating detail by the historian Damien Lewis in his canine biography, *Judy.* More than just a tale of one dog's sixth sense, it demonstrates how humans and animals are inextricably, mysteriously entwined by a bond of love that can survive the darkest of times.

By 1941 the British had declared war on Japan, and Judy and her fellow crew members were ordered to Singapore. The island city was no contest for the superior air power of the Japanese and fell in February 1942. It was hoped that foreign residents could be evacuated by boat, in a repeat of the miracle of Dunkirk. Judy circulated among the women and children on board, but alas, her usual alert warning—furious barking—couldn't stop the Japanese bombers. The gunboat was badly damaged. The captain gave the order to abandon ship. The surviving passengers made their way to a deserted island not far away.

There the situation looked dire. The survivors had salvaged some food and medical supplies, but they had no fresh water and wouldn't live long without it. An expedition headed to the interior in search of a spring or a stream. Although the sailors commanded Judy to go too, she lingered by the beach, pawing furiously at the sand, seemingly ignoring them. Yet she knew exactly what they needed. At the bottom of the hole she dug, water bubbled up. Clear, fresh water in a place none could have guessed.

The marooned shipmates were eventually captured by the Japanese. The men—along with Judy—were separated from the women and children. They were first imprisoned on the island of Sumatra. Judy's instincts as a hunting dog kicked in. She managed to sneak in and out of the camp, evading the guards, and would stalk anything that moved—rodents, birds, insects. Whatever food she caught she shared, and the men, even in their desperate hunger, shared their meager rice rations with her. The only way to get more food was to steal from their captors.

One of the men's biggest hauls was a bag of rice, which they hid under a blanket in a POW hut. As soon as the guards discovered it missing, they went on a rampage, searching high and low, brandishing their guns, bayonets fixed. The POWs were sure that they would be caught. But just as the guards came close to the bag, Judy appeared in the dim light, carrying something in her mouth: a human skull. The guards took one look at the dog and ran in terror. Judy seemed pleased with herself and no one could guess where she had found the skull.

The men loved Judy. One pressed his Japanese captors to add her to the official list of POWs. Amused, perhaps, the Japanese granted the request. Judy became the only registered canine POW of the war. More than a scavenger, more than a hunter and protector, Judy's true value was as a morale booster for the men. If this dog could survive in such brutal circumstances, they believed, they could make it too.

In 1944 the men were transferred back to a camp in Singapore. En route the boat was torpedoed by a British sub. As it began to sink, one of the men, Frank Williams, pushed Judy out a porthole. "Swim, Judy, swim!" he cried. She paddled valiantly through the waters. Soon she was seen helping one of the sailors to a rescue boat. Mere skeletons after their deadly experience, the POWs were pulled from the waters and hauled into a new camp. But where was Frank, Judy's rescuer? No one saw him get off the sinking ship. No one knew if he was still alive.

After searching for him at the camp, Judy sat and waited at the gate. Two days later, weak, exhausted, in terrible pain, Frank finally staggered into the camp. There he was greeted by a soft whine and a wet nose nuzzling his face. For days, Judy would not leave his side.

The captured soldiers' final test took them back to Sumatra, where they were put to work from dawn to dusk building a railroad in unforgiving terrain. With hardly any food, the POWs had to do backbreaking work and shield their four-legged companion from the guards, who were not given much to eat themselves and would have had her for dinner if they could. While the men worked, Judy scampered through the jungle, finding bones to gnaw on.

Once, her protective urges got her in trouble. One of the guards was mercilessly beating a prisoner when Judy emerged from the woods, snarling, her hackles raised. The guard reached for his gun and shot at her; she disappeared into the tropical underbrush. The bullet just grazed her shoulder.

At the end of the war, with rumors flying, the men were asked to dig long trenches in the camps, supposedly air-raid shelters for when the Allies bombed, but the POWs suspected otherwise—they were digging their own graves. On August 14, 1945, they finished the railway. It was the very day the Japanese surrendered, but it took time for the news to reach Sumatra. For weeks the men lived in limbo, all work suspended, their rations suddenly increased. Judy lay low, aware that something was up.

On the morning of September 4, Judy burst forth with loud, uncontrollable barking. Nothing could quiet her. The men woke to discover that all the guards had fled. Soon two heavily armed members of the Royal Marines appeared. Judy was the first in the welcoming committee. Frank Williams still had to hide her to bring her on to the troopship that would take them home. Official POW or not, dogs were not welcome on board. Back in England, however, she received the hero's welcome she deserved, with medals and celebrations.

Damien Lewis calls Judy a "dog in a million," yet she was not unlike others of her breed. Perhaps extraordinary circumstances brought out an extraordinary side in her, the way those same circumstances brought out the best in the men who loved her and protected her.

Judy moved with Frank to Africa and lived to the ripe old dog age of fourteen, dying in Tanzania in 1950, laid to rest in a Royal Air Force jacket and a simple wooden coffin. The plaque above her grave lists the places she spent her remarkable life, from Shanghai to East Africa. The final words are *They Also Served,* taken from the motto of the Royal Observer Corps, which watched for enemy aircraft in the skies over Britain.

Bella's Blessing
Michael Gordon

TALL PINES FRAMED AN ELEGANT outdoor amphitheater nestled in the Wallowa Mountains. This small ranch in Joseph, Oregon, was truly the ideal place for Kara and me to be married. We loved the outdoors. Looking out at the scenery on the morning of the ceremony, I marveled that this was everything we wanted when we got engaged. Well, almost everything, I reminded myself. There was one thing missing: Bella. And she was the reason we were here in the first place.

Six years ago to the day, I'd just finished competing in the Black Diamond Triathlon in Enumclaw, Washington. I was pretty proud that I'd raced well, having swam, biked, and run thirty-two miles. I was waiting to accept my award when a black Labrador retriever wandered over to me and licked my leg. "Bella! Come back here," another triathlete said when she saw what her dog was doing. "Sorry about that." Bella flopped down at my feet.

"No problem," I said. "My name's Michael." Kara introduced herself. We'd heard of each other before—the triathlon community is pretty small—but we might never have actually met if it weren't for Bella. As I got to know Kara, I got to know Bella. I got to love the way she jumped around me to get attention, begged me to play fetch or tug-of-war. The three of us became inseparable. We planned to make her a part of our wedding ceremony, but Bella died just two months before the big day.

"We'll just have to imagine her here with us," Kara said, coming up behind me. She couldn't even see my face, but she knew what I was thinking. "Let's get ready for the first part of the day."

Kara and I were both signed up to participate in a local triathlon just minutes from the ranch. Some of the guests thought we were a little crazy to compete in a multi-stage endurance race the morning of our wedding, but without Bella, we were glad for a special way to commemorate how we'd met.

"I like to think she will be running right along with us all the way," Kara said as we stretched and warmed up.

"She won't have trouble keeping up with us, now that she's got her angel wings," I said. I was trying to be cheerful, but I really missed her. The day that was supposed to be perfect couldn't be perfect without her.

I ran wearing my vest and tie. Kara attached a wedding veil to her bike helmet. A few members of the wedding party joined in as well. Some of them had raced in the same triathlon where Bella had brought us together. Friends and family cheered us on from the sidelines, and the locals loved our "formal" triathlon attire. Kara and I finished in the top tier.

We headed back to the ranch to make our final preparations for the main event. As we got out of the car, something on the grounds caught my eye. Something black with a long tail.

"That dog looks just like Bella," I said. Kara turned to look. The strange dog bucked excitedly whenever someone showed her attention and begged games of fetch from the kids.

"She acts just like Bella too," Kara said. "Those are her mannerisms."

One of the owners of the ranch hurried up to us. "I'm sorry," she said, gesturing to the dog. "Luna just loves being around people. We can keep her inside for the day if you want, so she doesn't bother anyone."

"No, she's great! I love having her here," Kara said. "She reminds me of my old Lab. She couldn't be here today. . . ." She smiled over at Bella's lookalike, who was now engaged in a fierce game of tug-of-war. *Just like Bella used to do,* I thought.

Kara and I went inside to shower and change in record time. We reemerged to find our guests settling themselves in the cool shade of the little amphitheater. I lined up with the minister and my groomsmen beneath the grove of pine trees that surrounded the ranch. Musicians played as my bride began her walk down the aisle.

Just as Kara reached me, I felt something touch my leg. I looked down. There was Luna, flopped at my feet, an exact likeness of Bella the day she'd introduced me to the love of my life. Luna lay there, pressed against my leg, while Kara and I said our vows and pledged to spend our lives together.

It was the perfect wedding. Bella might not have been there, but she'd found a way to give us her blessing by way of the Rainbow Bridge.

The Hummingbird
Rhoda Blecker

WHEN WE LIVED IN LOS ANGELES, my husband, Keith, and I—somewhat crazily for people living in a city—had four dogs. The big male, Elijah, was the alpha of our little pack, all of whom had been strays who seemed to have wandered up saying, *"I hear you have an opening for a dog."* When Elijah died suddenly, Perky, the smallest of the three females, thought she should take over. But she was an insecure alpha, and that made her aggressive. Of the two other females, the older never challenged Perky; she didn't care who was in authority. But the last, Jessie, bigger and stronger than Perky, wasn't going to stand for a smaller dog trying to boss her around. After weeks of posturing, one day they really fought, and Perky's chest was slashed open. I took her to the vet for treatment and stitches. When we brought her home, our dog trainer told us we could probably not reconcile them and should find another home for one of them.

But Keith and I didn't abandon one of our animals just because it might be easier on us. So for the next two years, Perky lived most of the time in my home office, where I spent many hours a day, writing or answering email, or sometimes just playing hooky from the rest of the house. Perky wasn't alone quite as much as she might have been. She had her "house" and backyard time when the other two dogs were shut in the master bedroom, but really, most of the time, she was in the office, where she had a bed inside an always-open crate, along with her food and water dishes. Unavoidably, however, she was spending much more time alone than the other dogs. I worried that she might be lonely.

One day I was working at my desk when I saw Perky put her forepaws on the sill of the open, screened window that looked out over our front lawn. Her nose nearly touched the screen. A few moments later, a beautifully iridescent green hummingbird flew down and hovered in the air directly in front of Perky's nose. I thought she might bark at the bird—she had a very distinctive bark—but she didn't move. For almost two full minutes, the dog and the hummingbird communed with one another as I watched, fascinated. Then the bird soared away, and Perky dropped down on to the rug and curled up at my feet. She had made a friend.

Because she lived nearly all the time in the office, there was a not unpleasant smell that hung in the room, like the scent of a dog's paw. I didn't mind it.

Several months after the hummingbird incident, Perky's spleen burst, and we had to have her put down. We took everything of hers out of the office, had the rug cleaned, and banished the doggie smell. But, strangely, at times over the next weeks, Keith and I would hear her bark. We would hear it at the same time, look at each other, and one of us would ask hesitantly, "Did you hear that?" It didn't happen often, but it was undeniably *her* bark.

Weeks after that, I was working at my desk, and I became aware that I was noticing that characteristic Perky smell. My head jerked upward. At the window, just outside the screen where Perky's nose would have been, hovered the hummingbird. It stayed in the same place for more than a minute, as I watched it, afraid to move. Then the bird flew off, and the scent vanished. We never heard Perky barking again. It felt as if we were being assured that she was all right, in the company of a friend.

When we moved to Bellingham, we took with us two cats, both of whom had known Perky, and a dog who hadn't. We put out feeders for birds, including a hummingbird feeder. Soon we had grosbeaks, nuthatches, juncos, towhees, sparrows, thrushes, finches, swallows, four different kinds of woodpeckers, and jays. But the hummingbird feeder remained unvisited. Every so often we would clean out the nectar, replace it, rehang the feeder, and wait hopefully. No hummingbirds came.

Some years after we moved into the house, we gave up and took the hummingbird feeder down. We reasoned that we might as well not keep looking in vain for the tiny birds when so many others were coming by all the time.

Then one of our cats died. It was not unexpected; Tau was twenty years old.

A day later, while I was sitting on the couch, I looked up to see a hummingbird hovering just outside the window. It stayed a short while, then darted off. I recognized it as a sign that Tau was at peace.

Of course, I immediately set out another hummingbird feeder. So far, no hummingbirds have visited it. I guess they have no messages from furry friends to pass along to me.

My Guardian Greyhound

Becca Hart

EVENING GOWNS CROWDED THE RACK in the dressing room. I took my sequined formal off its hanger. It was almost time to hit the stage for rehearsal. In a few days I would compete in front of an audience and a panel of judges for the title of Miss North Carolina USA 2015.

My dog, Mike, a lanky, brindle-colored greyhound, pressed against my leg. He'd be wearing his own costume on stage: a sign that said Service Dog. Mike had already helped me title in the Miss High Point Teen USA 2014 pageant. Without him, none of this would ever have been possible.

Up until five years ago, I was a normal, healthy girl. But at the age of twelve something went wrong with my heart. It beat too fast—over two hundred beats a minute, the school nurse said. My parents rushed me to the hospital, where I had emergency surgery to repair damage to tissue in my heart that was interfering with the signals telling it when to beat.

Things were never the same. I got sick all the time—colds, the flu, stuff like that—so my mom homeschooled me. Then I got achy. Every joint in my body hurt. Getting a hug from my mom or dad was plain painful.

Doctors did lots of tests to figure out what was going on, but it was years before I had a name for my problem: lupus. The disease caused my immune system to attack my body. Everything was affected: internal organs, joints, my skin—even my mind. I developed obsessive compulsive disorder, or OCD. Odd things gave me overwhelming anxiety. Like the feel of paper on my skin. Or being touched on my right shoulder. A change in temperature. Every day was full of obstacles.

If I competed in a contest like the Miss North Carolina USA pageant, I could tell everyone about service dogs and how important they are.

Mike thumped his tail in approval as I slipped the gown over my head and checked my reflection. The dress was beautiful—but glamour wasn't a priority. My real reason for competing for Miss North Carolina USA was the greyhound lying at my feet.

I remembered the day the two of us first met. I was fifteen. The doctor who was counseling me about my OCD explained how there were several ways a service dog could help. To give comfort when I was anxious, or lend balance when I was dizzy.

"You're talking about Labradors, right?" I said.

"Not always. In fact, greyhounds can be very good."

"Greyhounds?" said my mom. "Aren't those the dogs that chase little rabbits around tracks? We've got small dogs at home already. I don't want them to get chased or hurt."

"Actually, greyhounds like nothing better than to lie around," the doctor said. "They don't need as much exercise as some other breeds. That would be good if Becca winds up back in the hospital." Which was always a possibility.

My parents went on a quest to find just the right dog for me. It took a while, but I finally found myself visiting a greyhound-rescue group. Handlers brought out one greyhound after another. Some were stately. Some were bouncy.

And then came Mike.

He greeted me like a gentleman as his handler told his story. "Mike used to be a racer," he said. "He's been adopted twice since retirement because of changing circumstances for the families. They all loved him. I think he's got what it takes."

I reached out to stroke Mike's brindle fur. "Maybe you were just meant to be with me," I said.

Looking at the two of us in the mirror in the dressing room now, I knew I'd been right that day. Mike needed to go through extensive training to become a service dog. The trainer estimated it would take about a year. Mike graduated in three months.

One day early on, Mike and I were sitting in the waiting room at the doctor's with my mom. I was there to have a checkup echocardiogram for my heart. For no reason that I could see, Mike started pacing, like he was upset about something. "What's the matter, boy?" I said. We were still getting to know each other.

Mike put his paws on my knees, pressed his nose to my chest, and whimpered. "What's the matter with him?" Mom asked.

My chest suddenly felt a familiar, terrible tightness just where Mike was touching me. "Mom, it's my heart," I said.

Mom ran for the doctor. Tests confirmed what Mike had already warned me about. He knew before I did! My heartbeat was irregular, and I was treated immediately. From then on I trusted Mike to alert me when my heart had a problem. He also knew when I was in pain, pressing his face to the spot that hurt. When I got anxious he snuggled against me to distract me, calm me. He was more than a service dog. He was my guardian angel.

"Ready to go on stage, boy?" I asked, turning from the mirror. Mike jumped to his feet. "All eyes are going to be on us."

When I first got Mike I couldn't stand the attention. I hated the stares and questions. I wanted to blend into the crowd, but that was impossible with a big greyhound at my side. "You don't look sick," people would say about my having a service dog. "You don't have a cane or a wheelchair. Are you blind? Deaf?"

"Becca, you can be angry about it or you can turn it into something good," my mom said when I confessed my embarrassment over these encounters.

Something good? I couldn't imagine what.

A few weeks later, I was watching a beauty pageant on TV. Mike lay at my feet. One of the contestants talked about wanting to raise awareness for diabetes. "If I competed in a contest like that, I could tell everyone about service dogs and how important they are," I said to Mike. "There might be other kids like me out there who need one and don't know how to get one!"

I'd never competed in a beauty pageant in my life. Soon I was the first girl to compete in one with a service dog! I titled as Miss High Point in 2013. A fall that year kept me from going on to compete in the Miss North Carolina Teen USA 2014 pageant, but by now I was used to little setbacks. Here I was, the very next year, about to take the stage to compete in Miss North Carolina USA 2015.

I checked myself in the mirror one more time: hair, dress, makeup, service dog. What else did I need to face the world? Mike and I left the dressing room and headed for the stage. On the night of the pageant, the theater would be full and we would stand in the spotlight together. Maybe there was another girl like me out there watching who needed her own guardian angel dog. Mike and I were going to do our best to make sure she got one.

Flying through the Night

Rhona Westbrook

"READY TO FLY, GIRL?" I said, stroking the Arabian mare's mane. It was nighttime—pitch black. I'd just snuck out of the girls' dorm at my boarding school. If I got caught, I'd be in deep trouble. But sometimes a secret midnight ride on a horse named Sakie, pastured close to the school, was the only way to clear my head. At sixteen there was so much I couldn't control. I felt somewhere in the middle of being an adult and a kid. Everyday life could seem downright scary. My new boyfriend had broken up with me for another girl. I was nervous about a paper I'd just handed in to my favorite history teacher. But once Sakie and I were galloping along, flying through the night, everything was different. When we rode I was confident. I felt like I could take on the entire world.

I slipped a bridle over Sakie's ears and led her along a familiar path toward an abandoned airstrip near the school. As we got close Sakie tossed her head and sidestepped. We always took our midnight rides here. She'd never acted this way before. Why was she nervous?

"Easy, girl," I said into her ear. I scrambled up onto Sakie's bare back and pulled her reins toward the airstrip. She broke into a trot. The darkness made it impossible to see, but we both knew the way by heart. Once I could make out the wooden post that marked the beginning of the airstrip, I kept a tight hold on

Sakie's reins while she danced in place. Sakie reared a bit—but this time she was excited, finally ready to charge down the strip like usual. I wanted to let her too, but now something didn't feel right to me.

I tightened my grip on Sakie's reins. I had ridden down this airstrip dozens of times. What was holding me back now? I couldn't see anything wrong. I couldn't see anything at all in the dark. That's what made the airstrip so perfect. Barreling into total darkness, I just had to trust that nothing could hurt me. And I did. Complete trust. So was I scared of midnight rides now too? Like I was scared of what the kids at school thought of me? Or my teachers? No! I wouldn't let my insecurities ruin this too. I dropped the reins and clenched my knees against Sakie's side. *"Hee-yah!"* I yelled as she leaped forward. I wrapped my hands in her gray mane and held on tight as her hooves pounded the airstrip, galloping faster. I leaned down low on Sakie's back, the wind whipping through my hair. The old confidence I always felt on these midnight rides returned as Sakie and I flew through the night. There was nothing to stop us.

Then I thought I saw something up ahead. A mound of some sort barely visible in the dark. Like a big pile of…dirt? In a flash I remembered the construction workers I'd seen last week. They'd dug a deep, wide trench across the airstrip. The dirt pile in front of us was as high as Sakie's chest, and waiting on the other side was the trench. In my eagerness for a midnight ride I'd forgotten all about it. Now it was too late to stop!

Suddenly everything happened in slow motion: the pounding of Sakie's hooves on the ground, the thudding of my heart within my chest. *Dear Lord, we're coming up on it!* Sakie had never jumped anything before. Would she slow down when she saw the dirt pile? Swerve at the last second? Either way we were headed for disaster. What to pray for? I was certain we were both going to die. Closer…closer…I braced for the crash. *Sakie, I'm so sorry.* Sakie's strong body rose up, lifting me with her as she took to the sky. I clutched her mane with both hands, watching. We seemed to hang in midair for an eternity. We cleared the dirt pile, but the trench—I couldn't bear it. I shut my eyes.

Sakie landed on firm ground. I bounced on her back as she stumbled. She quickly regained her footing and resumed her stride. I turned to look behind me. The trench had disappeared in the distance. We'd made it! I tugged the reins gently to slow the horse down. I slid off her back when she came to a stop and tried to catch my breath. I walked her back around the trench and on to the stable. "How did you do that, girl?" I asked as I turned her out to pasture.

The next day I walked out to the airstrip and measured the length of Sakie's jump. A little Arabian mare, who had never jumped anything in her life, had cleared a four-foot-high, nine-foot-wide, nearly invisible obstruction. Was Sakie an angel in disguise, or had there been an angel looking out for Sakie and me on the abandoned airstrip that night? For some reason I felt complete trust barreling through the darkness.

But that seemed silly now. I'd put my trust in something real: the God who understands that I don't always make the best choices. Instead of judging me, He'd rescued me. There were plenty of challenges ahead. Life could still be scary. But I had a newfound confidence. A confidence that would stay with me long after I'd climbed down from a midnight ride with this angelic Arabian mare.

Tiny Twinkling Angels

Jennie Ivey

HEADING TO THE GREAT SMOKY Mountains National Park in June had become an annual tradition for a group of camping friends and me. That's the only time the species of firefly *Photinus carolinus,* the only known synchronous fireflies in the western hemisphere, puts on a not-to-be-missed show.

The darker the night, the more spectacular the experience.

On this particular evening, we were in luck. The new moon was just a pale sliver in the eastern sky as my friends and I crossed the footbridge that leads across Jake's Creek from Elkmont campground. We made our way up a steep, narrow road to distance ourselves from the gathering crowd. Because flashlights are discouraged and you must have the lens wrapped in red cellophane, only a couple of us carried one. When we found a spot we liked, we spread quilts on the rocky ground and spoke in hushed tones as the sky turned from gray to dark blue to black.

As total darkness finally descended, the synchronous fireflies began their magic. Dozens at first. Then hundreds. Then thousands. Maybe even millions, if it were possible to count them all. They didn't blink on and off in metronome-like fashion. Instead, a great cluster of fireflies twinkled like tiny white Christmas lights and then went completely dark. Six seconds later, the twinkling began again. Then darkness.

All up and down the mountain, as far as the eye could see, great waves of twinkling and then darkness swept past us.

I lay back on my quilt and watched in awe. I didn't mean to fall asleep, but that's exactly what happened. And my friends didn't mean to go off and leave me, but that happened too. When the firefly show was over after a couple of hours, they folded up their quilts in the quiet darkness and headed back to the campground. No one thought to call the roll to make sure everyone was present. We were, after all, grown-ups who knew it was important to stay together in the wilderness.

When I realized I was alone in pitch-black darkness, my heart began to race. I wasn't sharing a tent with anyone. Chances were that, once everyone got back to the campsite, they'd all crawl into their sleeping bags in their own tents and not even realize I was missing until I didn't show up for breakfast.

"Hey," I shouted into the black night, "where'd everybody go?"

My only answer was the rustling of the wind in the trees. I was all by myself, without a flashlight, in an ancient forest inhabited by all sorts of creatures I didn't want to run into in the middle of the night. Snakes. Skunks. Foxes. Bobcats. Coyotes.

And the animal that's the symbol of the Great Smoky Mountains—the black bear. I'd read that, over the past several years, black bears have made such an amazing comeback that it's estimated that there are at least two bears per square mile in the park. Bears who prefer to do their foraging at night. My heart began beating even harder.

"Hey," I shouted again, louder this time, "can anybody hear me?"

Again, no answer. I shuffled through the dew-wet grass until I felt the crunch of gravel under my feet. I had made it to the road leading back to the bridge. I strained my ears, hoping to hear human conversation. There was none. I wore no watch, not that I could have seen it anyway, so I had no idea what time it was. Perhaps the best thing to do was to curl up in my quilt and wait for sunrise, which could easily be hours away. But before I could act on that plan, a twinkling of light caught my eye.

It looked like a cluster of fireflies, which seemed strange because they, too, seemed to have abandoned me. Had they taken a break and were now tuning up for the second act of their nightly performance? I looked up and down the mountains but saw no other clusters of twinkling lights.

Only this one, hovering so close that I could have cupped some of the fireflies in my hand.

Slowly, the cluster began moving downhill. What could I do but follow? Though I was moving ever so slowly so as not to trip and fall in the pitch-black darkness, it took just a few minutes before the twinkling lights turned to the left.

I reached out my right hand and felt smooth wood. I had reached the footbridge that led to the campground! I placed my hand on the railing, moving more confidently now. The cluster of lights led me all the way across the bridge and then stopped. Suddenly, I realized I could see the flickering of campfires and hear soft laughter and conversation. It didn't take long for my eyes to adjust to the light shed by lanterns and campfires. My tent was only a stone's throw away.

I turned to see if the fireflies were going to follow me all the way to my campsite, but they were nowhere to be seen. God's tiny twinkling angels had led me to safety and then disappeared.

Night to Remember
Brenda Elrod

A BLUR OF MOVEMENT in the yard caught my eye on a recent evening. Another hummingbird headed over to my savannah holly tree.

I'd become accustomed to seeing these amazing creatures but never less surprised by their talent. Unlike most birds, whose wings flap up and down, a hummingbird's wings move back and forth—as fast as eighty times per second. So fast their wings become almost invisible to the naked eye. The hummingbird is also the only bird that can hover in midair, and the only bird that can fly backward. Their wings did things it seemed only the angels in heaven could do. And to me hummingbirds are heavenly. Seeing them always brings me back to the last night I ever spent with my husband, Jim.

We were enjoying an end-of-summer barbecue at Jim's brother's house. Hummingbirds were everywhere, darting around the flowers, circling the table. They had no fear of us humans. "They're so beautiful up close," Jim said as one hovered by his cheek, hanging in midair as if determined to get his attention. "Brenda and I have tried to attract them in our yard, but in twenty-seven years of marriage we haven't seen a one!"

"We're hoping the savannah holly tree we planted in spring just might do the trick," I said.

"Well, God is giving us a special show tonight," Jim's brother said. "We've never seen hummingbirds fly so close to people before."

Jim and I talked about it all the way home. Those hummingbirds made the night a memorable one.

The image of the tiny birds flitting around in the evening air was still clear in my mind the next morning—until I got a call from one of Jim's coworkers. There'd been a terrible accident on the job. Jim was rushed to the hospital in critical condition. By the time I got there it was too late. Jim didn't survive.

The next hours passed with me in tears, trying to comfort family, trying to comfort myself. I'd driven straight from the hospital to my daughter's. My sister drove in from out of town to meet me there. That evening I told her all about my last night with Jim. "You can't imagine how beautiful those hummingbirds were," I said. "I'll never forget them as long as I live." Somehow I got rest. When I woke I knew I wanted the comfort of my own home. My sister promised to follow soon.

Back in my kitchen I poured myself a cup of coffee. *Jim is gone*, I said to myself. There would be funeral preparations, decisions to be made. Family and friends would offer to help. I would have to learn to live without Jim. But how? The doorbell rang, and I was glad it interrupted my impossible thought. *How, God? How do I face the rest of my life without my husband?*

My sister was at the door. "I just saw the loveliest hummingbird in your yard," she said. "I wonder if Jim is giving us a sign that he's near."

I believed it was a sign, and a gift from God. And over the following weeks and months, the gifts kept coming. Each one made me feel closer to Jim. By the time I saw my most recent visitor at the savannah holly tree, I'd read all about hummingbirds and their special talents. But I also knew that the angelic little birds had a talent for healing.

CHAPTER 5

Guardian Angels of Children

"The caseworker carried the girl with dark braided hair into the living room. Her brothers introduced themselves gently. I took a seat on the floor. Dari looked around at us all, blinking her dark brown eyes. She seemed to make a decision. She crawled off the caseworker's lap, the feet of her lavender footie pajamas landing softly on the floor. Her eyes met mine. With a jolt I recognized the courage within them.

The girl from my dream!"

—MOLLY BROWN PENNINGTON

Meant to Be

Molly Brown Pennington

WAS THIS A CHURCH? The high, vaulted ceilings made it seem like one—almost but not exactly. That's the way things often are in dreams, and I was dreaming now. Deeply. A woman entered the room. With her was a small child, a little girl in soft, lavender footie pajamas. She was barely a toddler, still a baby in many ways. Her brown hair was braided, and her big, dark eyes were beautiful. But it wasn't their beauty that struck me so much as the quiet courage I saw reflected in them as the child took a tentative step forward.

I sank to my knees, putting myself at her level. *Don't be afraid*, I thought. The girl hesitated a moment, clinging shyly to the woman. Then, as if making a decision, she opened her arms and toddled to me. My own arms were open and waiting to catch her. Her little body was soft and warm and *right* in my embrace. Like she belonged with me. "You're fine," I said as I rocked her gently. "Everything's going to be just fine."

I opened my eyes to the sound of my alarm clock. Beside me, my husband, Val, rolled over and got up. Elsewhere in the house I could hear our sons, Dash, sixteen, and Phineas, six, stirring. I climbed out of bed. By the time the kids left for school and I started the breakfast dishes I barely remembered the details of my dream.

It was no surprise I was dreaming about children. After a lot of discussion, Val and I had decided to adopt a baby. A little girl, we'd agreed when we filled out the application. A little older than Phineas, so she would be in between the two boys in age.

Dash was already the best big brother anyone could ever ask for, and Phineas the friendliest, silliest kindergartner. We did laundry and yard work together, came up with family projects—we even had regular "family art days" in our craft room where Dash made duct tape wallets, Val sketched, and Phineas and I painted. There was plenty of room for one more in our family. We filled out piles of paperwork, underwent background checks, took classes on how to care for a child from foster care who'd potentially been hurt in the past. Neglected, surely.

I soaped up the dishes and thought about our daughter. I'd never met her. I'd only seen her in a photo, a grainy photocopy that barely captured her features. She was eighteen months old, younger than we had planned. "Can we handle a baby?" Val asked when the caseworker first told us about Dari. "Diapers? Middle-of-the-night feedings?"

He was right, but we decided to go to the interview anyway. "She's been without parents since birth," the caseworker explained when we got to her office. "She's in foster care now. But she needs a forever home."

Despite our misgivings, we applied to adopt Dari. Now we just had to wait. I dried the dishes and went upstairs to the nursery we'd fixed up for her. We refinished furniture, hung new curtains. Val painted a mural on the wall. I was excited to think about her coming to live here—but nervous too. Once the agency decided to move Dari out of foster care, we'd have a transitional period. We would meet Dari, get to know her slowly. She'd spend the night with us occasionally until she felt at home. I mean, there were four of us and only one of her. *We'll need that transition as much as she will,* I thought. As eager as we were to welcome Dari, it was scary too! With all my mixed emotions, I was thankful for the wait and the process. I wanted everything to be perfect for Dari.

The phone rang. It was Dari's caseworker. "There won't be time for transition," she said. "Your family is getting your baby *today*."

Today? We aren't ready! How can Dari be ready?

"The agency's decided to take her out of foster care immediately," the caseworker said. "For her own safety. I'm going to pick her up now. We'll be there in about an hour." The situation must have been dire.

I hung up with the caseworker and called Val. "I'll come home," he said. "Should I pick up the boys?"

"No time for that," I said. Val's commute was a long one. I called Dash on his cell. "I'll get Phineas at school and be right home," he said. "Don't worry, Mom. I got this."

How can he be so calm? My heart pounded in my chest. My hands shook. I wanted to hide under the bed. I wasn't ready to meet my new daughter! What if she didn't like me? What if she didn't like her room? What if we were the wrong parents for her? What if she belonged in another family instead? *God, I need to know we're doing the right thing!*

I ran around the house in a panic until the boys came home. Dash was grinning from ear to ear. Phineas jumped with excitement. Five minutes later Val arrived. "Is she here yet?" he asked breathlessly.

"You made it just in time."

The four of us gathered in the foyer together. "Everybody be calm," said Val. "We don't want to scare her."

He was talking to the boys, but I was the one who needed calming. Then came the knock on the door. Phineas pulled it open. The caseworker carried the girl with dark braided hair into the living room. Her brothers introduced themselves gently. I took a seat on the floor. Dari looked around at us all, blinking her dark brown eyes. She seemed to make a decision. She crawled off the caseworker's lap, the feet of her lavender footie pajamas landing softly on the floor. Her eyes met mine. With a jolt I recognized the courage within them. *The girl from my dream!*

I opened my arms. Dari toddled right to me in her familiar lavender footie pajamas. Before I realized it I was holding her, feeling how right this baby felt in my arms. A feeling that wasn't new to me at all. "You are fine," I heard myself whisper to her. "Everything's going to be just fine."

They were the same words from my dream. The ones an angel had spoken to reassure me. I knew Dari was just where she belonged. All of us were. Because, ready or not, we were a family.

Angel in the Intersection

Karen Kingsbury

IT WAS THE LAST DAY OF SCHOOL and Melba Stevens was waiting with fresh-baked cookies for her seven-year-old son, Mark, to come home. She sat in a chair by the window and thought about the conversation she'd had with the child that morning.

"Mom, are there really guardian angels?"

Melba had smiled. Lately Mark had been almost constantly curious about spiritual matters and this was merely the next in a list of questions he'd asked lately. "Yes, son. There really are."

He had taken a bite of his cereal and thought about that for a moment. "I'll bet my angel's huge, don't you think so?"

Melba had stifled a laugh. "What makes you think that?"

Because I'm the kind of kid who needs a really huge angel, that's why."

Melba chuckled to herself now, thinking of the way Mark's eyes grew large when he talked about his overly large guardian angel. *Silly boy,* she thought. Silly and sweet and tender enough to make up for the wilder side, the side that would never back down from a challenge.

Mark was their only child, a special gift considering the fertility problems Melba had experienced. Doctors thought she'd never be able to conceive and when Mark was born they'd had no choice but to perform a hysterectomy. There would be no other children, but that was okay with Melba and her husband. Mark was a very special child and more than enough to fill their home with love and joy and laughter. Melba smiled as she thought of the fun summer they had planned.

"Hurry up and get home, Mark... your mama's waiting," she whispered. Then she went to the kitchen to pour him a glass of milk.

Two blocks away, the children were walking home from school and Mark Stevens was in a particularly giddy mood.

"Summer's here!" he shouted.

"Yahoo," his friend shouted. Then the boy looked at the four lanes of traffic ahead of them. "Watch this!"

With that he ran across four lanes of busy traffic and jumped on to the opposite curb unharmed.

"Come on," the boy yelled to Mark. "Don't be a chicken."

Mark looked behind him at the sixth-grade neighbor girl who usually walked him home from school. She was distracted, talking to her friend. Mark glanced at his friend once more and hesitated. His mother had forbidden him from crossing the street by himself, but... He blinked hard. "Okay, here I come!"

Then, without checking for traffic, he darted into the street.

Suddenly Mark heard the children behind him scream and he froze in the middle of the road. A fast car was coming straight for him. He tried to outrun it but there was no time.

"Mom!" he screamed. And then there was a sickening thud.

Back at home, Melba felt a ripple of panic course through her. Mark was never late, but now it was seven minutes past the time when he usually arrived from school. She slipped on a pair of sandals and began walking toward the school.

She heard the sirens almost immediately and picked up her pace.

Two blocks away she saw an ambulance and a fire engine and a cluster of people gathered around a figure on the ground.

Her heart skidded into an irregular rhythm. *Dear God, don't let it be Mark.*

Melba began to run, convincing herself it couldn't possibly be her precious boy. He would never have crossed a street without looking for cars. But as she ran, a memory came to mind of a bad dream Mark had suffered through more than a month ago.

"I'm scared, Mom. Like something bad's going to happen to me." He had tears on his cheeks and she wiped them with her pajama sleeve. "I don't want to be alone."

"Mark," she said, "there's nothing to worry about. You're never alone. God has placed a guardian angel by your side to watch over you while you sleep and to protect you by day. You have nothing to be afraid of."

That conversation must have sparked the one she and Mark had earlier that morning.

Melba was almost to the accident scene and she scanned the crowd of children looking for Mark. *Please, God, put his guardian angel by him now. Please.*

At that moment she caught sight of the child on the ground.

It was Mark.

"Dear God," she screamed as she pressed her way to the front of the crowd. Terror racked her body and she fought to keep herself from fainting. "Is he okay?"

"He's conscious," one of the paramedics shouted. Then in a softer voice he mumbled, "This is incredible. The kid shouldn't even be alive."

Mark could hear the paramedics and his mother in the distance. He lay on the ground, not moving, but he couldn't figure out what had happened. He remembered being hit and flying through the air. But when he'd hit the ground, there had been no pain. Almost as if someone had carried him through the air and then set him gently down on the pavement. He looked up and saw a circle of people working on him.

"Check his pulse," someone shouted. "Check the reflexes."

"Don't move him yet," another cried. "Check for head injuries."

He could see his mother, standing nearby, tears running down her cheeks. He smiled at her and hoped she wouldn't be too mad at him. After all, he'd been told a hundred times never to cross a street without an older person to help him.

He looked at the other people gathered around and suddenly he gasped. There, hovering directly over him and gazing into his eyes, was a gigantic man with golden hair. The man was smiling and Mark understood by the look on the man's face that he was going to be okay. As the man faded from view, Mark's mother stepped closer.

Melba watched a smile come over her son's face and she knelt at his side. "Mark, are you okay?" she cried. "Honey, answer me."

Mark blinked, his face pale but otherwise unharmed. "I'm fine, Mom. I saw my guardian angel and I was right. He's so huge you wouldn't believe it."

Hope surged through Melba as a paramedic pushed her gently back from the scene. "He's in shock, ma'am. He's suffered a serious blow and he has internal injuries. We have to get him to a hospital right away."

They placed the injured child onto a stretcher and strapped him down. "He could have back and neck injuries, any number of problems," another paramedic explained to Melba. "You can ride in the ambulance if you'd like."

Melba nodded and began to weep quietly as they loaded her son into the ambulance. Before they pulled away, she saw four policemen and firemen examine the spot where the boy had landed.

"No blood," one of them said.

"Yeah." Another man approached the spot, shaking his head. "The car must have been doing forty plus and the boy sailed through the air. Came down on his head and there's no blood."

"I've never seen anything like it."

Melba felt a tingling sensation pass over her as she considered their finding. No blood? How was that possible? Then she remembered Mark's words: "I saw my guardian angel."

She closed her eyes as the ambulance pulled away and prayed the very huge angel had indeed done his job.

At the hospital, doctors did a preliminary check to determine whether Mark had feeling in all parts of his body.

"Look at this," one of the doctors said, running a hand over the boy's smooth legs and arms. "He doesn't have a single scratch on him."

"Didn't he get hit by a car?" The nurse assisting him studied the boy, her eyes wide.

"Yes. By all accounts he should have died at the scene. And I can't even find a bruise where the car made contact with him."

Within an hour the doctor had the results to a dozen different tests and he was stunned at what he saw. The tests were completely normal. The boy was neither scratched nor bruised, and he had absolutely no internal injuries.

"My guardian angel saved me," Mark explained. "That's why I need a huge angel, Mom. God knew I'd need one like that to keep me safe."

The doctor was in the room and at Mark's words he shrugged. "That's as good an explanation as any I have." He tousled Mark's hair. "I'll sign the papers so you can go home."

Today, Melba remains grateful for the precious faith of her only child. Mark is grown now but remembers the incident as if it were yesterday. After the accident, his young faith became vitally real, propelling him through his teenage years and into a career that still seems as natural to Mark as the idea of guardian angels.

That career?

Youth pastor, working with kids who pepper him with as many questions about spiritual matters as he once had for his mother.

Miracle in the Night

Lurlene McDaniel

THE BEING WAS WHITE, semiopaque, a glowing form with folded wings standing straight and unwavering at the foot of my bed. I was only six. I was terrified. I had been ill and feverish and was spending the night alone in my mother's room, far from the communal bedroom I shared with my cousins in case I was contagious. My father was on a navy battleship off the coast of Korea that year, 1951. My mother, brother, and I were living in Miami with my aunt and uncle.

I had always been a sickly child, struggling with colds, bronchitis, tonsillitis, and unexplained fevers. Even at birth I struggled. My mother loved to tell the story of my delivery. She said she remembered waking up from the anesthetic and looking over from the delivery table to see doctors and nurses huddled around her newborn infant. *I must have a beautiful baby*, she thought. *See how everyone's admiring her!*

Then she caught a glimpse of me, large and plump in the doctor's hands, a bluish cast to my skin. The nurses rushed me away. Later, when a nurse brought me in for a feeding, Mother took one look at the scrawny baby in the nurse's arms and announced, "There's some mistake. This isn't my baby. I saw her. She was big and fat."

"This is your child," the nurse replied. "She was stillborn; the umbilical cord was wrapped around her neck. She was bloated. For a while it was touch and go. We didn't think we were going to save her."

My mother thanked God for my survival that day and entrusted me ever after to His eternal care.

But I hadn't known God's care would mean the shimmering being I was staring at now. I'd never felt so alone and scared. I pulled the covers over my head and prayed to Jesus to help me. The humid night air closed around me until I thought I would suffocate. When I couldn't stand it anymore, I peeked out from under the bedsheet.

The great white being had not moved. I tried to cry out for my mother but could only manage the barest whisper. Not enough to hear over the thudding of my heart, much less the whirring fan on the dresser.

Could I ease out of bed and make a run for the door? Or cross the room to my mother's dressing table to turn on the lamp? What if I tripped and fell? I squeezed my eyes shut, hoping that when I opened them the figure would be gone. But the figure stayed put no matter how many times I tried it. What did the being want?

Slivers of moonlight slanted through the venetian blinds behind my head. *Maybe it's just a reflection. An illusion*, I thought. I grasped the cord and raised the blinds. Moonlight flooded the room.

I don't know how long I stared, hovering between terror and curiosity. Finally I got up the nerve to inch to the foot of the bed, closer, closer, until the being was only inches away. Where did she go? I reached out my hand and felt only air in front of me. Had I been dreaming all along?

I crawled back to my pillow, breathing fast, and said a quick prayer. When I turned around again there stood the being, as clear as before, splendid and white. She stayed there the rest of the night. I dozed off and on. Each time I awoke she was there, keeping her vigil.

Finally I awoke to sunlight and the familiar smell of frying bacon. My mother opened my door. I launched myself into her arms. "How do you feel?" she asked.

I could barely remember how sick I'd been. Instead the story of my nighttime adventure poured out. I described the large white being with wings. I confessed how scared I'd been. "What was it, Mom?" I asked.

"I believe you've seen an angel," Mom said, like it was exciting.

"But it was scary!" I said.

"Lots of people are scared by angels," Mom said. "That's why the angels in the Bible often warn, 'Fear not!' They know people aren't used to seeing something as awesome and powerful as a miracle right before their eyes. But angels are with us all the time, just like the Bible says." She felt my forehead. "See? The angel took your fever away."

I felt my forehead. She was right! I even felt a little proud, knowing an angel had been with me all night, and had even let me see her. Still, the next night I slept with the light on.

I never saw my guardian angel again. But many times when I've prayed, struggled, or faced despair and illness, I believe I've felt her presence near me. Perhaps one night she will return. And this time I will certainly fear not.

Rescuing Angels

Betty Malz

JIM AND ANGELA LOOKED UP from their renovation work on the second floor of their Texas farmhouse just in time to see their three-year-old daughter lean too hard on the window screen. Angela opened her mouth to call out when the screen buckled, and with a scream the helpless child slid out.

Paralyzed for a moment with horror, both of them breathed the word *"Jesus!"* It was a prayer, a gasp that cut through the terrifying realization that Penny would land on the concrete steps beneath the window. Nearly stumbling over one another, the parents rushed down the stairs and out the front door.

Their anguish turned to astonishment when they found Penny sitting on the bottom step. Scooping her up in her arms, Angela wept with relief.

"Don't worry, Mommy," piped Penny, "that big man caught me." Jim and Angela looked around but saw no one. What man? Where had he come from? Where had he gone? There was no place out there in the open Texas countryside for anyone to hide.

It would have sounded made up except for the fact that Penny was all right. When they examined their daughter, they could not find one scratch or bruise. And Penny did not seem a bit frightened by the experience.

After discussing the incredible event with other members of the family and my husband, who was their pastor, Jim and Angela were directed to Isaiah 63:9 (NIV): "In all their distress he too was distressed, and the angel of his presence saved them. In his love and mercy he redeemed them; he lifted them up and carried them." God must still use angels today, they decided, just as He did in Old Testament times, to rescue people.

Abby's Angels

Jane Kuhn

"Mommy, I want to go home."

It was heartbreaking to see my seven-year-old like this. "Honey, you *are* home," I said, stroking her face. "We've left the hospital. This is your bed. And I'm right here. You had a really bad fall and need a long rest."

"I don't remember falling." Abby sounded scared—my fearless tomboy was never scared. At least she never had been, until the accident.

"You were climbing the tree next door . . . ," I reminded her.

Even now, a week later, the memory of that day made my chest tighten. I was in the house when I heard Maggie, my nine-year-old, scream. I ran outside to where Abby lay on the sidewalk. Lifeless. Blood streamed from her ear. Maggie said Abby had reached for a branch that snapped. I looked to where Maggie was pointing. Abby had fallen thirty feet!

"Maggie, go inside and call 911," I said, barely aware of my own voice. I bent down next to Abby. Was she breathing? I prayed—no, begged—God to keep her alive. *Please, God, save her.* It seemed forever before the paramedics arrived. They strapped Abby to a backboard and lifted her into the ambulance. I called a friend to take Maggie. Then I called my husband at work.

At the hospital doctors and nurses worked over Abby's body, their faces grim. "She's coming to," I heard one of them finally say.

I stayed by her side for five days at the hospital. Abby had suffered multiple skull fractures and faded in and out of consciousness. Her father and I told her how much we loved her. But I wasn't sure she even knew we were there. I called a national prayer line. Friends and family prayed as well. It had been easy to believe God was watching over her when her every action was full of life. Where were her guardian angels now, while she was quiet, helpless?

The strong, confident daughter I knew was slipping away. After weeks of rest, her brain would begin slowly healing on its own. But she would need therapy to relearn the knowledge and skills she'd lost, and we might see permanent damage. It would take years to know for sure.

"Expect some memory loss," her doctor said, "headaches, trouble thinking clearly. It will be important to avoid stressful situations. I'm sorry. I wish I had better news."

Abby was discharged under strict orders to stay in bed for six weeks. How was I going to entertain her?

"I bought you a drawing pad and some pencils," I told Abby. "For now you just need to take it easy."

Abby never had much time for drawing before. She couldn't sit still long enough to do more than a few stick figures. But now things were different. I spread the drawing materials out on the bed. "I just want to go home," Abby said.

I guessed this was the kind of confused thinking the doctor had warned about. "Honey, this is your bed. This is your room," I said. "I'm going to put in a load of laundry. I'll be right back." Abby nodded and I slipped out of her room.

When I looked in on her five minutes later Abby was sitting up, the pad in her lap, busily drawing, intently focused. I thanked God for whatever it was that had captured her imagination and brought her peace. I went to make her lunch.

"Hungry?" I asked when I got back to her room. Abby was still engrossed in her artwork.

On the nightstand I noticed a piece of paper she'd torn from the pad: a drawing. I was astonished when I picked it up. The care, the detail—I never would have taken it for one of Abby's drawings. This was no stick figure. It was an angel with long, flowing hair, her arms open wide with beautiful wings that stretched across the page. "This is really nice," I said.

Abby looked up from her work and glanced at the completed angel. "That's Peace," she said.

"Peace? You did an amazing job of drawing her," I said. "Very creative."

"Not really," Abby said. "That's what she looks like." I took comfort in knowing that Abby was using her imagination. That was a good sign.

The next day Abby got back to her drawing. She didn't seem as afraid and worked with confidence. More like her old self. "You're busy," I said, picking up her breakfast dishes. On the nightstand were elaborate drawings of two more angels. *Why this sudden focus on angels?*

Above each of these angels Abby had written names. Ruth and Amy. Names more common than Peace, but still... "I see you are giving the angels names. That is very clever."

"They told me what their names were. When I saw them."

"Saw them? You mean in your imagination?"

"No," Abby said. "In the hospital. The room would get fuzzy and then suddenly there were angels all around me. In a giant circle. Mommy, they were so pretty. And happy. They made me feel happy. And safe. Mary, Jesus' mommy was there. And her cousin Elizabeth. And behind them, I saw God sitting on a big gold throne."

I didn't know what to say.

"I want to go back there," Abby said. "I want to go home."

I swept her into my arms and held her close. Instead of sending angels to Abby, God had brought Abby to Him for a glimpse of heaven, where the angels live.

"One day you'll go back there," I said. "But now God wants you here with Daddy and me and Maggie."

Abby squeezed me tight. In her six weeks of bed rest Abby drew fifty different angels. Each of them unique. Radiant. Good company in her recovery. She stopped drawing them when she was ready to go back to school. Not only that: she went back to drawing stick figures. But I didn't worry. I felt sure the angels would stay near. After all, Abby knew them each by name.

The Officer in the Yellow Slicker

E. Dann

SPOTTING A POLICE CAR in New York City with over eight million people living here is almost as easy as spotting a cab. When their sirens shriek nearby, I might clamp my hands over my ears, but I have taken their presence for granted just like the phone in my purse that I can take out to dial for help, or conjure directions from at a moment's notice. They're simply *there*, luxuries that I have long stopped classifying as such.

That certainly wasn't the case thirty years ago when I was just a little girl and my family lived in Omaha, Nebraska.

My mom and I were on our way home in our Ford station wagon after visiting family friends who lived just outside of the city. The sky had started out with a sickly pall that was worsening by the hour. By the time we said our good-byes that summer afternoon, raindrops had started to fall. The car was low on fuel and the roads only vaguely familiar, but Mom wasn't too concerned—we weren't that far from town and a gas station.

One wrong turn became two wrong turns, then another, then another. By now it had started to pour, and Mom had stopped indulging me in chatter. I could see the tension in her neck, rigid and straining toward the frantic windshield wipers, her hands white-knuckling the steering wheel.

A sudden barrage of hail came out of nowhere, *pinging* all around and on top of the car hood. As thunder cracked above our heads, the car sputtered and came to a stop right in the middle of the road.

I started to cry.

"Please don't cry," my mother begged. "Please, I'm already scared." But it was too late. Fear had taken over.

"Help us, Lord," she wept. "Help us. Help us."

But who could help us out here? We were on back roads and had passed no cars our entire ride. Even if a car did come, what were the odds that the driver would be a Good Samaritan and pull over in these conditions? Could we trust him or her? We could be there for hours, maybe even in the dark and long enough for the car battery to die and put us in even more danger.

And then, just as suddenly as it had arrived, the hail stopped. The silence was startling. But even more incredibly, a car's lights—seemingly out of nowhere—came into view behind us. And not just any car.

"It's a good thing I happened to be in this neck of the woods!" the police officer exclaimed when Mom rolled down her window, rain dripping off his nose and streaking his bright yellow slicker.

He was the first police officer I had ever seen up close. As he helped Mom guide the car to the side of the road and arranged to bring us back a can of gas, my young mind was still processing what had just happened, dumbfounded by the timing of it all. "Did the policeman *know* we were here, Mommy?"

"No, but God knew we were here. He sent the police officer. He has angels all around who don't even know they're angels—we have to ask Him to show them to us."

All these years and miles later, having swapped lonely Fords on country roads for crowded subway cars and sidewalks, I'm still comforted by the thought that one or two among the sea of faces are angels waiting for their chance to help an unsuspecting, but grateful, stranger.

A Knock at the Door
Ingrid Hofer

A HARD, ANGRY POUNDING came at the front door. I crawled underneath the bed and nestled into the space between the floor and the mattress. I curled up into a ball, trying to make myself disappear. My mother had hidden herself in a kitchen cupboard.

It was June 1945, and I was seventeen years old—too young to fully understand what was happening around me in Berlin, the city where I'd grown up. The war had ended a month earlier. Mutti, my mother, told me that life would go back to normal soon. Papa would come home any day now. We'd have more to eat.

But I'd heard other rumors. Stories of Russian soldiers hurting people. I was terrified that any moment now, a soldier would march into my room.

The banging at the front door grew louder. I held my breath. The knocking stopped. Maybe whoever it was would give up and go away . . .

The door burst open. Loud footsteps filled the apartment. I peered out from underneath the bed and saw two pairs of boots. *Soldiers!* The men paced back and forth in the living room, calling out to each other in harsh, angry tones, and worse, in a language I couldn't understand. I pressed my body closer to the wall, as far under the bed as I could get, and prayed as Mutti had taught me.

One man paused, his dirty black boots so close I could have reached out and touched them. After what felt like an eternity, the soldier turned and walked away. He and his comrade left out the front door, just as freely as they had come. I was safe. For now.

"Mutti!" I called, wiggling out from under the bed. I ran into the kitchen. Mutti emerged from her hiding place.

"Don't worry, baby," she said, wrapping me in a bear hug. "Everything is going to be all right."

It was the fifth time soldiers had entered our house in less than a month. How much longer could we survive like this? Alone. For over a year we'd waited for Papa to come back to us. Would he ever return?

Our lives had been so simple before the war. Papa was a professional organist and owned the apartment building we lived in. I grew up a savvy city girl and loved riding my bike around the neighborhood and visiting my girlfriends from school.

But the war changed all that. Toward the end of 1944, Papa devised a plan to get us out of the country. He took a train to northern Germany to scope things out. We were to join him once he was settled. We didn't know how soon the Russians would arrive, trapping me and Mutti in Berlin.

In the kitchen, Mutti and I comforted each other. We talked about the good times we would have when we were reunited with Papa. "Everything will be better once we're together again," Mutti assured me. "Things will get back to normal. Like they were before the war."

Before the war. That time seemed almost like a fairy tale. These days the streets of Berlin were mayhem: stores were raided. Women were abused. Children were terrified. We were all hungry. Try to leave the city? Mutti and I were afraid to leave the house. Trying to find Papa up north would be impossible.

The first time the soldiers broke in, they plowed through everything, overturning tables and chairs. They rifled through Mutti's jewelry box and china cabinet. What they didn't steal, they broke on the floor. What little food we had left, they took.

The raids and the chaos were scary, but the hunger was worse.

"Papa will be back soon. We just have to hold out for a little longer," Mutti repeated, patting my head. "Until then, God and His angels will protect us." I worried we couldn't hold out long enough. Sometimes I imagined Papa finally coming home, only to find it was too late.

The next day I woke up, still shaken from the raid. My stomach grumbled, but it was too risky to sneak outside to forage for food today. *Die on the street or starve to death in here,* I thought miserably.

I heard a knock at the front door. *Soldiers? Again?* But this knock was softer. Much softer. I tiptoed to the door, put my eye against the peephole, and looked out. No one there. Mutti stood beside me.

I opened the door and looked out into the hallway. A young woman stood there, holding a loaf of bread in her hands. Its heavenly aroma wafted up to my nostrils.

"I know you're hungry," she said. "Take this and eat."

I took the loaf. It was small but hefty, warming my hands. "Where are you from?" I asked. I had never seen her before. Not in the building or neighborhood. Why was she sharing this priceless gift with *us*?

"I live nearby," she said. She told us the name of her street. I turned to put the bread on the table. When I looked back, she was gone.

Mutti and I were too hungry to wonder what had just happened. We devoured a big hunk of the dense white bread and shared some with our neighbors.

But the next day, curiosity overcame us. We waited for a busy hour, when Mutti thought it would be safe, and walked to the street the woman had mentioned. As we came to it, we found nothing but an abandoned area. No houses anywhere in sight.

We ate from that loaf of bread for a week, far longer than I would have thought it would last. My Berliner angel had restored my hope. Mutti and I could manage to hold out just a little longer.

Soon the border opened and civilians were finally allowed to go in and out of Berlin. Mutti and I heard a car pull up and park right in front of our building. We looked out the window—Papa had come home! Just like Mutti promised. He was overjoyed to see us.

Not only were we together again, but Papa had filled the car with canned goods and wheels of cheese. He had a new plan for our family, and our lives were on the way back to normal.

The Message

Georgianna Demory Wheaton

"WHO DO YOU WANT TO SIGN IT, GEORGIE?" one of my friends asked that Friday as we stood in a circle in the schoolyard, holding our little autograph books for our friends and teachers to write in before eighth-grade graduation. It was exciting figuring out whom to approach next.

"Oh, it doesn't matter," I said, flipping through the pages of my book. "Just so long as I get all my friends and favorite teachers." The group nodded in agreement, but I wasn't being totally honest. There *was* one of those who mattered most: Mrs. Lucky.

She was my teacher in third grade, back when I attended Dante Public School. I'd had a lot of trouble with bullies back then. I was small and delicate, and a group of "popular girls" took every opportunity they could to harass me. They even threatened to beat me up! But no matter what they said or did to bring me down, Mrs. Lucky could always make me feel better. She was an older woman, short with gray hair and wire-rimmed glasses, but she was hardly frail like me. She had a reputation for being strict. Nothing got past her. And she thought I was special. She praised me in class, gave me gold stars, and generally let me know she saw how hard I worked to please her. With Mrs. Lucky on my side, I could face just about anything.

My eighth-grade friends passed around our books, scribbling jokes and messages we could laugh over for years to come. I remembered how, back in third grade, older girls used to come into our class at the end of the year to get Mrs. Lucky to sign their autograph books. She always took her time writing out a unique message. "Do not read it until you've left the classroom," she'd say sternly before giving the book back.

Too bad I can't drop in on her, I thought. After fourth grade my mother transferred me to Guardian Angel Catholic School. Mrs. Lucky was elderly when I left, so surely she'd retired by now. There was no way I could get that special signature I longed for.

My book was over half full by the time I got home. I'd made lots of friends at my new school. In fact, I ended up fitting in perfectly at Guardian Angel, and became more confident and self-assured—more like Mrs. Lucky. Bullies didn't bother me anymore, and I was excited, not scared, to start high school.

Would Mrs. Lucky be proud of how I've grown up? I wondered as I fixed myself an after-school snack. If I could see her again and have her write out a special message for me, I was certain I'd know. *Guess I'll just have to imagine what Mrs. Lucky would have said.*

While doing my chores and all through dinner, I thought about Mrs. Lucky. And that night I had a dream. I was walking down the street in a beautiful neighborhood. Trees with full, emerald leaves grew along the sidewalk, stretching their branches to the sky. Splotches of sunlight filtered down through the canopies, making patterns on the pavement at my feet. I felt dazzled by the scenery and walked a long time.

A noise from behind made me stop and turn. A sleek black limousine pulled up to the curb. The door to the backseat opened, and a familiar face looked out at me. Mrs. Lucky!

"Come on then, have a seat," she said, sliding in to make room and peering sternly at me from behind her wire-rimmed glasses. I quickly sat down next to her and realized my autograph book had been in my hands the entire time.

Mrs. Lucky took it from me, settled it on her lap, and began to write, choosing every word with care. After a while she shut the book and handed it back to me. "Do not read it until I've gone."

"Thank you!" I said, getting out of the limousine and clutching the book to my chest. "Good-bye!"

I woke up with a start. *Was that really a dream?* It had felt so real! I climbed out of bed and opened up my autograph book. No message from Mrs. Lucky, of course. But somehow, it felt like I really did get my chance to see her again.

I even felt like I knew what she'd have written. Maybe not the actual words but the way they made me feel: proud, loved, *special*. This was going to be the happiest Saturday of my life!

Walking on air, I got dressed and went out to run some errands for my mother. At the pharmacy, I noticed two teachers from Dante School talking at the counter.

I hadn't seen them in years, but with the dream still buzzing around in my head, I felt compelled to tell them about it. After all, Mrs. Lucky was as favored by her fellow teachers as she was by me.

They listened carefully as I spoke, never once interrupting and giving me their full attention. When I'd finished, they stared at me, eyes wide.

"What is it?" I asked.

"Well, it's just very strange," one of them said quietly, "but you see, Mrs. Lucky died last night."

Perhaps it wasn't so strange. Not to a child who'd felt such loving encouragement from this angel in her life. Mrs. Lucky *was* proud of me. She always had been, and my former teacher stopped by on her way to heaven to tell me one more time. That's pretty special.

The Touch
Jean Miller

Six years old was too young to understand something as terrible as cancer. All my son, Zac, knew was how much he hated going to the doctor for his annual checkups, which included MRIs and CAT scans to make sure his brain tumor hadn't returned. I wasn't sure which of us dreaded them more.

So far, my son had been in the clear, but I could detect a note of concern in the doctor's voice when he asked my husband, Wendell, and me to join him in his office to discuss the results of Zac's latest series of tests.

I thought back to the day Zac was diagnosed. He was only eleven months old. I couldn't imagine someone so tiny being able to beat cancer. The doctors weren't all that confident either. But they outlined an aggressive course of treatment.

The surgical team removed as much of Zac's tumor as they safely could. Then Zac began radiation therapy. Thirty-three treatments in all—the maximum he could safely receive. "If the treatment works but the cancer returns later," the doctor warned us, "we won't be able to do any more radiation."

The treatments worked. Zac went into remission. Wendell and I never took his health for granted, though. The head of pediatric surgery at the hospital said that Zac was still in danger. "I have rarely seen a child survive this type of tumor for more than ten years," he told us. "The tumor usually returns. I want you both to be prepared for that."

Prepared? How? In the five years since, every night before I took Zac to the hospital for a checkup, I'd toss and turn, unable to sleep. Even as he got older, I couldn't erase the ever-present apprehension. Sure, for now Zac was going to kindergarten, playing soccer, and tearing around the block on his bike. He didn't remember anything he'd gone through as a baby. He was the happiest of little boys, running and playing with the other kids in the neighborhood. One day the tumor could come back. One day we'd be out of treatment options. One day I could lose him.

The doctor came in with Zac's charts in his hand. Right away I could tell this wasn't like all the other tests. "We think we see a spot on the scan," he said. "We don't know what it is yet."

I did my best to stay calm. "What do we do now?"

"We wait a few months," he said. "Then we redo the scan. See if anything's changed."

Before we left the office, we quietly scheduled an appointment for a Monday afternoon three months away. I gave Zac my best happy smile. He had no idea anything was different or that he'd be coming back sooner than usual. But Wendell and I both knew what it meant if Zac's tumor returned.

I felt so helpless. Even more helpless than I'd felt when Zac was a baby. For the next three months I was in a nearly constant state of prayer. I read articles about miracle healings. Many of the people in them talked about using visualization to help the process. One afternoon I came up with my own visualization—or rather, one came to me. I closed my eyes and saw God reaching down to touch Zac's head, right above the area where the doctors saw the spot. At that touch the tumor melted away. I visualized this over and over and over.

I never mentioned it to anyone. Not even Wendell. He was praying just as hard for Zac as I was, but I didn't want him to think I was going around the bend.

That image became an obsession. Anytime I prayed about Zac—practically anytime I thought about Zac—I saw God's hand reaching down from heaven to touch him on the head.

Wendell and I decided not to tell Zac about the test. Not yet. We wanted him to enjoy being a kid for a little while longer, without something like this hanging over him.

"We'll tell him about it the Sunday before," I said. "That will give him some time to be upset about it but not too long."

We both agreed this would be best for him—and for us.

The Friday night before the test, my tossing and turning was so bad that I thought I'd be awake to see the sunrise. I finally nodded off, but sleep was short-lived. The creak of our bedroom door woke me. Zac.

Nobody gets up earlier on Saturday mornings than a six-year-old, I thought. It was still dark! I kept my eyes closed, pretending to be asleep.

"Zac, why are you up so early?" I heard Wendell asking him. "Go back to bed."

"Somebody touched my head."

My eyes flew open.

"You probably rolled over on your arm or something," said Wendell. "Why don't you go downstairs and watch cartoons? Mommy and I will be up in a little bit."

I heard Zac's bare feet patter out of the room.

"Someone touched his head?" I said. "Did he really just say that?"

"Yeah, why?"

I told Wendell about the image I'd been holding in my mind for months. Could it be...?

Later that day I asked Zac about it. If it was a dream, he probably would have forgotten it by now. "Why did you get up so early this morning, Zac?"

He didn't hesitate. "Somebody touched my head and woke me up!" he said, as certain as could be. "Was it you?"

"No, Zac. I was sleeping."

He frowned. "Then who was it?"

"Maybe it was God," I said.

"Why would God do that?"

"Because He loves you," I said.

He still had no idea about his test on Monday. He just knew what he had felt—a mysterious touch on his head.

On Sunday morning, as Wendell and I had agreed, we sat down with Zac and broke the news of the follow-up scan. He was upset and stomped around the rest of the day. I felt bad for him, but strangely, that terrible apprehension had evaporated. I felt...hopeful. Whatever our son was going to be facing, I knew he wasn't facing it alone.

On Monday we took Zac to the hospital for the scan. Shortly after, the doctor called us with the results.

That ominous spot? The one that had the doctors so worried? It had completely disappeared.

Stranger on the Plateau
Sylvia Zitting

BANG! THE DOOR SLAMMING jolted me awake. The sky outside my bedroom window was pitch-black. It wasn't anywhere near morning. Whatever time it was, my father was awake and furious.

"Those no good...they're gone!" he said. Then he yelled, "Everybody up!"

I scrambled out of bed and followed my older sister, Geraldine, into the kitchen, where my parents were. "The field hands have deserted us!" Dad said. "Snuck off in the middle of the night!"

Why would they do that? I thought sleepily. Then I remembered. The afternoon before I'd been tucked up in the hayloft and heard Dad fight with Allen and Jake by the corral. Dad wanted them to drive his herd of horses up Mount Home in the Unitas, across the wide plateau called the Blue Bench, then back down the other side, where our new farm was waiting for us.

"You're crazy!" Allen had said. "You want us to drive a hundred and twenty-five horses up a mountain pass for twenty miles, and another fifty across that godforsaken Blue Bench all in one day? It's impossible. You've got to truck 'em to your new place!"

"There's no money for trucking," Dad said. "You get your gear together. You're leaving at four o'clock tomorrow morning, so you'd better be ready. It's the only way to get those horses out of these here hills before it snows."

During dinner both Allen and Jake were silent. A terrible silence, louder than any angry words.

They sure were dead-set against crossing that Blue Bench, I thought now, standing in the dark kitchen in the middle of the night.

"We've got to move to our new place today, horses and all," Dad told me and Geraldine, his voice going gentle. "Your mom can't drive the truck or those horses. She and I will take your little brothers in the truck with our things. Geraldine, you and Sylvia will have to drive the horses up Mount Home and across the Blue Bench. Nobody's better with horses than you two. You're better than those field hands, even. Just move west to east. I'll meet you on the other side."

Life on a farm wasn't like life in the city, especially back then. We kids were used to hard work, and I was at home on a horse. But if two grown men didn't want to do it, how could Dad give such a job to Geraldine, at seventeen, and me, only twelve? Get all those horses up a mountain, across fifty miles of dirt, sage-brush, and sky in all directions? What if we needed help up there? *Don't you care what happens to us?* I wanted to ask, but nobody said no to Dad. And for good reason. He usually knew what he was doing.

Geraldine and I saddled up. I rode Hytone, my favorite, a big, beautiful palomino. As the sun rose, so did my spirits. We followed a mountain road lined with quaking asps, pine trees, and lots of grass for the horses to graze on. Trees canopied the road. Glimmers of sunlight danced through the dewy leaves. Geraldine and I giggled, sang songs, and yodeled at the top of our lungs. Two girls were doing what seasoned field hands couldn't!

We watered the horses at a creek, then Geraldine rode out in front to guide them onto the top of the plateau. I followed behind the herd. The Blue Bench was as desolate as I remembered, full of washes and ravines. Seeing it laid out before me, I wondered if we'd ever reach Dad on the other side. Maybe those field hands had the right idea by running away. It was just Geraldine and me, abandoned with the herd. "We have to be really careful," Geraldine warned me, "not to lose any of the horses back in those ravines."

The horses' hooves stirred up clouds of dust. We kept them close together. Too much space and some young renegade was sure to break ranks and race off to parts unknown, tail waving straight up in the air. Then we'd have to go racing after him. Looking out over their backs to the north, I saw the peaks of the Unitas glistening with summer snow.

We pushed out over the dusty land. There was no yodeling now. I was plain mad. My mouth was parched. My butt ached in the saddle. I squirmed from side to side, but it didn't help. My shoulders and neck hurt too. "Are we about there?" I cried out. "How much longer?" No answer. Geraldine couldn't hear me way out in front when I added, "My body feels like dying!" *Nobody would care if I did die up here*, I thought.

We pressed on, hour after hour, until the sun got low and the wind picked up. Heavy black clouds gathered over our heads. Now, as well as being tired, thirsty, and mad, I was scared. "Dad'll never find us in a storm," I yelled. "He cares more about his horses than he cares about us!" I laid my head on Hytone's strong neck and bawled.

But my bawling didn't stop the rain pouring down on us a moment later. The horses turned their backs to the storm, dropped their heads, and refused to move. *This is as bad as it gets*, I thought. Then it started to hail.

Geraldine rode her horse over to me. She looked as miserable as I felt. "This hail's beating us up!" she yelled over the wind. We huddled close to the horses' warm bodies for shelter. "I guess we know what hell is like, don't we?" Geraldine yelled. We sure did.

We pressed together in the thick black night as the wind battered us. When the storm finally let up a little, Geraldine said, "Let's get on our horses. We must be almost there by this time."

I climbed up on Hytone and tried to urge the horses forward. A flash of lightning showed they were wandering off, hunting for food. "Hey, I'm hungry too, but we've got to get off this godforsaken Blue Bench!" I yelled as Geraldine and I chased them back into line. I was shivering wet in my clothes. "Dad!" I screamed. "Where are you?" The wind pushed my voice right back in my face. I probably would have started to cry again if I wasn't so tired.

"I'm going to look for a way off this plateau," said Geraldine.

She disappeared in the darkness, and I felt like the last person in the world I could count on was gone. I was abandoned in this desolate place, lost. Lightning flashed again, showing only the same dirt and sagebrush I'd been staring at all day. "God!" I called out. "I need You now. Please! I'm farm-raised and tough, sure. But I'm still just a kid!"

Another bolt of lightning struck. It illuminated the sky—and something else. The outline of a figure. What was it? A man on a horse? "Dad!" My heart swelled. Courage surged through my body. *Dad's come for us!* I'd never loved my father so much as in that moment when I realized we weren't abandoned. Maybe I was just a kid, but I suddenly felt like I could do anything.

"Come on," I yelled to the horses. "We're getting off this plateau now!"

Another flash of lightning showed me our savior again. He was smiling proudly, like he was just as happy to see me as I was to see him. He motioned for me to come his way. Hytone trotted ahead like he was following the signal too, his tired muscles moving fast under my legs, stepping on to a narrow path I would never have found without Dad to guide me.

I met Geraldine at the bottom right beside a road. We'd made it off the Blue Bench, and we hadn't lost one horse. "Which way should we go?" Geraldine said, looking up and down the road.

That was a silly question—we would just follow Dad when he got down. But before I could say anything, a truck pulled up. Down rolled the window and out popped Dad's face.

"You made it!" he said. "Good work! Now just follow me down the road a bit and we'll be home." He started to raise the window and stopped. "I'm really sorry

I didn't meet you on the plateau," he said. "I couldn't find a way up there in this storm."

Couldn't find a way up? I thought. *Then who...?*

I twisted 'round in my saddle and looked back up to the Blue Bench far above my head. Lightning lit the sky. The man on the horse waved down to me, smiling and proud at what we'd done. I still felt him watching over me as I turned to follow Dad home in the truck. Dad had not been able to lead us down the mountain himself, but I was never alone on that plateau. And I would never be abandoned.

Tickets from Heaven

Tom Elliott

BASEBALL IS A TRADITION IN MY FAMILY. Some of my best memories growing up were the days when my dad took my brother and me on the ninety-minute drive to San Francisco to see the San Francisco Giants play at Candlestick Park. We saw a lot of baseball history being made, like when Willie Mays and the Giants won the National League pennant in 1962.

When I had my first child, Zach, Paw—as Zach called him—had another youngster to school in all things baseball. Unfortunately, by the time Zach was old enough to go to games Paw could no longer go. He had Alzheimer's and had to move into an assisted-living facility. Zach couldn't understand that Paw would never "get better" or why we only saw him in his "new home."

"Why don't we take Paw with us to a Giants game, Dad?" Zach asked me one day as we drove home from a visit. He wouldn't understand a medical explanation; I barely could. The permanence of this disease seemed completely unfair, the situation utterly painful. But I could not bear to dash my son's dream. I just couldn't. "Maybe someday we'll all see a game together," I said. Maybe someday.

Even if we couldn't attend any ball games together, our bond of three generations stood strong. Paw was Zach's biggest fan until he passed away. After he died, the world seemed pretty gray for all of us but especially for Zach. "Now we'll never see that game together," Zach said on the day of Dad's funeral. *I should never have raised Zach's hopes*, I thought. *I always knew it couldn't happen. I should have told the truth.*

Several weeks after Paw died, a good friend who was related to a Giants player offered us some complimentary tickets. I hesitated. Since his death, even baseball had lost some of its flavor. On the other hand, maybe it was just what we needed. *It's what Dad would want us to do*, I thought. *He'd want Zach to go.*

After thinking it through, I accepted my friend's offer.

We drove to the game in high spirits. "I can't wait!" Zach said as we entered the stadium. Pleasant memories of my father swirled around my head. *I went to see the Giants when I was Zach's age with you, Dad*, I thought as we walked up to the will-call window. *Now it's Zach's turn.*

"First and last name with some ID, please," the attendant said.

I slid my driver's license under the partition and ruffled Zach's hair. The attendant flipped through a stack of envelopes. She looked worried.

"I'm sorry," she said finally. "There aren't any tickets here for you."

"There must be some mistake," I said. She checked again and still came up empty. We backed away from the window in shock. The game was sold out, and I didn't have the money for scalped tickets. *Lord, I should have been straight with Zach.* We weren't ever going to see a game with Dad, nor did it look like Zach and I would see this one.

I didn't know what to do. Zach looked down at the ground, upset, when someone walked over to us.

"Are you taking your young son to the game?" a kindly old gentleman asked. He nodded to Zach.

"I was planning on it," I said, "but there was some sort of mix-up with our tickets. We don't have any."

The man held up two. "Here," he said. "Why don't you take these?"

I blinked. Was he kidding? People didn't just give away tickets to sold-out games. Must be selling an extra. "I'm sorry," I said. "I don't have the money for scalped tickets."

The man shook his head and waved the tickets at me. "Take them," he said. "I want your boy to see the game."

He put the tickets in my hand and walked off with a smile. I stared after him, still confused. "Thanks!" Zach hollered as the man disappeared into the sea of sports fans milling around the entrance. I felt Zach tug at my hand. "Come on, Dad. Let's go!"

Inside the stadium I led Zach toward the "nosebleeds," assuming we were seated up there. But when I looked at the box and seat numbers to guide us, I stopped short and my mouth fell open. Zach bumped into me from behind. "What's the matter, Dad?"

"These seats are right behind home plate," I said. "Only a few rows up! I've never been this close!"

"Unbelievable," I muttered to myself all the way down to the seats. The seat next to us was empty. But I assumed that wouldn't be the case for long. "The man who gave us the tickets must be coming," Zach said. "We'll buy him a hot dog!"

It was one of the best games I ever saw. The Giants came back late with a grand slam to tie it up. They won in the bottom of the ninth with a slide around the tag at home plate. Zach and I were exhausted from all the hooting and hollering we'd been doing. When it was over I took a good hard look at the empty seat next to us. "I can't believe nobody ever sat there the whole game," I said. "What a waste of a good seat."

"But, Dad," Zach said, "someone *was* sitting in the seat next to us."

Wow, could I really have been that caught up in the game?

"I didn't see a soul. Who was it?"

Zach grinned. "It was Paw, Dad. He was sitting right here with us the whole time. We finally did get to see that Giants game, the three of us."

I pulled Zach close. People around us must've thought we were feeling very emotional about the Giants' win. But only the two of us knew the truth: we were living a gift from above. Well, maybe three of us knew it. "Maybe that old man had it all planned all along," I said as we were leaving the stadium.

"I think that angel flew back up to heaven with Paw," said Zach. "They're probably rehashing the game." Just like Zach and I did all the way home.

Far Away from Home

Doug Holmes

ANY MINUTE NOW, I WAS GOING TO DIE. I gripped my blanket and peered out the hospital window, the cold December wind howling in the darkness. My heart thumped in my chest, fast and erratic. Not the strong, steady heartbeat of a normal eighteen-year-old. But I wasn't normal.

Three weeks earlier, I'd had a kidney transplant at Children's Hospital Los Angeles, where I was still recovering. I had hydronephrosis, a disease that damages the kidneys. When I had one of my kidneys removed at the age of four, my doctor warned my parents I'd eventually need a transplant. We weren't prepared when the other kidney gave out during my senior year in high school. I had no choice but to defer admission at my first-choice college, the University of Southern California, and have the operation. I would remain on dialysis until my new kidney started working on its own.

I heard a knock at the door, and a nurse stepped in to administer my nightly medication. I'd grown close to the nursing staff over the past few weeks. I tended to be more blunt with them about my fears, rather than worry my parents. I was absolutely certain I was going to die. Soon. It didn't matter what the doctors said.

"You're making great progress," the nurse told me. "You'll be home in no time." I washed the pills down with the icy water, wishing I could believe her. I tried to imagine my new kidney working to cleanse my blood. Healing me. But all at once, I felt dizzy. The room spun around and my heart rate surged, pounding faster than it ever had before. I looked up at the nurse in panic. She ran out to call for help. *What now?* A reaction to the medicine? A heart attack? *This is it. I'm dying.*

The doctor and nurse rushed into my room and prepared a syringe. They managed to bring my heart rate down but warned that I'd need further treatment. "For now, you need a good night's rest, young man," the doctor said, closing the door behind him.

Sleep? That was the last thing I wanted. If I fell asleep now, I was sure I'd never wake up. I pictured my friends off at their first semester of college, starting their lives. My heart raced faster and faster. There was still so much I wanted to do. Go to college. Meet the love of my life. Find my dream job. My eyes welled up. I missed Mom and Dad. Everything was slipping away. I was used to health problems but this? I needed more than a good night's rest. I needed a miracle.

There was a knock from outside, and the door to my room creaked open. A new nurse poked her head inside.

"I'm sorry to disturb you," she said with an accent I couldn't quite place. "Are you still awake?"

"Yes," I whispered. My voice cracked. The nurse was middle-aged, with lovely brown hair. In all my time at the hospital, I'd never come across her.

"How are you doing, my dear?" she asked sweetly.

I was too scared to lie. "Not good!" I blurted out, tears running down my cheeks. "I'm afraid I'm going to die. I'll never go home again!"

She reached for my hand and patted it gently. "I'm far away from home too," she said, looking into my eyes. "My native country is Ethiopia."

There was something comforting about her eyes, and I relaxed. My tears stopped.

"You're strong," she said. "Don't worry, okay? Let me read you something." She held up a book, opened it, and leafed through the pages until she seemed to find her spot. "It's from the Bible," she said.

I listened to her delicate accent, not necessarily focusing on her words but on the soothing sound of her voice. I found myself lulled into an incredible sense of peace and warmth, almost as though I had floated out of the room. Everything was bright, and I felt the presence of something greater than myself. I thought of family and friends I had loved in my life. I thought of my parents resting at home until they returned to my side in the morning. For once, I felt calm. Serene. As my heart rate steadied and I drifted off to sleep, I caught one last glimpse of the nurse's wavy brown hair.

"Good night, Doug," she said.

Then I fell asleep.

My heartbeat was stabilized in treatment the next day. My new kidney started working only a few days later. I was taken off of dialysis and released from the hospital. The doctors and my regular nurses had been right.

But I knew that my going home only partially explained the peace I had finally found. So a week later I returned to the hospital and headed straight for the nurses' station. There was someone I wanted to see again—and thank.

"I want to at least write her a note," I said. "She really helped me when I felt so desperately alone."

The nurse listened to my description of a middle-aged woman from Ethiopia and shook her head. "We don't have anybody like that here," she said. "Never have."

"But she visited me . . . ," I stammered. "What about one of the other floors?"

"No," she said. "I'm the head nurse here. I would know."

I couldn't stick around too long to investigate. I had family to spend time with, friends home for winter break, and a meeting with my advisor at the University of Southern California to plan my school year.

I went on to finish college, marry the love of my life, and find my dream job as a pastor. But I've never forgotten that night I thought my life was over—or the one woman who assured me it was just beginning.

CHAPTER 6

Angels Unaware

"I couldn't wait to tell my husband how our car was saved

by someone who reminded me of my Arizona home.

I never learned the cowboy's true identity, and these days,

even with GPS, I still get lost. Yet I'm certain that

even when life tries to drive us over the edge,

God can send an angel,

even one wearing a ten-gallon hat."

—LINDA S. CLARE

Angel in a Ten-Gallon Hat

Linda S. Clare

SIX WEEKS AFTER MY SECOND BABY'S BIRTH, I was exhausted, depressed, and lonely. My husband and I had recently moved to San Diego, where we now had two young sons. But I was a native Arizonan, and I felt like a fish out of water. With few friends and no family nearby, I was overwhelmed. My husband tried to help me, but what I really needed was the support of other mothers.

Some women from our church invited me to a weekday mini-retreat at one of their homes. At first I was hesitant about taking my little ones out for an entire day, but the ladies encouraged me. I accepted the invitation and wrote down directions to the retreat leader's home—in 1981, GPS and computer maps were nonexistent.

The morning of the event, I got up extra early to pack a diaper bag, feed my toddler, and nurse the baby. As I leaned over to strap the children into their car seats, I frowned at the snug reminder that I was still carrying "baby weight." *These women aren't there to judge me*, I reminded myself. *Besides, if I stay home, I have only myself to blame for the cabin fever and feelings of loneliness.* From the rear seat, my two-year-old, Nathan, asked, "Mommy, are there friends at the meeting?"

"Yes." I smiled. "We'll all make new friends."

Trying to read the directions and figure out which way to turn was hard enough, but then I had to answer my toddler's questions and try to keep the newborn's pacifier in place. The road to the house was at the top of a hill. I'd have to navigate through canyons and rugged terrain to get there. Apprehensive, I drove toward the right neighborhood.

Soon the road narrowed, and several turns later, we were on a dirt road. *This can't be right*, I thought. I glanced at my watch. The event had already started and I was still driving in circles. Baby Christian started to cry.

After turning around several times, my blouse dripped with sweat and my waistband squeezed my midsection like a boa constrictor. My heart pounded in my ears. "You can find it," I muttered.

"Are we there yet?" Nathan asked.

My hands shook as I reached yet another dead-end dirt road. *Should I just give up and go home?* I bit my lip. *No.* I longed to make new friends in this strange town. Hills or no hills, I'd find this place, even if it took me all day. And at this rate, it just might.

Turning the car around again promised to be a tight squeeze. I backed up, carefully avoiding the steep little canyon on one side of the road. Between two houses on one side and the chasm's steep walls on the other, there was little room to maneuver. *Concentrate!* I told myself.

Without warning, the car lurched backward. The back tires slipped off the gravel and hung over the edge of a hundred-foot cliff. The car teetered dangerously. I cut off the engine, threw on the emergency brake, and leapt out. I raced to unbuckle Nathan and then lifted out Christian's infant carrier. "Mommy needs help," I said.

"Maybe God can make angels come," Nathan said.

Kids in tow, I yelled for help and pounded on the nearest home's door. Nathan rang the doorbell, but no one answered. Inwardly, I was a quivering mess, but for the kids' sake I tried to appear calm. "Guess nobody's home. Come on." How would I explain all this to the churchwomen? Or tell my husband that our car had rolled into a canyon?

Nathan tugged my sleeve. "Are all the angels busy?" he asked.

"Honey, God has plenty of angels." I pointed to the only other home in sight. "Let's try that one." My arms ached from carrying the baby as we marched to another seemingly deserted house. If no one answered, how far would we have to go to reach the nearest pay phone?

As I rapped on the door and shouted for help, I noticed Western-themed décor. A pair of bulls' horns hung on the door and potted cacti adorned the entryway. It brought me peace, reminding me of my Arizona home.

I was about to give up when the door jerked open. A tall man, wearing pointy-toed boots and a cowboy hat, stood in the doorway. He touched its brim. "Howdy, ma'am. You look like you could use some help."

I quickly outlined the problem, and he followed us to where my car still dangled. The cowboy smiled. He climbed into the car, started it, and then rocked it back and forth from drive to reverse. I held my breath. The wheels spun, but the car wouldn't budge. I closed my eyes, expecting the worst.

When I looked again, all four wheels were on solid ground. The cowboy tipped his enormous hat as I thanked him. He wouldn't take any payment, and instead clearly explained the directions to the retreat. Then he strode back toward where he'd come.

Soon we arrived at the hilltop home. Still shaking, I told the hostess about the cowboy and how he'd kept my car from plunging into the canyon.

She seemed puzzled. "Which house did you say?"

"The door had bulls' horns on it."

"But no one's lived there for years. That house is vacant."

"Wait a minute," I said. "You mean there's no cowboy?"

The hostess shook her head.

That evening, I couldn't wait to tell my husband how our car was saved by someone who reminded me of my Arizona home.

These days, even with GPS, I still get lost. Yet I'm certain that even when life tries to drive us over the edge, God can send an angel, even one wearing a ten-gallon hat.

The Best Partner

Joan Johnson

"Excuse me. Ma'am? Excuse me!" A man was hustling my way.

My eyes narrowed slightly. In my small town, I knew almost everyone, if not by name then by sight, so when I saw him I knew he was most definitely a stranger. *What does he want?* I wondered. I hurried to put my bags in the car.

It had been two years since I'd lost my husband, and while I'd always done most of the errands, there were things that had remained to be done. This trip to Lowe's was supposed to be a quick stop to grab some flowers for the front beds, and now I was wondering if it had been a mistake.

When Lloyd was living, he loved errands. Not a day passed that he didn't make his way to Walmart for something. He happily managed the car's maintenance and dropped off prescriptions at the pharmacy. Any chance to get out and visit with people made him happy, plus it took something else off my own to-do list!

When he died, I prayed to God that He would be my partner now and remind me of all the little things that I'd relied on Lloyd to help with: locking up at night, running the errands, and taking care of the house. It was easy to look back and see how faithful He had been!

"Ma'am." The stranger spoke to me with such purpose, he snapped me out of my reverie. "I don't want to bother you, but your tires are really bad. They're practically bald. See how you can see the belt? You really need to get them swapped out." He seemed genuinely concerned. I appreciated it.

"Thank you," I replied, but the man was already hurrying away. I tried to see which car he got into, but he turned behind a sedan and I lost sight of him.

It was only midafternoon, so I swung by the filling station on the way home. "You're lucky," the technician said. "These tires could've blown any minute. What made you come in?"

The flower planting would have to wait. I stayed in the shop until near closing as the team there helped outfit my car with new tires, changed the oil, and outlined a service schedule that I could easily follow.

In everything I'd picked up since Lloyd died, taking care of the car had completely fallen off of my list. Luckily, God's messenger knew better.

Angel at Westbridge
Jeff Hill

MY WIFE AND I WENT on a planned extended vacation overseas. When we returned I had an urgent message to get in touch with Gary, my former employer. Before we left, I'd been working in a temp position, filling in for someone on a leave of absence. The woman was coming back and they had no other openings. However, Gary appreciated the work I'd done for them and was active in helping me secure another opportunity. "The people over at Westbridge want to talk to you. You need to contact them and set up an interview," he said.

I called Westbridge the following morning and got an appointment for 1:00 p.m. I made sure I was there ten minutes early. When I walked through the main door, only a third of the hallway lights were on. Most of the work areas were dark, and no one was seated in the main office. *I must have come to the wrong building*, I thought. I wasn't sure where I should wait or *if* I should wait. My watch told me I had better make up my mind pretty soon. At the peak of my indecision, I saw someone coming down the hall to my right. He was slender, almost gaunt, a couple of inches shorter than me, with pepper-gray hair.

Too old to still be working here, I thought.

But he was wearing dark blue pants and a light blue shirt with the company logo on the pocket. Above the pocket *Bill* was embroidered in heavy red thread.

A small crescent wrench handle was sticking out of one back pocket and a rag out of the other.

"Everyone is out to lunch. You must be the new guy they're hiring in product development," he said. He greeted me warmly and held out his hand. They were hands that had worked in oil and grease and dirt and dust for years. Honest hands.

I shook it gladly.

"I haven't been hired as of yet," I replied. "I haven't even had an interview."

"I can tell you the job will be yours if you want it. John, the boss, isn't bringing in anyone else to interview unless you turn it down."

Why would a custodian know the employment decisions of the head of the company? I wondered.

"You know," the man continued, "sometimes he doesn't have anyone to talk to. So he talks to me once in a while. I know a great deal of what goes on around here."

"Sounds encouraging," I replied, still a bit suspicious about the quality of his information.

"You should wait for him in his office," he said.

"I don't think that's such a good idea. I'll just wait in the reception area."

"Okay. But you should at least have a look inside. The door's open. C'mon."

I followed him in.

The office was modest. A small round table with four cloth upholstered office chairs was squeezed in one corner. Two straight-back leather chairs faced the desk. But it was what filled the entire wall behind the desk that brought me to a halt. It was a gigantic bronze bust, a relief of Christ from the shoulders up. It was stunning. How someone could create such a warm facial expression, penetrating gaze, and flowing hair out of metal was a mystery to me. Underneath the artwork, the well-known words of John 3:16 were etched on frosted glass.

When I was done surveying the room, I looked over at Bill. His eyes were smiling.

"I'd better get back to work," he said. "Good luck."

I sat in the outer office and waited for my interview.

John finally arrived. He shook my hand firmly. "Glad to finally meet you," he said warmly.

The interview was nothing like what I had expected. John showed me around the building, explaining what went on at different locations and detailing how he saw me fitting in to their plans. He even showed me where the private coffee stash was, the good stuff. At the end of the tour, we sat in his office and had an informal chat. We talked about business philosophy, where I saw myself in ten years, family, and even hobbies.

He offered me a contract. It was fair so I signed it on the spot.

Later, as I was pulling out of the parking lot, I caught sight of Bill working on an outside water faucet. He turned and saw me. He flashed a big grin and waved.

My second day on the job during one of my breaks, I wandered around trying to find Bill. I wanted to say hello and thank him for his encouragement on the day of my interview. I also wanted to find out why he had been so confident I would be offered the job. He was nowhere to be found. *Must be on vacation*, I surmised. When I still hadn't seen him after a week, I went in to talk to John.

"Where's Bill?" I asked.

"Bill who?"

"You know, Bill the custodian. I never caught his last name. He's an older guy, slender, gray hair, wears frameless glasses. He told me you talk business with him occasionally."

John adjusted his seat and sat up a bit straighter. He looked at me questioningly. "The only custodians we have here are Tony, Ray, and Lisa. They're all younger than I am. I can't say I actually talk business with them," he said.

"But I met Bill on the day of my interview. He was working here. He had the uniform, with the company logo and everything. He told me everyone was out having lunch, which was why the building was dark when I arrived. He even told me the job was mine for the taking and that you weren't planning on interviewing anyone else unless I turned the job down."

John's eyes widened. I could tell he was thinking. "I thought those thoughts," he finally whispered. "But I never spoke them out loud to anybody."

We let that hang about for a few seconds. And then as if on cue, we both looked at the huge Jesus sculpture on the wall, and then back at each other.

I'm not sure if it stemmed from reverence, confusion, or what, exactly, but neither of us spoke about Bill again.

"You Shouldn't Worry"

Stephanie Thompson

A TWENTY-FIVE-DOLLAR CAB FARE from the airport? I frowned at the travel paper that contained instructions for my weekend workshop. With an obligatory tip, that would be about sixty dollars to the hotel and back to the airport. I'd budgeted five hundred dollars. And I still had to pay for my flight, hotel room, and meals.

My husband and I weren't broke, but I worked only part-time so I could be home with my first-grade daughter after school. My husband's income was sufficient if we were careful when it came to extras. I'd prayed for more money, enough so that things wouldn't be as tight, but so far that hadn't happened. So I resorted to coupons at the grocery store, dinners at home, waiting to buy clothes on sale—whatever I could do to pinch pennies. Still, I worried that we wouldn't have enough money at the end of the month to pay all the bills.

The workshop would help me with my job, but I wondered if what I would learn would be worth the expense.

That Friday afternoon, the plane landed in Austin, Texas. I followed the signs for ground transportation. A rotund man with a quick smile sat at the information booth.

"I need to get to my hotel, but the taxi fare is a little over my budget," I confided. "Do you know if there's a shuttle? Maybe I could even share the cost with another traveler."

He nodded his head and traced the shuttle's route on a brochure.

"But the bus runs downtown," he suggested. "And it stops right across the street from your hotel. If you want to ride it back to the airport, you must walk down the block, but at one dollar you can't beat the price."

Quickly thanking him, I hurried through the automatic doors and waited under the awning. Within a few minutes, a long blue and white bus chugged to a halt. I stepped on, proud that I'd saved twenty-four dollars.

The workshop was productive. On Sunday morning, before leaving for the airport, I counted up my cash. Thirty-six dollars—enough for a cab. But for a one-dollar ride, I certainly didn't mind walking the block to the bus stop.

The downtown streets were deserted as I pulled my carryon toward the bus stop. A bright orange, laminated sign was attached to the bench. I tried to read it, but the words were in Spanish. *Probably just a schedule.* I fished the bus brochure out of my purse and double-checked the departure times. *The bus should be here any minute.*

I tapped my foot as worry bubbled up. The appointed time came and went. I unfolded the schedule and double-checked it. Another bus should arrive in fifteen minutes. I still had enough time to make my flight, but anxiety churned in my mind. *Will I be able to find my way around quickly once I get to the airport? How are my husband and daughter doing back home?*

A man with a backpack rounded the corner. Obviously a homeless person, his dirty blue jeans hung on his thin frame. A beat-up T-shirt peeked out from his ripped wind jacket. He gently sat on the edge of the bench and sighed. Something in his bright blue eyes made me relax. I gave him a quick smile. He nodded.

I checked my watch. *That second bus should have been here by now.* "Excuse me," I said. "I'm worried that the bus might be late. Does it always run on time?"

The man stared at his well-worn sneakers. "You shouldn't worry," he replied slowly as he ran his fingers through his grimy hair.

"But I'm concerned that the bus isn't coming. I'm going to the airport. I don't want to miss my flight." I tried again to make him understand.

He hesitated for several seconds. Lifting his face, his crisp blue eyes fixed on mine. He shrugged and smiled. "You shouldn't worry."

He stood, slung his backpack over a shoulder, and started up the sidewalk.

Maybe if I try, I can remember enough high school Spanish to figure out what's going on with the bus schedule. I stooped over the neon sign. Now the words were big, bold, and *not* in Spanish, but English: *No runs from this stop on Sundays.* I looked up the street, but the homeless man was gone—as if he'd disappeared into thin air.

I pulled my suitcase behind me and waved for a cab, but this time I didn't mind the expense. I'd asked God to send me money, but instead I got free advice from a mysterious down-and-out stranger. Indeed, I shouldn't have worried.

The Lady at the Service Station

Geraldine Cerrone

ONE UNEVENTFUL EVENING my husband and I were driving down a frontage road in our native Oregon. I was at the wheel while my husband slept. It was a quiet night, and the road was practically empty. I didn't think anything of it until suddenly I realized that our car was very low on fuel. The deserted road became a bit more intimidating as I began looking for a place to pull over and wait for morning. I figured it was our best bet since it was late at night and it seemed unlikely we would be able to find a place to get gas.

But as I started to pull over to the side of the road, I saw the glow of lights up ahead. I drove a little farther and saw that it was a gas station. I couldn't believe my luck!

The attendant emerged from the station door. She was a small, frail-looking woman, and a sight for sore eyes. She came up to the car window. I couldn't help noticing her flawless features and her calming, soft voice as she asked, "Fill 'er up?"

My husband is a light sleeper, so I figured I would get money from him when he awoke once I stopped the car. He, however, continued to sleep soundly. I noticed a twenty-dollar bill in the cup holder. I handed her the bill and she quickly got to work. It took no time for her to fill up our tank.

My husband remained blissfully asleep as I drove away. I glanced down at him, smiling at the fact that we'd avoided spending the night on the side of the road, then I looked back toward the gas station through my rearview mirror. The station was not there!

Was it just a dream? I wondered. Then I looked down at my gas gauge. It read full!

The Red Lettuce Angel

Vicki Cool

WHAT WAS I THINKING? On top of my night rotation as a nurse, I'd volunteered to manage First Lutheran Church's Thursday night Share a Meal program. It was a worthy cause—we'd provide a balanced meal to more than fifty people. And I was just filling in for a friend this one week. But I was already overwhelmed by my work schedule, and I didn't completely trust myself not to mess up.

"Don't worry," I'd told my friend. "You can count on me." At least I hoped so.

In the days that followed, my calendar became a balancing act. I hadn't factored in the amount of time spent collaborating with the other volunteers in a whirlwind of preparations. We had to figure out the menu, find affordable ingredients for the casseroles, coordinate our shopping lists, cook, and then make sure we had enough hands on deck Thursday night to serve. It was a lot to organize, but driving over to the church Thursday afternoon, still groggy from a long shift at the hospital, I was sure I'd remembered everything on my to-do list.

All of the volunteers showed up on time, and after praying together we settled into an assembly line in the basement kitchen, preparing casseroles like a well-oiled machine. *Looks like we pulled it off,* I thought as we loaded the last of them into the oven. *Wait a minute,* I thought, *just casseroles? Something's missing.* The salad!

I'd decided it would be more efficient for me to just take care of that myself, instead of involving the rest of the group. I looked at the wall clock. It showed 4:30 p.m. Dinner was set for six o'clock! Not nearly enough time to add another item to our menu. So much for a balanced meal....It looked like my friend couldn't count on me after all.

"Hey, Vicki!" One of the volunteers poked her head into the kitchen. "There's a lady in the church parking lot asking to see you."

What now? I hurried upstairs and out the door. A woman waved at me from beside her car. I jogged over.

"You're in charge today?" she asked cheerfully. She opened her car door to reveal several loads of crisp, fresh red lettuce. "I picked it from my garden this morning," she said. "It's all washed and ready to go. Can you use some extra salad?"

I couldn't believe it. "Yes, we can! Thank you!" It took a few of us to carry it all into the kitchen. I went into high gear chopping up head after head and concocting a simple oil and vinegar dressing. Everything came together by dinnertime. Each one of our guests left with a full stomach, and several even stopped to comment on the most delicious salad they'd ever had.

The woman with the red lettuce had saved the day, but no one knew who she was, and I never came across her again. Not in town or at church. All I can figure is, God had sent an angel with just what we needed. I could always count on Him, and that's what counted most of all.

The Man with the Black Umbrella

Rita Liles

IT WAS EARLY ON A LOVELY spring day back in 1990. The pleasantness of the day, however, was overshadowed by how stressed I felt. I had rushed around all morning cleaning the house, doing the laundry, and laying out the children's school clothes. I was also now caring for my older brother, who was mentally challenged. Since my parents had passed away, I'd inherited the duties of cooking for him, cleaning, and tending to his laundry—things he simply couldn't do on his own. Adding the extra duties on to my already packed schedule made peaceful mornings a challenge, and on this day my brother was especially impatient with me. I usually took time during the day to pray and talk to God, but my brother's meltdown was all I could handle.

That evening I had to work a shift at a hospital about thirty miles from my home. I needed to get there at least fifteen minutes early to receive a report from the nurse whose shift was ending. All of the nurses were asked to park in designated areas of the parking lot, which were some distance from the entrance, in order to allow patients and their families to park in the closer spots.

While driving down the road on my way to work, I began to pray and talk to the Lord. It seemed like a good time while everything was finally quiet. *At least I won't be interrupted in here*, I thought. Suddenly there was a downpour. I could barely see the road through the sheet of water and had to slow the car down to a crawl. I glanced around to look for my umbrella, and realized I had left it at home. The thought of walking into the hospital soaking wet was so frustrating after the crazy day I'd already had. Now I had to freeze through my whole shift?!

Suddenly I heard a still, small voice say, *Don't worry, you won't get wet; just trust in Me.*

Wow! I was so excited to hear the Lord speak to me with such calming and reassuring words. So I relaxed and resumed praying and worshiping the Lord.

When I pulled into the parking lot, the rain hadn't stopped, but as soon as I opened my door to get out, the storm faded away. I walked into the building completely dry and thankful to God for what He had just done for me.

Later that night, when my shift was over, the rainstorm returned with a vengeance. We were giving reports to the incoming nurses, but all they could talk about was the stormy weather and how badly we were going to get soaked on the long walk out to our cars. As they stirred up worry in my colleagues, I remembered the Voice telling me not to worry and I stayed calm.

When I made it outside to the drive-through overhang, people were huddled up, some trying to cover their heads with bags and others holding umbrellas, waiting for the rain to let up. As I moved toward the middle of the crowd, I was wondering what I should do since the rain was coming down so hard. That's when I noticed a tall man walking toward me from the right side of the parking lot. He was wearing a dark poncho and carrying a large black umbrella. At first I thought maybe he was a security guard.

He motioned for me to come. Without hesitation I went over to him. I felt very safe and secure as he walked me to my car, but I noticed that he never said a word. When I opened the car door to get in and turned to thank him, he was gone. He'd vanished. I looked all around, but he was nowhere to be seen. Again, I remembered what the Lord had said to me.

With tears streaming down my face, I thanked God that He loved me enough to send an angel, a gentle reminder that even my smallest concerns are significant to Him.

Angel in a Pickup

Karen Kingsbury

THE TWO DOCTORS HAD BEEN friends and partners for twenty years. Their mannerisms and mind-sets were so similar, they often joked that even their wives could barely tell them apart.

"Kindred spirits," William Sutter sometimes said.

And his best friend, Harry Bateman, would laugh and nod his head. "Kindred spirits."

Ten years after starting their practice, the two men found land in a remote canyon outside Cottonwood, Arizona. The drive was long and winding, and during monsoon season it could get treacherous, but the friends found the extra effort worth every minute.

They bought properties a few miles from each other and moved their families out into the desert.

One night in late August, Harry and his wife were watching a movie at a theater in Sedona when Harry was seized by a strange and sudden thought. Will was in trouble; he was sure of it.

About that time, a clap of thunder sounded above the movie theater and he jerked in his seat.

"It's just a storm, Harry." His wife took his hand, her voice barely a whisper. "Why so jumpy?"

"Will's in trouble. I have a feeling."

Both doctors had been Christians forever. Therefore, though their region was given to New Age philosophies, neither of them paid heed to the energies or feelings their patients sometimes talked about.

But this…this was something Harry simply couldn't deny. He grabbed hold of his seat's armrests and leaned close to his wife. "Let's go. I have to find him."

Twenty-one miles away, Will Sutter was in a world of trouble.

His wife and daughter were out of town visiting family on the East Coast, so he'd gone out by himself for bread and milk. On the way home, just as he turned on to the canyon road that led to his house, a monsoon unlike any Will had ever seen before let loose.

Signs bordered the canyon warning of landslides and flash floods, but in the ten years the families had lived off the road, neither had happened. Now, though, Will began to worry. Rain was coming down in sheets, and he couldn't be sure but it looked as if the earth along parts of the hillside had given way.

He moved slowly along, determined to make it home before the roads grew any worse. At that exact moment a car came from the opposite direction. As it neared, it halted and flashed its lights. Will stopped and rolled his window down just enough to see the driver, a white-haired man with light eyes that almost glowed in the dark of the stormy night.

"Can't get through," the man shouted at him. "Part of the road's gone."

Will had a sinking feeling in his gut. He had to get through; where would he spend the night if he didn't get home? Besides, the road couldn't be that bad. Whatever was wrong with it would be fixed the next morning, and everything would be fine.

As long as he managed to get home.

Will stuck his hand out the window and waved at the man. "Thanks," he yelled. "I'll take my chances."

The man looked hard at him and showed no signs of leaving. Will pulled himself from the man's stare and hit the gas pedal. *Strange guy*, he thought. And what was he doing on the remote canyon road, anyway? Will had never seen him before.

Will kept driving, going slower with each turn. After a few minutes, the strange man in the pickup truck was forgotten. Suddenly, without warning, a wall of water and mud crashed against his Suburban and pushed it toward the edge of the canyon. The drop was more than two hundred feet in that area, and Will could do nothing to stop his vehicle from heading closer toward the edge.

"God! Help me!" Will shouted the words, glancing quickly at his surroundings. He had a few seconds at best before the flash flood and flowing hillside pushed him into the canyon. "Please, God...help!"

Then, suddenly, his Suburban jolted to a stop.

Will blinked, his fingers in a death grip around the steering wheel. What had happened? He looked out his driver's-side window and saw that the water and mud were still flowing against his car, but not as strongly as before. Every few seconds he could feel his front tires slip a little toward the edge of the canyon, but still his vehicle held.

When it looked as if the flow had stopped, he tried to open his door and escape. But the movement of his body caused his Suburban to lurch a few feet closer to the edge. *Okay, God.* His heart pounded and he forced himself to stay as still as possible. *Give me a miracle, please. Get me out of this.*

Back at the theater, Harry and his wife had just climbed into their Explorer when a pickup truck pulled up next to the driver's door. Harry was trembling now, desperately worried about Will without any real reason for feeling that way. He rolled down his window and looked at the man. Something about him seemed strange, otherworldly. His hair was bright white, and his eyes held an unnatural light.

Harry frowned at the man. "Can I help you?"

"Do you have a winch?" The man motioned back down the road. "There's a guy off of Old Canyon Highway stuck in the mud. He's gonna need a winch."

Old Canyon Highway? That was the road he and Will lived on. Harry struggled to find his words. "I'm headed that way. I'll see what I can do."

The entire drive back toward Cottonwood, the feeling that Will was in danger only grew stronger for Harry. But as he turned on to the highway, he looked for a car stuck in the mud, since he'd promised the guy in the pickup he'd help.

"Do you think maybe this is a little crazy?" Harry's wife took his hand and gave him a curious look. "Will is home tonight, remember? His family's out of town."

"I don't care." He met his wife's gaze and hoped she'd see how serious he was. "I've never felt like this is my life. He's in trouble, and God wants me to help him. That has to be it."

They kept driving, and Harry noticed sections of the road that were nearly buried in mud. The rain had stopped by then, but the damage it had caused was evident everywhere. "Flash floods," he told his wife. "That must be what that guy in the pickup was talking about."

One more turn and another straightaway and Harry's breath caught in his throat. There, ahead of them, was Will's car, the headlights flashing. It had slid sideways off the road toward the canyon's edge, and though a bank of mud remained wedged against the driver's door, a tree stump on the passenger side kept the Suburban from going over.

"Dear God, let me help him." Harry pulled over but stopped short of wading through the mud toward Will's car. "Will! It's me. Are you in there?" he called out loudly.

"Yes!" Will's voice was higher than usual, tense and worried. "Stay there. I'm not stable. One wrong move and . . ."

At that instant, Will's car slid another few inches away from the stump, closer to the canyon's edge.

"I've got a winch. Hold on!" As Harry said the words, a chill ran down his spine. Suddenly he could picture the man in the pickup asking him if he had a winch, telling him that a man was stuck on Old Canyon Highway. How had the man driven from the remote canyon spot where Will was stuck to the theater parking lot in search of someone with a winch?

He had no time to analyze the situation. Cell phones didn't work on that stretch of the road, so a rescue would be up to him. If he left for help, it could be too late. Moving as fast as he could, he found his winch and, using a nearby tree for support, braced the Suburban in six places. Just as he attached the last rope, the Suburban pulled away from the tree stump and slid freely toward the edge of the canyon.

But Harry's ropes held, and the vehicle stopped a few feet short of going over.

"Praise God!" Will shouted from inside his car. "I'm getting out." He climbed through the backdoor, and using the ropes for support, he made his way over to Harry's car.

There the two men compared notes and realized something strange: they'd both had an encounter with the same man in the pickup—a strange man with white hair and glowing eyes, whom neither of them had seen before that night.

"Do you think maybe..." Harry's wife was the first one to make the suggestion. "Could he have been an angel?"

The more the three talked about the possibility, the more it seemed the only answer. How else would Harry have felt driven to find his best friend at the very moment of his greatest need? And who else would have known where to find Harry at the theater, and in which direction to send him?

For a long moment no one said anything. They didn't have to, really. God in His miraculous wonder had said enough for all of them.

The Last Ride

Linda Winn

FOR OVER A YEAR, I prayed one of Moses's blessings for my husband, Earl, and me: "The bolts of your gates will be iron and bronze, and your strength will equal your days" (Deuteronomy 33:25, NIV).

I'm so thankful God answered that prayer for Earl.

He had been through a rough time with atrial fibrillation, an irregular heartbeat that can lead to a stroke or heart failure, and living with constant fear had dulled his will to live. He tried all the medicines available before insurance finally approved a procedure to correct it; the procedure worked beautifully. Six weeks later he was off the clot-preventing blood thinners and enjoying his active life, which meant riding his motorcycle again. So he and his buddy Mitchell planned a trip to Florida for a motorcycle show.

The morning they left, our conversation was different than usual. In the past, Earl always told me his itinerary and where they had reservations. And typically when I reminded him to be careful, he always responded, "That's the plan."

But he didn't have this trip mapped out; he hadn't made reservations anywhere; and he didn't say, "That's the plan," when I told him to be careful.

When I reminded him to call me when they settled in the first night, he didn't even respond with, "Okay." So I grabbed him by the lapels and said, "Call me tonight."

We hugged, shared a brief kiss, said, "I love you," and he walked out the door with my prayer, "Lord, keep him safe and bring him home."

Later that day I read, "See, I am sending an angel ahead of you to guard you along the way and to bring you to the place I have prepared" (Exodus 23:20).

Somehow I understood. Earl was under the direction of God's angel sent to escort him home.

Two hours later the Tennessee Highway Patrol and sheriff pulled into my driveway, their faces solemn. "There's been an accident," they said.

My mind fast-forwarded beyond the overwhelming sadness of Earl's death to my concern for Mitchell and for the two officers who had to deliver the bad news. They assured me that Mitchell was not involved in the accident.

Later Mitchell told me he witnessed the same peculiar prelude to Earl's home going. "Earl didn't come out of your house as talkative as usual," he told me. "We usually had good conversations, but he didn't talk at all when we stopped at the store. Then, when he led us onto the interstate, I wondered what we were doing. He never rode the interstate."

The story was coming together for me.

The law enforcement officers then called the hospital and put me in touch with the medical examiner who saw Earl when his body was brought in. He comforted me with the information that Earl had had a massive heart attack before the crash, and there wasn't a scratch on him. To me, that meant the Lord kept him safe and took his spirit to heaven before his head hit the highway.

God was merciful in the way He took Earl home; and in doing so, God was merciful to me too.

Every time Earl had left on a motorcycle trip, I wondered if it would be the last time I would see him. But this time, God blocked those thoughts.

He knew Earl was going to ride his motorcycle all the way to the other side of eternity, and He spared me the anxiety of anticipating Earl's death.

He orchestrated the events of that day to ease Earl's transition from here to there without causing harm to anyone else.

He surrounded me with people He chose to comfort me and ease my transition from life with Earl to life without him.

And He sent Mitchell back to tell me of an interesting occurrence that would assure me God ushered Earl all the way home: "Earl's body came to rest face down at the base of an iron post that supports the guardrail on the left shoulder of the interstate. As he lay there, a little lady appeared out of nowhere, placed a rosary on Earl's back, and prayed for him. Then she simply disappeared. I don't know where she came from or where she went."

Sometimes we are not aware of the angels in our midst—those spiritual beings God created to assist, protect, and deliver His people—but Mitchell saw this one. And as if to assure me that God kept Earl safe and led him home, the rosary stayed with his body until I received it with the rest of his belongings.

To me, that rosary represents a tangible sign of God's presence as His angel watched over Earl and guarded him all along the way to the place God had prepared especially for him.

The Skeptic and the Turnpike

Edward Joseph

AT OUR HOUSE it's my wife, Susan, who's the big believer in angels. She has enough angel pictures, statues, and assorted doodads to start her own mail-order business. I'm a skeptic. During trying times, though, I have to admit I've asked angels to lend a helping hand, the way Susan says they do.

Like the week after my father died. I had driven over to New Jersey to take care of some business related to Dad's will. Afterward, I met my sister for dinner. We had lots to talk about. Close to midnight I pulled onto the New Jersey Turnpike and headed back home to Yonkers, New York.

It was a blistering cold January night. Wind pounded the car, and it was as dark as ink outside. *Susan's probably praying I get home safe.* As I finished that thought, the lights on the dashboard went out and the pedals locked up. My car had lost power. I drifted to a halt on the snow-packed shoulder of the turnpike.

Now I understand why people carry cell phones, I thought and looked at my watch. *I wish I had Susan's angels with me now.*

I got out of the car and zipped up my coat. I waved my arms frantically, but it was no use. No one stopped. I wouldn't want to stop on the turnpike after midnight either. Not these days. But I knew Susan would call my sister and get worried when she learned what time I'd left. No doubt she'd turn to her angels.

If You really do listen, God, send half of the angels to comfort Susan and the other half to get me home.

I shivered and willed a state trooper to come by and help me, but none did. My teeth chattered. The later it got, the less likely it seemed someone would ever stop for me. Especially because the cars were now few and far between. *Guess I have to abandon the car and hoof it over to a roadside motel.*

I was about to walk the mile or so to the next exit when I heard the crunching sound of tires on snow. The car wasn't coming up behind me but backing up toward me. Just two red taillights on the shoulder. *A car in reverse on the turnpike?*

The car stopped right in front of me. The door opened and out came a young man. Or, at least, the man made a youthful impression on me in the darkness.

"Trouble?" the stranger said. I told him my electrical system was shot.

"I found you a tow truck," he said. "Help is on the way."

What a stroke of luck. The guy smiled, got back into his car, and pulled away, this time in the right direction! I was so relieved, I hadn't asked to borrow his cell phone—if he had one—to call Susan. Or how it was he knew I was in trouble, since I hadn't seen him pass me on the road. As promised, a flatbed tow truck pulled up, and I was able to tell Susan not to worry.

Back home, I told her the whole story. She just looked at one of her angels and smiled. *That's my Susan*, I thought. But that night, in the wee hours of the morning, when I finally slipped into my warm bed, I had to wonder. Perhaps my wife was really on to something.

"Maybe I'm rethinking my position on angels," I told her the next morning. Susan didn't say, "I told you so," but she did spend the day dusting the house and adjusting her angel collection. I didn't expect to describe the various pieces as doodads ever again.

The Second Stewardess
Marci Alborghetti

MY HUSBAND, CHARLIE, and I were congratulating ourselves on our decision to avoid planes in future travels. After we'd gone through all the terrible memories that had caused us to embrace plane-less travel, Charlie asked, "What was your worst flight alone?"

"When I was coming back to you," I answered promptly. When his eyebrows shot up, I added, "Fortunately, an angel showed up."

The winter after we'd first met, I'd left Connecticut to spend a few months in Key West, Florida. This had already been my winter routine, but I also needed to clear my head and figure out if I should give up my vaunted independence to spend my life with Charlie.

I was miserable from the instant I boarded the plane in Connecticut until the moment I decided three weeks later to cut my trip short and return to Connecticut...and to Charlie. Unfortunately, it was one of the stormiest Februaries Florida had ever had; Key West had seen power outages, torrential rain, and high winds, which meant I wasn't the only one who wanted off the island. It was chaos at the tiny Key West airport. I was booked on an already crowded flight that got canceled because the small plane scheduled to fly us *to* Miami hadn't arrived *from* there. There was still one small plane, booked to capacity, on the runway as more storm clouds threatened. Thankfully, they had a seat for me.

As I was about to board, I heard as clear as day, *Do not get on that plane.* It was my aunt Dearie's voice. Though I'd seen her just twice in my life, long ago when I was a child and she was, well, alive, I'd know her voice anywhere.

Aunt Dearie was superstitious, and though she was many miles away, her dictums came through loud and clear in the many phone calls and letters she exchanged with my mother, a much-younger sister she clearly felt needed her long-distance counsel. She was particularly superstitious, not to mention plainly suspicious, of airplanes. "If God had meant us to fly, He would have given us wings," she'd proclaim, using that old chestnut to good advantage, but she had plenty of her own: "Mildred said that before they got on the plane, they met the pilot and *he had liquor on his breath!* She spent the whole flight sick to her stomach!" "I don't even like being on the ground during Florida thunderstorms. Can you imagine being in one of those things *thousands of feet in the air?*" "Pete [her husband] heard from one of the managers that he wouldn't set foot in one of those tin-foil contraptions. *And he'd been a pilot in the Air Force!*"

Bound and determined to get home, I ignored my long-dead aunt's voice. Because I was traveling alone, I got squeezed on to a flight where I ended up buckled in between some luggage and the flight attendant's station. Instead of Miami, we were flying into Atlanta, which theoretically would allow us to fly higher and over the storms.

Theory met Mother Nature on that flight, and Mother Nature won. We struggled to gain altitude in the heavy storms and air pockets, but to no avail. At one point, the plane was falling so fast that people's food and drinks (and they *were* drinking now) ended up airborne. Even the elegant flight attendant looked alarmed as she tried to keep up with passengers' cries of fear and demands for information. A few had started to pray. Someone was shrieking in terror.

By the time the second stewardess returned from trying to calm other passengers, I was scrunched over in my little seat in terror. She leaned over me, taking my hand firmly in her own cool fingers. "We fly in weather like this all the time," she said, smiling. Her face was calm and plain, without the carefully applied makeup that was sweating off the first flight attendant's face. The tiny airline pin on her collar looked reassuring. "Really," she told me, "we're used to this. And we have a really experienced pilot."

She didn't let go of my hand, even though she was being buzzed by other passengers. "Okay?" she asked. And, for some reason, it was. I nodded and straightened up as best I could in my cramped perch. She returned to her duties, and I closed my eyes and prayed quietly. I didn't open them until the pilot announced we were about to land in Atlanta.

As we deplaned, I looked for my helpful friend, but she wasn't standing with the still-shaken first flight attendant who had a grim smile plastered on to her face. "Excuse me," I said, "but could you tell the other stewardess thank you for me? She really got me through that."

She narrowed her eyes at me, barely maintaining the painted smile. "I'm the only attendant on this flight," she said, not quite unclenching her jaw. "It must have been another passenger."

I started to protest but then thought about the wings pinned to the collar of my helper's uniform. "You're probably right," I said, but she was already looking past me at the next person in line.

When I finished telling Charlie the story, he said, "I can't believe you didn't tell me that when I picked you up at the airport!"

"I probably didn't want you to think I was crazy."

He was quiet for a moment.

"What are you thinking?" I asked.

"I don't know...maybe we shouldn't give up flying just yet."

The Four Strangers

Carolyn J. Decker

WHEN I TURNED FORTY-EIGHT, I fell in love with my life! I was single again, my children were adults, and my career required that I cavort back and forth to Europe and all over the United States. I was thrilled to be living my personal and professional dreams, traveling to places I'd never believed I would visit. I was exactly where I wanted to be! I was a runner, even running in races, and I adhered to the guidelines of a healthy lifestyle. I was fit and felt like a million dollars.

Then one day that all changed. My energy began to diminish little by little.

I blamed my lethargy and too-thin body on my busy schedule, everyday stress, and work demands. But I began to notice that getting out of bed in the morning took great effort. I had no appetite, and my skin was noticeably pale. The career I had enthusiastically embraced had become laborious, although the position duties had not changed. I went to doctors of all disciplines, seeking a diagnosis, but every test result was "within normal range."

Despite their words, I knew something was seriously wrong.

One evening I was meandering around my house when I sensed what I would equate to an electrical buzz, just above my right breast. The buzzing didn't hurt…it was *just there,* and it didn't relent until it got my attention. I haphazardly touched the spot the first time, and the buzzing stopped, each time, *until*

I removed my hand. This pattern repeated several times: I would feel a buzzing sensation, I would touch the spot, and the buzzing would cease. Finally when I touched the place where I felt the buzzing, I discovered an area that was as hard as a rock. A quick comparison to the left breast confirmed an obvious difference. And then the buzzing was gone; it never returned. Notice had been served.

I was so terrified I waited a couple of weeks before going to a surgeon. He confirmed that there was indeed a mass in my right breast. He offered the standard options: I could wait three months to see if the mass enlarged before pursuing the cause, or I could opt for a biopsy, which was the only way to determine what the mass actually was. I had been getting progressively more and more ill for months. I wanted to know as soon as possible what I might be dealing with. The doctor left me alone while he checked the hospital schedule for the next available surgical suite to perform the lumpectomy. He seemed stunned when he informed me he could perform the procedure the next day. "Available Johnny-on-the-spot surgical suites never happen here," he said.

I left the surgeon's office in somewhat of a daze. I was scared. Was my life about to end? As soon as I got home, I turned on the TV. Daytime television has never appealed to me, but on this day, I needed the distraction. My mouth dropped open. There lay Mary Tyler Moore in a hospital bed, portraying a woman recovering from a mastectomy! She'd had breast cancer. I was stricken with fear. In that moment I knew I had breast cancer too. I felt angry. I couldn't sit still. Adrenaline coursed through me. I began cleaning furiously, organizing drawers, doing anything to keep from thinking about cancer.

But the next morning when I arrived at the hospital for the lumpectomy, I had somehow come to grips with what I knew was my fate. I was calm, easing myself into the acceptance stage.

Immediately following the lumpectomy, I was amazed at how much healthier I felt! The mastectomy was scheduled for three weeks away. Three days before that was my lifelong best friend's birthday. Life needed to be celebrated. So our group of close friends went to a conservative club we frequented to celebrate. *Ironic*, I thought, *celebrating another year of life when fate could have me facing an early death.*

Our group knew most of the patrons at the club. So when three middle-aged men with dark hair, olive complexions, all wearing black slacks and long-sleeved beige shirts approached us that evening, we were caught off guard. We assumed they were new to the oldies club, had noticed the birthday celebration, and wanted to pay respects to the birthday girl. But instead they sought *me* out. Without any introduction, they stood in a horizontal line before me. Each man in turn asked for my hand to gently kiss it, then bowed and said, "We wish you well." And then one of them presented me with a long-stemmed red rose. Then they simply walked away. We had never seen them before, and we never saw them again.

A couple of months after my mastectomy, my friends escorted me to the same club to listen to oldies music. I needed a change of scenery after the grueling chemotherapy treatments. On that particular night, another man was there; he had an olive complexion and was dressed in black slacks and a long-sleeved beige shirt. He was much taller than the previous three men from before, but a close lookalike. He approached our table several times to ask me to dance. He appeared to be alone, yet he never stopped smiling. We watched him interacting with others, but he never settled at any one table or with any single group.

I tired quickly and was preparing to leave when this distinctive young man dashed up to me and said, "Are you leaving now?"

"Yes," I replied.

"Will you please wait?" he asked. He said he wanted to give me something. "It will only take a moment. Please wait."

I agreed.

Then he asked me for my first name. By this time my friends and I were curious. Just a couple of minutes later, the man returned with a napkin in his hand.

He handed it to me. On it he had written, "Dear Carolyn, stay close to the angels. They will watch over you and protect you." He smiled broadly at me, then he left.

None of us ever saw him again. We asked if anyone knew who he was, but no one had ever seen him, or the previous three gentlemen for that matter.

I kept that napkin in a special place. The words provided me months of hope, support, encouragement, and blessed serenity. I frequently took the napkin from its safe place where I kept it and reread it; repeatedly those words settled my fears and lowered my anxiety during the months of difficult treatments.

One day I went to take the napkin from the place I had always kept it, to read it again... and it was gone. I searched everywhere. But I never was able to find it. I was devastated. It had disappeared... just as suddenly as the four mysterious visitors who had appeared unexpectedly at the club. It still saddens me that I don't still have that napkin for comfort. But I know the purpose of the napkin and the written words have been served.

I have been in remission from breast cancer since 1992, and I am forever grateful for the four mysterious angels that keep watch over me.

God's First Responders
Malvina Middleton

SHATTERING GLASS, CRUNCHING STEEL, everything a blur—our SUV rolled until we reached the bottom of the hill. Somehow, we landed upright. I breathed deeply and turned to my husband in the driver's seat. His face was scratched and glass shards sparkled in his hair, but he was alive and conscious.

Ralph and I were driving north on the expressway toward the campground in Oscoda, Michigan, where we spent our summers. A semitruck sped past us, clipping our side-view mirror, jolting our SUV to the right. Ralph fought to control the wheel, but the trailer fishtailed. We ran off the road and tipped over. But we survived.

We were still gathering our wits when two young men appeared in the backseat. Witnesses to the accident, I assumed. One put a hand on Ralph's shoulder; the other put his hand on mine. "May we pray for you?" one of them asked.

"We can use all the help we can get," Ralph said.

Soon we heard sirens. We turned away from the good Samaritans and watched emergency crews. "You okay?" asked the first one to reach us.

"We are!" I looked behind me. The two young men had gone.

The emergency crew tried to open the doors, but power saws were needed before they could climb into the backseat to get us out.

Ralph and I wondered: *How did those two young men get in?*

Angels of Christmas

"Maybe it was my imagination, *I thought.*

But deep down inside I knew I had never seen anything so real.

When I closed my eyes I could picture my vision—vividly—once again.

And how could something I had imagined take away

my fear so completely? I no longer had trouble joining in with the choir.

I lifted my voice up to God and sang with all my heart.

Now I knew that I was singing with the angels."

—HELEN WALKER

A Host of Christmas Angels

Helen Walker

FRIGID WIND STUNG MY CHEEKS as I walked up the steps to Chicago's St. Hyacinth Basilica near my hometown of Evanston, Illinois. I barely felt the cold. My head was still spinning from the news. I steadied myself on the icy railing. It was December 7, 1941. I was sixteen years old. I knew I'd never forget this day as long as I lived. *How could it have happened?*

Less than an hour ago, my family had been cozy at home enjoying Sunday dinner. We were all dressed up, my little sister in shiny patent-leather shoes and my four older brothers looking smart in matching ties. Right after the meal we would head over to St. Hyacinth, where Evanston Township High School was hosting our annual Christmas concert for the community.

Our school was known for its musical program, and I was honored to be one of the singers in the chorus. I couldn't wait to perform. We'd been rehearsing for weeks. I knew every note. Singing was my passion, and my refuge. My mother said singing was like praying twice. I intended to send my prayers soaring up to heaven at the concert this evening!

But then, while we were finishing up our meal, the phone rang. My father left the table to answer it. "Hello?" he said. "Yes, I'm listening." His eyes widened and he fell silent. He hung up and turned back to us. "The president just made a radio announcement," he said. "Japan has bombed Pearl Harbor."

The dinner table went quiet. Everyone seemed to hold their breath, unsure of what to do. According to my father, details were still trickling in from the White House. But a few things were already clear—American military personnel had been caught completely by surprise and thousands on the island naval base had died.

The radio broadcasters warned that nothing could be gained from hysteria, but my mind was jumbled and I felt dizzy. I could see the same shock reflected back at me in the faces of my brothers and sisters, my mother and father. I knew we were sharing the same thought: *How could this have happened? How can this be real?*

My mother's voice finally broke the silence. "Helen, sweetheart, get your coat. We don't want to be late for your concert."

I did as Mother said, and the family drove to the church in silence. All of my excitement had vanished. Worry and doubt crowded my head. Would the United States now enter the war? What would that mean for my older brothers?

An icy chill went through me at the thought, and I pulled my hand from the church railing. For now I had to concentrate on the concert. My mother hurried me up the rest of the stairs. I quickly put away my coat and found my place in the chorus on stage.

I looked out at all the people in the audience. Were they afraid too? How would the war affect them all? My brothers, my family, my community, my country—would we ever be, or feel, safe again?

Before the program began, one of the teachers from the music department came to the head of the audience and repeated President Roosevelt's announcement for the crowd. I felt sick. How could we be expected to perform after hearing such news?

The orchestra struck the first notes, and my classmates began to sing. I tried to lose myself in the music, but I couldn't push away my anxieties. I looked up at the grand dome of the basilica, praying silently for strength. *Singing is like praying twice,* I told myself.

I mouthed the words to the music, but it was as if I had no voice to sing with. I kept my eyes focused on the dome, its exquisite mural of saints and angels stretching around the base. Bright clouds floated above them, fading into a sky-blue backdrop that led up to a stained-glass window in the center, patterned in azure and gold.

Music filled my ears—orchestral instruments, the voices of my friends. I felt like I was part of a celestial concert. The dome appeared suddenly to me like the inside of an observatory, opening up to reveal the heavens. Glittering stars and rainbow galaxies burst into life, casting colors across the walls of the church. A glorious white-gold staircase shimmered into view, spiraling down from the infinite beyond. On its steps descended a host of angels, their faces bright and joyous. They danced up and down the stairs, their divine song joining our chorus. I realized I was singing too. As our song came to a close, the ceiling above solidified again. The vision vanished. But I was left with a peace I couldn't have expected. Especially now.

Maybe it was my imagination, I thought. But deep down inside I knew I had never seen anything so real. When I closed my eyes, I could picture my vision—vividly—once again. And how could something I imagined take away my fear so completely? I no longer had trouble joining in with the choir. I lifted my voice up to God and sang with all my heart. Now I knew that I was singing with the angels.

After the concert I rushed around to my friends in the chorus, asking if they had seen the angels too, or the staircase—or perhaps anything unusual at all. I asked my parents, my brothers, and sister. They all shook their heads.

Why the heavenly vision was for me alone, I cannot say. But as we sang I believe I saw Christmas angels, carrying our prayers up to God and carrying God's blessings back down to all of us.

My Sister's Gift

Judith Preston

THE SALESCLERK REMOVED the pair of chandelier earrings from the glass case and dropped them in my waiting hands. They felt real, but I still had trouble believing it. Thin, hand-forged hoops and dangling, delicate chains, all in shimmering gold. I was mesmerized. Time seemed to stop. The department store clatter faded into the background. Enraptured, I held one up to my ear and looked in the mirror. "A terrific Christmas gift," the clerk said cheerily. "For your mother, maybe?"

The spell was broken. The crowd clustered by the shoes and handbags grew loud again. Out of the corner of my eye, I saw my mother walking over from the perfume counter. "They're…they're not for anybody," I murmured to the clerk. How could I explain to her when I couldn't even explain it myself? I hadn't told anybody about the dream, not even my mother.

It was the strangest dream I'd ever had, on the strangest, most terrible night. One month ago, close to midnight, I'd just returned home from a party when the phone rang. My mom was on the other end of the line, breathless, panicky. I held the receiver close to my ear, straining to make out her words.

"It's your sister," she said. "She had a brain aneurysm."

"I'm on my way," I said, reaching for my keys. It was snowing and the hospital was more than two hours away, but I had to see her. "There's no point risking the drive at this hour," my mother said. "The doctor says she's not going to wake up. Come in the morning."

I sat on the edge of my bed long after we hung up, desperate for sleep but scared of waking to a world without Jan. She was only forty-three. Never again would I hear her voice. Or sit at her kitchen table, eating home-baked treats from her little cookie tin. I crawled under my comforter. I wanted to talk to my sister again, but I wouldn't get the chance. Instead I spoke into the darkness: "Forgive me, Jan, if I've ever hurt you. I love you dearly."

Sleep came in fits and starts, one odd image breaking into my consciousness. A human ear—shaking, vibrating almost violently. The ear was pierced, and dangling from it was a beautiful gold earring: smooth, perfectly round hoops and fine, tightly linked chains. Was this Jan's way of letting me know she had heard me? The thought was as confusing as it was comforting.

Jan died five days later, never waking up. In those hard days that followed, it was the vision—strange as it was—that I held on to. I played the dream over and over in my head. The shaking ear and the dangling gold earring that adorned it.

Exactly like the pair of earrings the salesclerk had put in my hand. What did it mean?

"Find anything?" my mother said, joining me by the jewelry counter.

"These earrings," I said. I lifted them up so she could get a better look. "I... I had a dream about them. The night that Jan..."

Mom gasped and covered her face with her hands. She was so upset, I put my arm around her. "I'm sorry...," I began to say.

"Judith, you don't understand," my mother said. "I have those earrings at home. Jan bought them to give you for Christmas."

Three Lumberjacks

Jon Poehner

APPREHENSION? EXCITEMENT? My wife, Rosland, and I didn't know what we felt more while we packed our belongings into the rented U-Haul trailer. We'd married young, even for the freewheeling 1960s—and at eighteen we'd already added a new baby to our family. I'd just completed my basic training at Fort Ord in California, which meant I could eventually expect a tour in Vietnam. Already I worried who would take care of my young family then.

For now, though, I was in charge. We were leaving Southern California for my first duty station at Fort Riley, Kansas. We hitched the trailer on to our 1958 Rambler station wagon and set off, making good time until we hit New Mexico.

"Snow!" Rosland said, marveling at the pretty white flakes falling outside. "It's certainly going to be a white Christmas in these parts." Not something we were familiar with. Soon we seemed to be enveloped by flurries. It was getting hard to see the road as the sky darkened. I turned on the radio and scanned for a weather report.

"I hope this snow doesn't keep us from getting there on schedule," I said. Being late was simply not an option when you were in the army during wartime.

Rosland pulled out a map and found a mountain pass that would cut hours off of our travel time. "We'll take it."

I quickly regretted the decision. Towering trees on either side of the road made everything even darker. The snow was falling faster and heavier, pummeling against the windshield. The temperature had dropped below freezing. But we'd passed the point of no return—the trailer behind our car made going back impossible.

I inched along at a snail's pace, gripping the steering wheel and trying not to slide off the road. Sometimes, without warning, the rear wheels spun in place, leaving us holding our breath until they caught solid ground again. The heater in the Rambler was on full blast, and I prayed it would continue working.

Then, the car came to a stop. I pressed on the brake, but instead of holding steady, our station wagon slid backward! I couldn't see out the back window. Would we roll until we hit a tree? Rosland held the baby tight to her. We didn't say a word. After what felt like a lifetime, the car halted. Rosland turned to me, her eyes wide with panic. I knew mine must have looked the same.

"Here, get in the driver's seat," I said, trying to keep my voice calm. "I'll see what happened."

"Be careful," she said, squeezing in next to me, our little son on her lap.

Outside the car I was blinded by icy wind and snow. When my eyes adjusted, I saw the trailer had jackknifed, folded against its hitch until it was nearly parallel with the car. Its rear wheels were near the edge of a cliff! I couldn't let my wife and child get out in this cold. The baby, especially. I groped desperately around in the snow until I found rocks big enough to brace against the wheels. I tried to rock the trailer until I was convinced it was secure. Then I rushed back to the car.

"We're stuck in a ditch," I lied. No need to scare Rosland too. "Stay here, I'll walk up the road to get help." The car was already losing its warmth.

They just need to hold out until I get back, I thought as I trudged through the snow. But what did I hope to find? We'd been on the mountain for at least five miles and hadn't seen a single house along the way. The road stretched out before me looked the same—black and empty.

"Lord, I don't know what to do. How can I keep my wife and baby safe?" Everything felt out of my control—the war in Vietnam, the blizzard conditions, the cliff. We hadn't made it to my first post and I'd already failed to protect my family.

I was still praying out loud through chattering teeth when I stepped right into a deep snowdrift. "Help!" I screamed, trying to claw my way out. I could barely hear myself over the howling storm.

Then a soft sound drifted to my ears on the wind. I strained to listen. Was that a Christmas carol? "Joy to the world!" a chorus of men sang off in the distance. "The Lord is come."

I yelled for help again, and out of the snowy white curtain stepped three lumberjacks. They were tall and barrel-chested, dressed in suspenders, red plaid, and thick wool caps. Each one had a bushy beard and kind eyes. If I was hallucinating, this was mighty vivid!

"Help me!" I said, talking a mile a minute, explaining the danger my family was in. Through it all the lumberjacks remained stoic, their faces radiating strength and composure. I felt warmer just looking at them.

"Show us where the car is," one of the men said. His voice was jovial—as if he wasn't worried at all. The three pulled me out of the snowdrift, and I led them back to the cliff edge. Rosland and the baby were still settled inside.

"Put it in gear and we'll push," one of the men instructed. I nodded and climbed into the driver's seat. The three positioned themselves behind the station wagon and gave me a signal to press on the gas. Slowly we inched forward, until we found ourselves back on the road, moving forward. Behind us we saw the lumberjacks waving good-bye, but we couldn't stop to thank them. I couldn't help but think they'd saved our lives.

We picked up speed and the snowstorm eased up. The road became less slippery. By the time we descended the other side, we could see sunny skies and signs for the highway in the distance. I knew God had protected my family when I couldn't—just as I knew He always would.

My Blue Spruce

Rosemarie McManus

THANKSGIVING HADN'T ARRIVED, and yet I couldn't wait to decorate for Christmas. This year, in addition to our big family tree, I wanted a smaller one decorated entirely with angels.

I could see it in my mind as I browsed the Christmas aisles of my favorite department store. A blue spruce strung with little white lights, just like the trees of my German childhood, with a white cotton cloth underneath to simulate snow. I was admiring the angel tree toppers when I ran into my friend Fran. "I tried to call you earlier," I said. "How is Ralph?"

Fran explained that her husband was at home resting after his hospital stay. "We have an appointment at the National Institutes of Health the day after tomorrow," she said. "Things don't look good for Ralph."

"Come to our house for lunch tomorrow," I said. "Ed would love to see him."

"I think that's just what Ralph needs."

But when Fran and Ralph arrived the next day, Ralph had something more important on his mind than lunch. "Ed, you ever have a PSA test? It checks your prostate gland."

"Never heard of it," Ed said. "I'll remember it if I don't feel well…"

"Don't wait until then," Ralph said seriously. "The benefit of this test is that it can detect a problem early. I don't know how things are going to turn out for me, but I want to inform every older man I know. Promise me you'll get the test."

"I'll ask my doctor," said Ed.

I thought that would be the end of it, but Ralph was relentless. Ed promised to make an appointment for the test. "I guess I should be flattered that you care about me so much!" he said as the two shook hands before Ralph left. "I'll call the doctor tomorrow. Count on it."

Always a man of his word, Ed made that doctor's appointment. We thought he was just keeping a promise to a friend. But the test results indicated a problem. After more tests Ed was diagnosed with prostate cancer. "It's got an extremely aggressive cell structure," the doctor warned us as we sat in his office, stunned. "That means every second counts." I thanked God for Ralph. Even in a fight for his own life, he was concerned for his friends.

Ed was scheduled for surgery right after the holidays. The shadow of it hung over all of our Christmas preparations. It was hard to enjoy anything when I didn't know whether Ed would be all right. Still, we got two trees: a full-size pine and a smaller blue spruce. Back home I set up the little tree in the corner and decorated it with lights and icicles. One by one I hung angel ornaments from its branches, breathing in the comforting smell of pine. *Ed needs at least this many angels this Christmas*, I thought as I reached into the box of ornaments. And, of course, there was our dear friend Ralph, whose own battle was nearing an end.

Our three sons and their families visited for Christmas. The house was so filled with family and angels that Ed's condition didn't seem real. When I looked at the grandchildren playing with their toys or my daughter-in-law who was expecting a new baby soon, I saw the promise of new life.

All too soon Christmas was over. Then New Year's. I left the angel tree up in the corner. I couldn't bear to take it down. I still needed all the angels I could get, and I was too busy to worry about it, what with Ed's trips to the doctor to see whether the cancer had metastasized.

Days went by without my even remembering to look at the angel tree in the living room, much less water it. The scent of pine that I found so comforting had long since disappeared.

One afternoon at the end of January, a couple of friends, Sally and Paz, came to visit. As we chatted in the living room, one of them reached out to touch the tips of the branches. My eyes followed her fingers to the nearly forgotten angels, the white lights and icicles, the...

"What's that?" I said, going over to look. I could have sworn I saw a spot of bright green at the end of the branch. I examined it closely.

"It's a new shoot!" said Paz. "Sprouting out of the branch."

"There's more over here," said Sally, peering 'round the other side.

The green shoots were everywhere. It was as if the neglected tree was suddenly bursting with new life. "But how is that possible?" I said. Had the shoots been growing all this time while I was too worried about Ed to notice? Or had they sprung up suddenly like a message?

"The tree has new life," said Paz. "Like we hope Ed will have too." When everyone left I sat down beside the angel tree. *Is it really a sign, God?* I wondered. I caught the faintest scent of pine on the air.

Ed's tests were encouraging. The cancer had not metastasized. A radical surgery might indeed remove it all. On February 19, when we left for the hospital, the angel tree was as bright as ever, still sprouting fresh green shoots from every branch. I tried to picture it in my mind as I sat with my sons in the waiting room during the surgery.

Finally the doctor came out to see us. He believed the operation was a success. With Ed safely in recovery, I returned home to rest. When I walked into the house the scent from the little spruce was stronger than ever.

Closing my eyes and breathing it in, I almost felt like I was back in the Black Forest of my childhood surrounded by the giant trees. How could such a small tree produce such a strong fragrance? Only the angels knew. I drifted to sleep on the couch beside the tree, the little white lights seeming to warm me all over.

The angel tree continued to sprout shoots for another week, until the day Ed returned home from the hospital—the same day our new granddaughter was born. After that the green tips turned brown. The needles fell and scattered on the cloth beneath the tree. The pine smell disappeared. I took the ornaments off and laid them in their boxes until next year. The promise of the angel tree had seen us through.

The Light That Never Fades

Marci Alborghetti

A GOOD FRIEND'S DAUGHTER DIED RECENTLY, leaving behind confused and grieving children and grandchildren. I watched helplessly while the little ones tried to cope, and it made me wonder, *How do you explain to children the death of someone they love?*

Then I thought back to my childhood best friend, Carol. I was only seven when she died.

She'd had cancer, but I didn't understand that then. What I did understand was what I could see: while the rest of us grew bigger, she grew smaller. When I got a big-girl bed, Carol went back to a crib. When my mother and her mother, also best friends, got together, they cried instead of laughed. On the swings now, Carol had a special harness to keep her from falling. While we gobbled hamburgers off the grill, Carol wasn't hungry. While the rest of us kids rejoiced in staying up late, Carol couldn't wait to go to bed.

In the long months when Carol was sick, and then very sick, I saw things that I couldn't forget. I saw her perfectly round, luminous little face grow gaunt, and her crazy-joy smile fade. Carol was the family baby, and I saw her two sisters and brother become quieter and more cautious, a marked change given the family's love of music, antics, and fun.

Through the eyes of a seven-year-old, I watched everything grow dim.

Then there were the things I didn't see anymore. I didn't see her bounding down the hallway whenever we came to the house; eventually, I didn't even see her waiting with quiet happiness just inside the front door. I could barely see her at all when I was led softly down that dark hallway to the closed door of the darkened room where she slept shadowed in her crib, in the middle of the day. I couldn't see her through the window of her hospital room. Though I told my mom that I could.

And then I didn't see her at all.

The first Christmas after Carol died, I was a different little girl. Gone was the chatterbox who'd followed people around asking questions and talking nonstop. I'd become quiet, withdrawn.

Christmas had always been a huge deal in both my house and Carol's. We were Christmas families, lavishing great care on decorating the tree ("You've moved that same ornament twice in the last hour," my father would say to my meticulous mother), baking hundreds of cookies, not to mention making fudge and candy. And both of our households placed electric candles in every window; every night during the Christmas season, my sister and I would race to see who could turn on the most candles. Oh, the spark of delight when that small, cool glass bulb would flare and bring Christmas to the December night.

But the Christmas of Carol's death I didn't compete, except in the bedroom my sister and I shared. I spent a lot of time there now, staring out the window at the early falling darkness. I considered the candles in that room my property, lighting them alone every night with none of the joy of previous Christmases. I'd stare at them, thinking how little they could do against the darkness inside me.

One night that December we had company. The tree was lit, an early dinner had been consumed, and cookies were set out on the special tablecloth in the dining room. I was in my room, staring at the candles against the darkness. I heard our guests arriving, and then my mother at my door. "Marci!" she whispered. "Everyone is here. Come out now and say hello!" I just looked at her until she sighed and left, shutting the door behind her. I returned to the window.

Abruptly the noise from the party faded, and I could hear the night outside my window: its silence, its waiting, its chill. Our windows were ordinary, but now the candlelight seemed to reflect outward, in multiple windowpanes, mirrors of candles, each a little less bright than the last but never completely disappearing.

Like Carol, I thought sadly. *She just kept getting dimmer and dimmer. Until she faded away.*

Then suddenly the light changed. Each reflection shimmered and took on a shape—an angelic form—and in each reflection the angel pointed to a new scene. Each scene showed a memory of Carol, but not of a bad thing, not of a *cancer* thing. In one reflection, I saw the Christmas when her aunts came from Massachusetts and danced with us around the tree until the room shook and we were dizzy with laughter. Then I saw Carol's sisters letting us play with their hamster, and I saw again the pure smile on Carol's face—unadulterated by pain—when the hamster ran up her slender arm. Then in scene after scene, I saw Carol and me: searching for peepers in the hollows by her house's foundation; Carol eating ice cream; Carol being swung into the air by her mother; Carol playing on the swing set in our yard; Carol plunking on the keys of the piano that crowded her living room. Each time, the shimmering form pointed to a new scene, and I recovered a memory of Carol that I'd forgotten. After a minute—or an hour?—the scenes faded, and the shimmering angelic form flared up and turned back into candlelight.

The angel had given me what I hadn't known was mine: memories of Carol before cancer that would for the rest of my life remain sharp and joyous counterpoints to what I saw that last year. I looked at the candle reflections once more before going out to the party. Every light looked a little like Carol to me, and this time she didn't fade away.

That bittersweet memory gave me a new perspective on how to talk to my friend's grieving children. I called her right away. "I thought of something to share with the kids," I began. "Do you remember when we went dancing with Gi-gi and she made us laugh so hard?" My friend responded to my question with a soft chuckle and no doubt a fresh smile.

Dad's Message of Peace
Rita Hodges

WHEN MY FATHER PASSED AWAY in December 2007, I was crushed. I went through the motions to accomplish what had to be done. But peace eluded me.

Shortly after my mother called with the news of Dad's passing, I made the three-hour drive from Huntington, West Virginia, to my parents' country home in the small rural community of Summerfield, Ohio. When my sister, Reva, and I went to the funeral home and florist to make the necessary arrangements, we decided to do the casket spray in fragrant, woodsy pine (to celebrate Dad's love of the outdoors), exquisite pink roses (in honor of his love of that hue), and Christmas ornaments (in memory of his favorite time of the year). To be sure, Dad loved, loved, *loved* Christmas. The two-story white frame home with black shutters he shared with Mom looked like a Norman Rockwell painting. And it was never more joyously alive than during the holiday season.

At a small discount department store in nearby Woodsfield, Reva and I sorted through countless cartons of red and green balls (too flashy for a casket, we decided) until we found serene silver ones. Two boxes of ornaments featuring white doves also caught our attention. "I sure wish we could find three of these," I said to Reva. "That way, we could both have one for our trees, and we could give one to Mom." But as we combed the entire store for more of the dove ornaments, clerks confirmed there were absolutely none to be had.

Doves had always been symbolic of Dad. If there ever was a more loyal, devoted man who cared for his young like doves are known to do—one whose very heart centered on peace—that was Dad. (To our never-ending amusement, he even loved Dove soap, and he always brought a bar with him when he visited Reva or me, just in case we didn't have one on hand.)

After the funeral, everyone headed back to Mom's home. Folks brought in flowers, comfort shawls, and other tokens of affection from the hearse. It had snowed during the night, and the entire surrounding landscape was a pure, unspoiled white. The white frame house was bursting at the seams with family and friends, when we heard the grandkids yell: "Come quick! Outside! You won't believe your eyes." Everyone congregated in the front yard, where a pristine white dove was stationed front and center atop the white hearse, as if choreographed by angels. We watched, transfixed, as it flew to the porch and perched on the red Amish swing, Mom and Dad's evening destination after dinner. Next, it made a trek to Dad's trusty fishing pole. When the front door opened, the dove headed straight to the fireplace, the center of our parents' existence, where it landed on the hearth. Finally, it waddled into the kitchen and rested under Dad's chair at the head of the table. Not long after, it flew back out the front door and away.

The vision of the dove stayed with me in the coming days as I tried to wrap my head around what it all meant. Back home, I hung the dove ornaments on my Christmas tree. But my heart still hurt that there were no dove ornaments for Mom, Dad's eternal sweetheart.

The next morning as I was backing out of the garage en route to work, I noticed an identical third box of dove ornaments on the small refrigerator we kept in there. *That's strange*, I thought. I hadn't shared my desire for another box with anyone else after we left the store. Certain I was losing my mind, I got out of the car, went back into the house, and tracked down the sales receipt. Yes, I'd purchased only two boxes of dove ornaments, not three.

It appeared to be something my peace-loving Dad had orchestrated. With the help of angels, Dad had delivered his heavenly message to my heart: *I've found* my *peace, Rita. Now you find yours.*

And in God's perfect time, I have.

Glimpses of Eternity

"The air had a brilliant clarity that made small details stand out

in a new light: the orchard in translucent white and pinks,

startling shades of greens, reds, yellows, and russets—

for there were both fragrant blossoms and ripe red fruits on the trees.

As I sat there drinking in the beauty,

gradually I became aware of a Presence:

a Presence of joy, harmony, and compassion.

My heart yearned to become a part of this beauty."

—Julia Phillips Ruopp

The Window of Heaven

Julia Phillips Ruopp

THIRTY YEARS HAVE PASSED since the experience I am about to describe, thirty years of active life as a minister's wife and a mother. But it remains, to this day, the most vivid and extraordinary happening in my whole existence.

When our first son, "Phipsy," was four years old, I became ill with a glandular condition and was told that I must have a thyroid operation to save my life. Accustomed to entrusting all of my cares to God, I did not fear the operation. It was far harder to come to terms with the future of our child, should I not be there. After a heart-wrenching night, peace came when I knew that his Creator loved Phipsy more than I possibly could, and He would guide his future. I knew also that he would be happy with his earthly father, so I could let go of him and pack my bag for the hospital.

My husband, Harold, took me to Crile's Clinic. Dr. Crile himself was to operate. As only a local anesthetic was used during the surgery, the doctors kept me talking and singing in order to more readily locate the vocal cords.

I was feeling rather pleased about my ability to think of things to say and sing in spite of the unpleasantness when suddenly, to my amazement, I seemed to be looking down at myself and the group around the operating table from a short distance just over their heads. The nurse was saying with a startled expression,

"Doctor, her pulse is going." Then I started moving through what seemed to be a long, dark passageway, and as I went along I thought calmly, *This must be what they call dying.*

This journey continued uneventfully for some time, and I was beginning to wonder how long it would last when I emerged into an overwhelmingly wide space of light—a pulsing, living light that cannot be described in words. Here my body felt light and free, and for a little while I drifted about with no apparent destination. Finally, it was with great relief and pleasure that I found myself sitting on what seemed to be a cloud, or some kind of heavenly island, looking into an enormous convex window that resembled one-half of a huge crystal ball. I knew that it was not glass, for I could easily have stepped through to the other side; at the same time the thought came to me that I must be looking through a window into one bright spot of heaven.

What I saw there made all earthly joys pale into insignificance. I longed to join the merry throng of children singing and frolicking in an apple orchard. The air had a brilliant clarity that made small details stand out in a new light: the orchard in translucent white and pinks, startling shades of greens, reds, yellows, and russets—for there were both fragrant blossoms and ripe red fruits on the trees.

As I sat there drinking in the beauty, gradually I became aware of a Presence: a Presence of joy, harmony, and compassion. My heart yearned to become a part of this beauty.

But somehow, I could not bring myself to go through the window. An invisible, tenacious restraint pulled me back each time I leaned forward with that intention. I remember thinking that I had lost consciousness of my identity, and that my name no longer mattered. All I needed to do was to keep my eyes wide open and step through the window to be a part of what I saw. I frowned at my inability to move, and gradually, unable to bear the light and vibrant life of this small corner of heaven, my eyes closed tight. As I squeezed them tighter, I seemed to recede farther and farther away from that convex window.

After another long journey through the passageway, I returned to the bed, upon which a body was lying, motionless and limp, while nurses and doctors were working over it. Reluctantly I entered it through what seemed to be the natural door, the former soft spot at the top of my head, at the same time asking myself, *Why must I return? Do I have to come back? Can I ever get that weak frame back into action again?* Experimentally, I moved one finger, wondering at the same time who "I" was.

One of the nurses exclaimed, "Glory be; she's coming to. It's been fifteen minutes." I tried again to remember my name, with no success, but another name did come to me—"Harold," and then "Phipsy." They were the ties that had pulled me back, and I needed them now if I was to stay. With great effort I whispered my husband's name.

Then suddenly I knew—I was Julia.

Am I Julia? Can this be Julia? This flattened-out figure with the bandaged neck? I did not want it to be Julia, and yet I did—if there was a Harold and a Phipsy waiting. But to have left all that glory, for this painful return, was almost unacceptable. Then a dearly loved voice spoke—a hand held mine—I did want to stay.

The rest of that day and the next, that other world was far more real to me than the one to which I had returned. I insisted that my husband hold my hand day and night; when he had to leave from sheer exhaustion, my sister came. I sensed that there was some mysterious link between my soul and the palm of my hand, and I felt that my staying in this life depended upon the pressure of love through the hand of another holding mine. The lure of that heavenly place that I had glimpsed was very strong. But their firm grasp, even though they did not entirely understand, kept me from escaping again to its freedom.

During the next twenty-four hours, while I was hovering between two dimensions of life, all the meanings of life and death seemed to pass before my inner eyes. Awareness came strong that the dying of the earthly body was not a calamity. Death was a natural transformation into another phase of living, where one could go right on joyfully progressing, if ready. One graduated from this room of learning into another, just as real and important.

I believe there is a comparison to be drawn between the birth of the spirit and childbirth. We know that if the infant has ready the equipment for breathing—nostrils, lungs, and air passages, then he is able to live in a world of air. However, if the fetal development is incomplete or faulty, he is unprepared for a world where he has to breathe on his own. In like manner, in this life, if one's soul or spirit remains undernourished, underdeveloped, and unrelated, then it cannot enter into or function freely in the highest form of life to which it is capable of attaining. It came to me with certainty, then, that one began there in the next world, where he leaves off here in this life. And if one is unprepared, or unable to "breathe" the atmosphere of that state, or bear the light of a more intense or luminous quality, then one would have to go through a period of waiting or adjustment.

This seemed to give a deeper meaning to suffering, to all experience, and to one's everyday relationships. Not to grow spiritually, seemed to me then, and still does, the real death of the individual.

Thus, I believe that my brief glimpse through the window of heaven was a flash of revelation about the meaning of life itself.

Now I watch eagerly as each new day brings its lessons and its blessings, and I am at peace in the belief—no, the conviction—that in the sight of God the world we live in and the world of my vision are really one.

Wrapped in Light
Mitch Finley

DIANA'S GRANDMOTHER DIED at the age of ninety-five. "Although I knew she had lived a long life," Diana said, "it was still very painful to see her go. We had a very close relationship with each other. I grew up with the blessing of having her live with us throughout my childhood and into my adult life."

Diana believes that her grandmother loved all of her grandchildren, but Diana always felt like she was her grandmother's favorite. "I think the bond between us was so strong because she served, unplanned, as my mother's midwife when I was born at home."

When Diana's grandmother passed away, Diana was twenty-five years old and still living at home. Six months before her death, Diana's grandmother was no longer able to speak, then she became ill and was taken to the hospital, where she quickly went into a coma.

One week after her grandmother's death, Diana had a dream. "In my dream," she said, "I was walking out of my bedroom and looked into her bedroom, which was right next to mine. And there was Grandma sitting on her bed with a big smile on her pretty face. Her cheeks were rosy, and there was a bright light glowing all around her. I ran as fast as I could and threw my arms around her, hugging her as tightly as I could. Then I said, 'You're back—I can't believe you're really back. But how can this be true? You're dead!'"

Diana kissed her grandmother's cheek and told her how much she loved her and how much she missed her. "Then Grandma looked at me and said, 'I can't stay. I must return. I just wanted you to know that I'm fine and happy.'"

"Please don't leave me," Diana replied. "If you can't stay, then please take me with you."

"Where I am going," Diana's grandmother said, "you cannot go because it is not your time. But someday we will be together again."

"With that," Diana said, "she gave me a kiss and, wrapped in light, she flew out the open window. I looked out the window as she flew higher and higher until the heavens opened up, and she went in; and all that remained in the sky was a beautiful white dove."

When Diana awoke, she wondered if all this had been a dream because it had seemed so real. "This experience brought me great comfort," she said. "I believe God allowed me to have this experience for a chance to say good-bye to Grandma."

A Guardian for Bambi

Lyn McConchie

WHEN I WAS IN MY TWENTIES, I worked for a riding stables just outside of a major city, and unlike the other staff, I lived in a tiny cottage on the grounds. At the stables we bred children's ponies, sheltered a few boarders, and rented out mounts by the hour or day. Both the staff and those who spent a lot of time at the stables were devoted to the horses. We were in it because we loved each horse and pony as if it were our own.

The mild weather leading up to the weekend made one Saturday in particular especially busy. Thankfully we'd anticipated the rush, so several of the horses had been conveniently left in the corrals with food and water, ready for the first early customers, and a couple of the others that were being broken and trained were on standby.

When I finally returned to my cottage after the long day, I was dog-tired and turned in early. The bright moonlight spilled through my window, making it easy to see the horses down in their enclosures, dozing in the half light. I crawled into bed and went to sleep almost at once, only to be awakened abruptly about three hours later by one of the boys who spent a lot of time at the stables. He shook me by the shoulder. I stared up, recognizing his face in the moonlight. "Jeez, Craig," I said, "what's the emergency?"

"It's Bambi. He can't breathe. Come quick!"

Bambi was the name of a two-year-old palomino colt that Craig adored. They had a real bond. Bambi would stand for Craig, allowing him to sit on his back and would trot after him begging for treats and attention any time he was loose. He wasn't an aggressive animal, but I guessed that if Bambi was in real trouble, he'd become difficult to handle. Small though the animal was, he was still a colt, and young male animals tend to become dangerous when they fear they are in danger.

Craig urged me to get up. "Hurry, he's dying. *Do something!*"

Still fuzzy with sleep, I pulled my jeans and a jumper on over pajamas, and I ran after Craig down the slope and across to the corrals to Bambi.

Craig was right. Bambi was in genuine peril. One of the staff had dumped a long rope over the corner of the fence instead of putting it away in the tack shed as they were supposed to do. It had a spliced loop at one end. But when the staff member had coiled it to hang over a post, they'd tucked the rope's loose end through the loop as it was coiled. Bambi, endlessly curious, must have been nosing the rope, got his head through the noose the rope had formed, and jumped back. The noose had tightened, and in his subsequent panic he'd become entangled.

There had been a light wind blowing all day, which after dark had increased a little, muffling any sounds so that I'd heard nothing. Bambi had been thrashing about for some time. At last he must have gotten down on the ground and rolled in a final effort to free himself, so that now he had the long rope coiled around his body, while the noose tightened every time he thrashed about. His eyes were bulging, and he was unable to breathe. In seconds, a minute at the most, he'd be dead.

Craig pointed to a pocketknife sitting on top of the fencepost. I didn't hesitate. I dodged flailing hooves, hooked the knife's blade through the noose at Bambi's neck, and jerked up hard. I watched the rope fall away and sighed in relief. Bambi gulped in air while I rubbed his neck and spoke gently to him. The poor little colt staggered to his feet again—he would be all right now. I turned to reassure Craig that his friend was fine and would recover. Craig was gone.

I stopped in my tracks. I was finally awake enough to remember: Craig had been dead almost two weeks. He'd died in a motorcycle accident the previous month. I stared down at the pocketknife. It was my personal knife that I'd placed by my windowsill when I'd emptied my jeans pockets just before going to bed.

I looked at the knife, the rope, and the panting palomino, then I nodded to Bambi. "I didn't know horses had their own guardian angels, boy. But it looks as if you do. I hope he sticks around if you keep doing things like that."

Maybe he did, since Bambi lived a very long and healthy life. He was close to thirty when he died. I like to think that he met his angel again in heaven.

"Get Up and Walk"

Ruthie K. Harbaugh

I REMEMBER THE EXACT DAY that I got the call from the doctor's office: April 12, 1999. "You should go immediately to the nearest hospital for more bloodwork," the doctor's nurse told me. I had just been to the doctor for a routine exam, and as part of the exam I gave a blood sample. The news that the results weren't good was shocking. After all, I was a healthy, active sixty-year-old. I certainly didn't feel sick.

"I don't have time today," I said. "My husband and I have a busy day planned."

"It could be life-threatening," she said.

That got my attention. I headed back to the doctor's office. "Ruthie, you have leukemia. I'm sorry," he said. I sat in disbelief. How could this be?

I immediately went to the hospital for more bloodwork. Tests revealed that I had a very rare large granular lymphocyte leukemia. It was so rare that only fifty-six cases in the world had even been reported. My immune system was almost nonexistent. I was offered the usual treatments—chemotherapy and radiation—but after praying about it with my husband, Don, I refused the treatments. We believed that we should trust God to heal my body.

I was subject to many infections because of my fragile immune system, and hospitalized with pneumonia more than once because of it. Time and again doctors sent me home with "no hope," but Don would nurse me back to health.

Over the next few years, the fight got harder. I grew extremely tired and began sleeping most of the time. Months later, our daughter Susie, a nurse, came to see me. Afterward, she told the doctor she believed that I was dying. The doctor came to visit me every week in my home to monitor my care, and he confirmed that I was steadily declining. Don took total care of all my needs, faithfully staying by my side. My friends covered me in a blanket of prayer. But I was totally helpless. Eventually my weight dropped to eighty-four pounds. One day, I overheard some friends discussing with Don that they needed to plan for a funeral for the coming weekend. *Who in my family has died?* I wondered, then realized that the funeral they were planning was for me.

It wasn't long before the Lord called me home. I fell into a deep sleep and saw a bright light, warm and welcoming. Then I heard my mother's voice calling me to come in, my favorite uncle Baldy was standing at the entrance smiling, and I saw my daddy, walking without a limp for the first time, in a field full of blue corn-flowers with his dog, Ginger. And there was my husband's best friend, Charles. He was smiling and his body was no longer wasted away from cancer. I hovered at the entrance for days. I don't know why I didn't cross over.

Then, a few nights later, I felt a dark presence at the foot of my bed. From above, a voice said, "She is a child of God. Be gone." Then I heard another voice say, "She has had enough. Ruthie, you are healed. Get up and walk." I believed the two voices belonged to Jesus and an angel.

The next morning I asked my husband to lift me out of the bed, and I took three steps into his arms.

Slowly I began to regain my strength. I set a goal to see my granddaughter, Rebecka, graduate from high school in 2008, and I made it there. I set another goal that I would see her graduate from college, and I made it to that date too!

On May 3, 2014, nearly fifteen years after my initial diagnosis, I met with my oncologist to go over my latest blood test results. "Your blood tests are normal and the cancer is gone!" he announced. "A higher power, higher than any doctor, deserves the credit for your healing."

I know that God sent an angel and His Son to me to give me hope—and a miraculous healing.

Our Angel Tedi

Denny and Sheila Linn

LIKE MOST PARENTS WITH CHILDREN, we have had our share of animal burial services, ranging from birds that hit our glass windows to the most recent one of Spot, our beloved and very intelligent guinea pig. Many of the burials came with the question, "What happens to Spot (or whatever animal we were burying) when he dies?"

Our friend Harrel wondered the same thing the day the vet arrived to put down Tedi, her fifteen-year-old golden Lab. Tedi was blind, deaf, and in intense physical pain. Harrel was sobbing and holding Tedi as the vet injected her with the medications. A moment later, Harrel, who is adamant that she is not a visual person, experienced both herself and her dog going into the light. She saw Tedi enter a beautiful grassy field, where she was immediately jumping and playing with the other dogs. Her golden hair was waving in the wind. Tedi communicated to Harrel how happy she was to be free. Harrel felt a great sense of relief that Tedi was happy and well. She wondered, *Why was I so hesitant to have Tedi put down?* Although she grieved Tedi's loss, she said that it was very different from the grief you would expect if you had just put your dog down. Her experience with Tedi has helped Harrel bring comfort to those making the painful decision to let go of their pets, as well as to those grieving their pet's death.

At important times, Tedi returns to comfort Harrel. For example, four days after putting Tedi down, Harrel's husband, Jerry, was in critical condition in the hospital ICU unit. That night, Harrel woke up crying with concern about Jerry. Tedi came to her and said, "Put your face in my fur. Put your arms around me." Unexpected as this was, it was just what Harrel needed.

When Gypsy Came Running

Lyn McConchie

I'VE ALWAYS LIKED DOGS, but because of my disability it isn't practical for me to have one of my own. So I didn't mind when the tenants on my farm got a puppy. She was a small, fat, golden bandy-legged pup. There was nothing to worry about. But after a while I found out that Gypsy was actually a pit bull/Staffordshire terrier cross. Unfortunately neither breed has a great reputation. In fact, they're downright intimidating. That made me a bit wary. She grew into a nice dog, but still I remained cautious whenever she was nearby. She hadn't done anything to make me nervous, but neither had she done anything to soothe my concerns. We lived in distant harmony.

One day I was taking in firewood when a sudden commotion jolted me. I dropped the wood and circled the house to see what was happening. I discovered that my bantam and her seven tiny chicks were cornered under a hayrack by a dog that looked like some sort of German shepherd mix. It was snapping at the chicks as they huddled and peeped in terror.

I yelled at the dog threateningly and moved toward it, not thinking about my own safety. I expected it to run away. But instead it turned to face me, snarling, making it clear it would attack me if I got in the way of it and its potential meal! As it started to approach the chicks again, I screamed with a combination of fear and anger. It must have been heard as a cry for help.

From around the corner of the house, Gypsy came running, low to the ground, a golden streak of outrage that hit the stray dog with a dropped shoulder, taking it right off its feet and knocking it down. Before it could rise again, Gypsy had it by the throat. Then she held it and looked at me. It took a few seconds, but I soon realized that she was waiting for instructions. The stray dog was squealing in a small muffled voice, and I thought—I hoped—that it had learned its lesson. "Let it go, okay, Gypsy?" Her jaws opened slowly and the stray raced away, whimpering and crying as it ran.

Gypsy beamed up at me, her tail waving wildly with pride. She'd heard a friend call for help, and she'd come running.

She turned in the sunlight and her golden fur seemed to glow. I knelt down and said quietly, "Good girl, Gypsy," as she wagged her tail. Then, very slowly she faded into the sunlight.

Suddenly I remembered that she had died almost ten weeks ago, and was buried only yards from where I now knelt. A guardian angel had been sent as a testament to God's never-ending care.

A Note from the Editors

WE HOPE YOU ENJOY *The Best Angel Stories 2016*, created by the Books and Inspirational Media Division of Guideposts, a nonprofit organization that touches millions of lives every day through products and services that inspire, encourage, help you grow in your faith, and celebrate God's love in every aspect of your daily life.

Thank you for making a difference with your purchase of this book, which helps fund our many outreach programs to military personnel, prisons, hospitals, nursing homes, and educational institutions. To learn more, visit GuidepostsFoundation.org.

We also maintain many useful and uplifting online resources. Visit Guideposts .org to read true stories of hope and inspiration, access OurPrayer network, sign up for free newsletters, download free e-books, join our Facebook community, and follow our stimulating blogs.

To learn about other Guideposts publications, including the best-selling devotional *Daily Guideposts*, go to ShopGuideposts.org, call (800) 932-2145, or write to Guideposts, PO Box 5815, Harlan, Iowa 51593.